Care of the Aging

RECENT ADVANCES IN NURSING

Already published
Current Issues in Nursing
Edited by Lisbeth Hockey

Forthcoming Titles in the Series
Cancer Nursing
Edited by Margaret C. Cahoon

Nursing Education
Edited by Margaret Steed

Primary Care
Edited by Lisbeth Hockey

Research Methodology
Edited by Margaret C. Cahoon, Laurel Archer Copp and Lisbeth Hockey

Patient Teaching
Edited by Jenifer Wilson-Barnett

Communication
Edited by Ann Faulkner

Clinical Nursing Practice
Edited by Alison J. Tierney

SERIES EDITORS

Margaret C. Cahoon RN PhD

Dr Cahoon is Rosenstadt Professor of Health Research at the School of Nursing, University of Toronto, Canada. She has wide experience as a teacher, adviser and author. She is a former Fellow of the World Health Organisation and of the Ontario Ministry of Health and a past president of the Ontario Public Health Association. Health care research has been of major interest to her throughout her career, and at present she is the principal investigator in the Sunnybrook-University of Toronto Project for the development of a collaborative nursing research demonstration unit. She has made important contributions through her work in community health and oncology; she has been involved in studies of patient care and coping and has recently embarked upon a project for the Bayview Clinic of the Ontario Cancer Treatment and Research Foundation. In addition to her own publications on research in books and periodicals, she is a member of the editorial board of *Research in Nursing* and of the overseas panel of the *Journal of Advanced Nursing*.

Laurel Archer Copp RN PhD FAAN

As Dean and Professor at the School of Nursing, University of North Carolina at Chapel Hill and a Fellow of the American Academy of Nursing, Dr Copp is an established nursing authority, having contributed over sixty articles to international nursing journals, instigated ten research studies and served on a number of important advisory committees. Her main interest is the psychology and philosophy of pain and suffering but her studies have ranged widely to investigate many aspects of research and the nursing curriculum. She has maintained close links with work being carried out in other countries and in particular, her association with nursing research centres in the U.K. has meant a valuable exchange of views and knowledge. Her current appointments include Chairman of the Alumni Council of the Harvard Program on Health System Management and Chairman of the Task Force on Research of the American Association of Colleges of Nursing. In 1981, she received the Alumnus of the Year Award from Dakota Wesleyan University.

Lisbeth Hockey OBE PhD SRN BSc FRCN

Dr Hockey, a Fellow of the Royal College of Nursing, is well known as the Director of the first Nursing Research Unit established in the U.K. at the Department of Nursing Studies, Edinburgh University, in 1971, a post which she still holds. She gained extensive practical experience as a district nurse, midwife and health visitor before specialising in teaching, administration and, above all, research. She developed a Research Department at the (then) Queen's Institute of District Nursing, undertaking and guiding research in community nursing. Her present post involved her in research in the wider field of nursing. She is currently a member of several national committees and Chairman of the Royal College of Nursing Research Society. She is also a member of the Advisory Board of the *Journal of Advanced Nursing*. Lecturing and visiting Professorships have taken her to Canada, Australia, the U.S.A. and several European countries. She has made valuable contributions to international nursing and paramedical journals as well as being author and co-author of important textbooks and research reports.

RECENT ADVANCES IN NURSING 2

Care of the Aging

Edited by

Laurel Archer Copp
RN PhD FAAN
Dean and Professor, School of Nursing,
University of North Carolina at Chapel Hill,
U.S.A.

Foreword by

Thelma J. Wells RN PhD
Associate Professor of Nursing
University of Michigan School of Nursing
Ann Arbor, Michigan, U.S.A.

GRANTHAM HOSPITAL
LIBRARY SERVICE

CHURCHILL LIVINGSTONE
EDINBURGH LONDON MELBOURNE AND NEW YORK 1981

CHURCHILL LIVINGSTONE
Medical Division of Longman Group Limited

Distributed in the United States of America by
Churchill Livingstone Inc., 19 West 44th Street, New
York, N.Y. 10036, and by associated companies,
branches and representatives throughout the world.

© Longman Group Limited 1981

All rights reserved. No part of this publication may be
reproduced, stored in a retrieval system, or transmitted
in any form or by any means, electronic, mechanical,
photocopying, recording or otherwise, without the prior
permission of the publishers (Churchill Livingstone,
Robert Stevenson House, 1-3 Baxter's Place, Leith
Walk, Edinburgh, EH1 3AF)

First published 1981

ISBN 0 443 02187 2
ISSN 0144-6592

British Library Cataloguing in Publication Data
Care of the aging. — (Recent advances in nursing,
  ISSN 0144-6592;2)
  1. Geriatrics   2. Geriatric nursing
  I. Copp, Laurel Archer   II. Series
  618.97'0024613   RC952

Library of Congress Catalog Card Number
81-7700

Printed in Great Britain at The Pitman Press, Bath

Foreword

Care of the aging is an ancient function entrusted to those who occupy nursing roles in a society. But over time the concepts of both aging and nursing have changed. Life span as measured in years has steadily increased from about a fifty year average in 1900 to more than the biblical three score and ten. Seemingly odd terms such as 'young-old' and 'old-old' have social meaning with families commonly including grandparents and great grandparents amongst their living kinship. Nursing, originally thought to be solely a set of intuitive behaviors transmitted by genetic happenstance, has become not only a structured educational program but a questing research endeavor. Still nursing is a practice or 'hands on' behavior and today those hands are mostly likely to be working with the older patient or client. It is timely that this book should focus on progress within this domain. Such progress is even more noteworthy when seen against the backdrop of common ill-founded comments about nursing care of the aging.

One innocent sounding opinion is that nursing care of the old is 'just good basic nursing'. This comment typically arises from two sets of false assumptions: (1) that aging is a time of illness and incapacity and (2) that nursing's major role is providing total care to dependent people. Studies have found that most elderly people consider themselves healthy and live in the community with little or no assistance. The most significant role for nursing surely is preventing incapacity and maximizing self care in this group. Of course nurses provide care and comfort for those who cannot manage by themselves, but the means for doing this are more likely to be rehabilitative than custodial.

Nursing care of the old is 'just lots of dull, dirty work' represents either an angry or an apathetic view. This comment is often heard amidst the stench of urine in stark back wards designated as being for 'chronic care'. What is typically chronic about such settings is the lack of qualified staff, adequate equipment, and basic amenities. And those who make the comment have been neglected as much as those in their care. The care, while usually valid given the circumstances, should be a call to change the underlying deprived settings through competent and courageous nursing leadership.

'There isn't anything to nursing care of the old' is a frequent comment from those who have had positive personal experiences caring for an older person, typically a relative. A restricted perspective, it flourishes within a philosophy that proclaims most of nursing just as common sense anyway. The basic difficulty with this opinion is that it does not even suggest a course of action for genuine complex care issues such as urinary incontinence and mental confusion.

This book will help to quell these views. By focusing the attention of nurse scholars from around the world on significant clinical issues in nursing care of the old it spreads knowledge to dispel myths and clarify concepts. This is a landmark book, overdue in the sense of having been long needed. The international tone is a tremendous strength as different backgrounds generate new stimuli and provide contrasting challenges. This is a hopeful book; it suggests a promise that sharing across cultures will not only be rewarding in itself but will yield solutions to difficult problems. Nursing care of the aging has advanced; here is its rallying standard.

1981   Thelma J. Wells

Preface

The title *Care of the Aging* for this volume in the *Recent Advances in Nursing* series is appropriately in the present and active form of the English language. Care of the aging is going on even as these words are read, and going on in many countries and in a variety of care settings. And it is hoped that wherever possible, there is a caring, nurse professional involved. This publication is intended to communicate not only an 'in process' skill and art, but to demonstrate the way in which nursing care of an aging population is changing, growing, and developing.

Ten other nurse authors from ten other settings might have given insight into yet other evolving aspects of care designed to improve the quality of life for the older person. Those presented here, however, are representative and timely. Each presents an area of expertise. Each views a setting in an individual, educated, scientific, and inquiring way. Each writes, speculates and discusses a topic for which there is not only interest, but intense and genuine involvement.

None of the studies presented is in any way finished. These reports describe a stage of development in a specific area of nursing activity or inquiry. In many cases the contributor has continued the development of thought and posed new researchable questions long after the manuscript has been submitted. The settings are as diverse as the countries in which these authors work. Forms of government, health care financing and delivery, organization of nursing services, and patterns of nursing education — all differ. For this reason it is believed that the ideas presented here can be applied to a variety of settings and will stimulate the reader to consider the meaning of the study in his or her own context.

Aging is an ongoing process which binds us to clients, health workers, family members, and professional colleagues.

Whether we value it, dread it, deny it, or harbor an increasing interest in it — we are all doing it. And for that reason we have a vested interest in the evolution of the art of the care of the aging, for its effects will most certainly involve us in personal as well as professional ways.

The bibliographies provided by the contributors at the end of their studies, and that provided by the editor at the end of the book, are designed also to speak in the active voice. Although they are only representative of a larger body of knowledge, reflective publications, and research findings, they are cited to accomplish two purposes: (1) they serve as a guide to increasing one's reading along a developmental line of topics which deal with issues of the aging, and (2) they serve as a method whereby researchable topics can be interfaced and cross-referenced, and they expand the options for professional inquiry.

Many of us involved in this volume have persons we would like to thank. They include Thelma Wells for her Foreword, and the staff at Churchill Livingstone for their patience and professional skills. Each author would like to thank those who work in their settings and who listened, retrieved, read, typed, edited, and posted the manuscripts.

One last comment. It would have been ideal if we contributors could have met but the vast miles which separate us made this impossible. Fortunately, ideas overcome the problems posed by distance. And it is hoped that our ideas will encourage further debate and discussion among our colleagues everywhere.

Chapel Hill, N.C. 1981   Laurel Archer Copp

Contributors

Faye G. Abdellah RN, EdD, ScD, LLD, FAAN
Assistant Surgeon General, Chief Nurse Officer, U.S. Public Health Service, Department of Health and Human Services, Washington, D.C., U.S.A.

Dosia Carlson PhD
Coordinator Social Services, The Beatitudes Retirement Campus, Phoenix, Arizona, U.S.A.

Laurel Archer Copp RN, PhD, FAAN
Dean and Professor, School of Nursing, University of North Carolina at Chapel Hill, North Carolina, U.S.A.

Anne J. Davis RN, PhD, FAAN
Professor, School of Nursing, Department of Mental Health and Community Nursing, University of California, San Francisco, California, U.S.A.

Helen K. Evers BSc, MSc
Senior Research Fellow, Department of Sociology, University of Warwick, Coventry, U.K.

Val M. Hardy RN, RM, DNE, FCNA
Director of Nursing, Bendigo Home and Hospital for the Aged, Bendigo, Victoria, Australia

Miriam J. Hirschfeld RN, DNSc
Tel-Aviv University and Kupat Holim, Israel

Margaret F. Hudson RN, MAEd
Assistant Professor, School of Nursing, University of North Carolina at Chapel Hill, North Carolina, U.S.A.

Dana C. Hughes RN, PhD
Assistant Professor, School of Nursing, University of Virginia, Charlottesville, Virginia, U.S.A.

Sally J. Redfern PhD, SRN
Lecturer, Department of Nursing Studies, Chelsea College, University of London, London, U.K.

Greta Wiseman RN, BSN
Coordinator of Home Health Care, Hospice of the Valley, Phoenix, Arizona, U.S.A.

Contents

PART ONE

1. New directions in the care of the elderly 3
   Faye G Abdellah

2. Ethical issues in gerontological nursing 38
   Anne J Davis

3. Tender loving care? – patients and nurses in geriatric wards 46
   Helen K Evers

4. Role stress reported by Directors of Nurses in skilled nursing homes 75
   Dana C Hughes

5. Modifying attitudes toward geriatric nursing in Australia 92
   Val M Hardy

6. The older adult, primary care, and the geriatric nurse practitioner 114
   Margaret F Hudson

7. Hospice concepts applied to the aging 137
   Dosia Carlson and Greta Wiseman

8. Families living and coping with the cognitive impaired 159
   Miriam J Hirschfeld

9. Evaluating care of the elderly: British perspective 168
   Sally J Redfern

10. The protection of aged human subjects in the clinical research setting 192
    Laurel Archer Copp

PART TWO BIBLIOGRAPHIES

General sources of reference 208

Specialised bibliographies 210

INDEX 233

PART ONE

1
Faye G. Abdellah

New directions in care of the elderly

INTRODUCTION

In the field of aging the beginning of a new decade offers an opportunity to assess problems and examine new challenges. For the elderly person, whether patient or client, significant advances, particularly in research, will have a direct impact upon how policy makers and planners assess ways in which the needs of the elderly in the Eighties can be met.

The incredible increase in the proportion of older people 65 and over will have far reaching effects upon health systems of delivery of care and upon those who provide these services, particularly nurse practitioners.

Substantial declines in two of the three leading causes of death, heart disease and cerebrovascular disease, account for most of the decrease in mortality of the elderly (Kovar, 1977).

Reductions in mortality and fertility have markedly changed the age distribution in the United States. While the total population increased 2.5 times from 1900 to 1970, the number of persons aged 65 and above increased 7 times. Persons aged 65 and over now constitute about 10 per cent of the total population, but over the next 50 years, they are expected to make up between 12 and 16 percent. There are now about four persons under the age 20 for every person over age 65.

About one-third of the older population is very old, 75 years or above. This proportion will stay about the same for the foreseeable future if mortality rates remain constant. If they do, there will be about 12 million of the very old by the year 2000. If mortality rates decline, however, the numbers of the very old may grow as high as 16 or 18 million.

A 65-year-old man can now expect, on average, to live to 78, a woman of 65, to 82. By the year 2000, life expectancies for 65-year-olds may increase by another two to five years.

The gain in life expectancy during the twentieth century represents an outstanding achievement, but it brings with it substantial changes in the society as a whole and enormous challenges. There are increasing numbers of persons in the late 50s, 60s and early 70s, who are retired, relatively healthy, vigorous, and who seek meaningful ways to use their time. Policy issues are how best to utilize the talents of the 50-70-year-olds, both to enrich their own lives and to improve the society at large.

In addition, there are striking increases in the numbers of persons in the mid 70s, 80s and 90s. An increasing minority remains vigorous and active but the majority needs a range of supportive and restorative health and social services. The old-old of the 1970s represent a disproportionately disadvantaged group. The reasons are several, including the fact that this group includes many immigrants who were poorly educated and who have spent their working years at low-paid jobs. Many have been unable to accumulate savings or to build up sufficient equity in the social security system to sustain them adequately through their years of retirement.

Future populations in the Eighties will have different characteristics. They will have been better educated, will have received better health care throughout their lives, and will have been provided with the benefits of an improved social security system. Because their life experiences will have been markedly different from the present population of older people, their expectations of life, including their expectations of old age will be different. As a result, programs suited to the elderly today will need continuous revisions if they are to meet the needs of future populations (DHEW, 1978).

Long-term care defined

Long-term care is the provision of that range of services — physical, psychological, spiritual, social and environmental, including economic — needed to help people attain, maintain, or regain their optimum level of functioning. It includes health maintenance throughout the life span as well as care during acute and protracted illness and disability. Long-term care affects patients, clients, families and communities.

In their older years, patients often experience overwhelming effects of disease, residual pathology, and irreversible disability. Eighty-one percent of those 65 and over suffer from some chronic physical distress.

Until individuals everywhere are convinced that helping people maintain optimum health takes precedence over other types of care, the country will continue to be faced with expensive illness and disability that could be prevented. Until we accept that premise, long-term care at best will be a catch-up effort rather than a direct attack on the problems.

KEY ISSUES AND PROBLEMS IN LONG-TERM CARE

Long-term care (LTC) is not currently provided in an optimal way. The development of better ways to provide long-term care services to the elderly and disabled in need of care has proven difficult.

The basic issue is that we do not know enough about what are the most effective and efficient ways of providing a diverse range of LTC services, within both institutions and community-based settings to a fast growing elderly population.

The costs of LTC services have mushroomed since 1965 and are still continuing to rise rapidly. State and Federal programs that provide fund for LTC services are fragmented making it difficult to estimate the total costs of care. The best available estimate, however, and a conservative one, is that over $11 billion in public and private funds were spent on LTC services in FY 1975. This represents a 200 percent increase from 1970.

The unexpected large growth in the elderly population, particularly the very old (those over 85) will greatly increase the population at risk for LTC services.

Most of those requiring long-term care services are elderly, alone, and often without means of support. Whether or not they receive care and the kinds of care they receive often reflects the availability of financing. Long-term care services are not now the province of any single program, agency, level of government or articulated service delivery system. The relationship within each of the various programs on issues of finance, administration and service delivery and between programs has resulted in overlaps, gaps, inconsistencies, confusions in the provision of care and a lack of flexibility in meeting a wide array of individual and family needs.

Many individuals are inappropriately placed in costly acute care institutions because of a lack of community alternatives or the failure to develop systematic mechanisms to provide access and link existing community service programs. There has been reluctance to implement a national or state program of comprehensive long-term care services without being better able to predict the costs and potential demand for services. Deinstitutionalization has been a major objective for many states. Both state policymakers and client advocates have made it a priority.

In addition, a growing trend in recent years has been to transfer older patients out of costly State mental hospitals into less expensive boarding homes. Very often, these homes lack adequate medical, nursing, social, and psychiatric care. Residents of these facilities are not included in epidemiologic studies of the prevalence of mental disorders among the elderly, which base their conclusions on data from mental hospitals and community mental health centers. The rate of mental illness among the old, therefore, is vastly underestimated (Butler, 1975).

Mental illness is more prevalent in the elderly than in younger adults. An estimated 15 to 25 percent of older persons have significant mental health problems. Psychosis increases after age 65, and even more so beyond age 75. Twenty-five percent of all reported suicides in this country are committed by elderly persons. The chronic health problems that afflict 86 percent of the aged and the financial difficulties faced by many clearly contribute to increasing stress (Cohen, 1977).

Preventing entry or getting individuals out of institutions, whether hospitals (general or psychiatric), skilled nursing or intermediate care facilities, involves the realignment and/or development of new community resources and service delivery systems to ensure appropriate placements, service and quality of care.

The difficulty experienced in developing new approaches to long-term care financing, administration and delivery is in part because of the multitude of medical, social, economic, ethical and political issues which are relevant. For example, there is the persistent concern that the expanded availability of publicly financed community long-term care services will displace existing informal arrangements and family support networks. Another concern is that a system needs to be developed with effective cost controls and quality assurance mechanisms. An important issue which impinges on resource allocation decisions is how one defines the population in need of care and who, how and when a decision is made in favor of institutional versus in-home care.

Issues of health care assessment in determining need, financing, administration and delivery and training of health professionals and consumers are closely linked and must be adressed if the needs of the elderly are to be met.

Health care assessment — too limited

Health care assessment efforts should be designed to address the unique needs of the chronically ill, we know that many individuals, particularly the aged, have several chronic conditions. Thus, health care assessment must not be limited to only diagnostic-specific criteria, but must use functional status as a measure. The long-term nature of the patient's condition and frequent fluctuations in physical and mental states require that treatment and care plans vary. Patients/clients may require differing levels of care within a short period of time ranging from acute hospital care, skilled nursing services, intermediate care services, home health services to periodic office visits. Health care assessment needs to include all sources of care and should consider the impact of care on the patients'/clients' expected and actual ability to function in daily life.

Since 1950, several instruments have been developed to measure a client's physical functioning in one or more areas. Due to the state of the art, psychometric data are often limited.

A source of difficulty in functional measurement is the absence of concise conceptual and operational definitions of specific terms. For example, how is self-care maintenance to be measured? And how are the conditions handled that may affect a client's rating or score, e.g. an individual's need or lack of need for assistance in activities of daily living? How are terms such as range of motion, decubitus ulcer, assistance needed defined?

Few instruments have been validated and tested for reliability. Many instruments have not been used with samples with different populations that vary by race, socioeconomic status, age, educational background. Another limitation is that equal weighting of the items or dimensions comprising the scale for some instruments is assumed while others assign varying weights based on some assumed relationship such as the amount of staff time required as a function of the degree of disability.

Some instruments include one or more activity or function that are not within the scope of those being measured. Others include multidimensional assessment such as the OARS methodology. (Pfeiffer, 1975) This variance makes it difficult to obtain one overall total score. Instruments also need to make it possible to measure incremental changes and the length of time between measurement points.

General approaches to assessing an individual's functioning may include observation by one or more raters of a person's behavior/performance, over a period of time; a questionnaire approach where self-report data are used; and performance of specific tasks in a test situation.

Selected instruments
Several instruments or assessment techniques have been developed for use in long-term care settings and/or for specific research and demonstration projects. Examples of these are:

Patient Classification for Long-Term Care (Jones, 1973) and the *Patient Appraisal and Care Evaluation (PACE)*. The Patient Classification for Long-Term Care and a further developed instrument PACE represent a systematic, comprehensive approach to patient assessment and classification.

PACE is a systematic process based on utilizing an instrument for assessing and evaluating a patient or client's care in a long-term care facility. Using the PACE tool, the appraiser (provider of care in a nursing home) observes and records data about patient characteristics and his/her functional capacity, develops a plan for the individual's care in a logical and comprehensive manner, including time-limited goals, and then determines whether or not those goals have been met. The PACE instrument has been incorporated into a *Patient Care Management System* thus coordinating the total assessment process (DHEW, 1978).

Monroe County Long-Term Care Program, Inc. The Pre-Admission Assessment Form and the Access Unit Home Review Form include physical self-care maintenance, instrumental activities of daily living, mental functioning as well as other appropriate data items. Instrumental self-maintenance requires further specification and expansion.

Geriatric Functional Rating Scale (Grauer, 1975). This instrument includes some demographic data and items on physical condition, mental condition, functional abilities, support from the community, financial status, place of residence, and family and friends. The measure was developed as a guide for evaluating the need for institutional care for older persons. It was used in the Wisconsin Community Care Organization Project.

Testing the reliability and validity are needed. Also, the selection of areas to be measured and the weighting scheme need further specification and testing.

OARS Multidimensional Functional Assessment Questionnaire (Pfeiffer, 1975). The OARS methodology was developed at the Center for the Study of Aging and Human Development, Duke University. It has been used in other studies.

The following five major areas of functioning are included in the instrument: social resources, economic resources, mental health functioning, physical health, and activities of daily living. Data for each area can be summarized into a single functional rating. These five ratings can be combined to obtain a single Cumulative Impairment Score.

The instrument is comprehensive in coverage but needs further research particularly with reference to the sensitivity of the instrument in assessing function of chronically ill older persons; the validity of the questionnaire; and the appropriateness of summary data to produce a single score for each of the five areas of functioning.

Patient Status Instrument (PSI). This instrument was developed by Medicus Systems Corporation for the Public Health Service's National Center for Health Services Research. It was used to evaluate a number of long-term care demonstrations under the Section 222 provision of the Social Security Act. The instrument includes such areas as risk factors, range of motion, and joint motion.

Mental Status Questionnaire (MSQ). The Disability Scale from the Minnesota Quality Assurance and Review Program (PMR Scale) includes physical self-care activities, as well as items in communication, orientation, and behavior; and a scoring approach based on a time motion study relating each activity's disability points to minutes of required nursing care. It is considered to be a valid and reliable instrument.

Philadelphia Geriatric Center Morale Scale is another useful instrument that has been fully tested and is applicable to a target group for home care services (Lawton, 1975).

Long-term health care data

The importance of long-term care in human services complex is increasing. With improvements in living conditions and advances in medical technology, the major burden of illness in the United States and other industrialized countries has shifted from acute infectious and parasitic diseases to chronic and degenerative conditions. The population is aging, and the elderly, who are at highest risk of long-term illness and associated disability and dependency, have been the fastest growing segment of the population.

A serious limitation in furthering progress in obtaining comprehensive long-term care data is the need to identify a minimum data set. Considerable progress has been made, however, by the report of the Technical Consultant Panels on the Long-Term Care Data Set (DHEW, 1979).

As the concept has evolved in the United States, a uniform basic data set is a recommended set of minimum specifications for public and voluntary information systems. It accomplishes two things: first, it defines the central core of data about a given dimension of health and health services needed on a routine basis by the majority of users; and second, it establishes standard measurements, definitions, and classifications for this core. Minimum data sets deal primarily with the content of data systems, not their structure and procedures. Information does not begin to flow until organizations are set up and procedures adopted to record, report, process, and distribute the recommended data.

All parts of the health service system contribute to the care of the chronically ill. The Minimum Data Set, however, has been designed primarily for providers who specialize in long-term care. They include rehabilitation, psychiatric, chronic disease and other hospitals where the average length of stay exceeds 30 days; nursing homes; health-related residential facilities; and a variety of community-based services for long-term care clients like home health agencies, mental health clinics, special education and other health-related day care and treatment centers.

The Minimum Data Set for Long-Term Health Care sets the stage for the development of comparable, comprehensive, and relevant information about a sector of the population and of the health service system that is growing in size and importance.

Data sets are an essential means of communication. They permit variety and flexibility in health information systems without loss of the essential ability to make basic comparisons. In addition, through arrangements like the Cooperative Health Statistics System, they make it possible to share data and keep to a minimum the demands made on health providers by external agencies and associations. Finally, uniform data are needed for policy decisions.

Fragmentation of Federal, State and local funding
Existing financing for long-term care services complicated by a fragmented array of categorical Federal, State and local programs. Major programs providing funds for one or more long-term care services include Medicaid, Medicare, SSI, Title XX (Social Services), Administration on Aging's Older American Act, Veterans Administration, and Community Action programs. In addition, Vocational Rehabilitation services, housing programs, general revenue sharing, mental health and community development programs in many instances support some aspects of long-term care services. Each program has its own regulations, eligibility criteria and administrative mechanisms that govern the amounts and kinds of services available. The flow of funds within each program and between programs is complex.

Institutional model predominant choice
Quality and overutilization problems exist with institutional care. These problems, however, are more controllable in an institutional environment than when services are provided in an individual's home.

These reasons have contributed to the reluctance of planners to establish full-scale community long-term care service systems.

Because of the administrative simplicity of providing institutional care, the need for some individuals to receive a wide array of services on a frequent basis and the preference or need of individuals to live in a group arrangement, alternative living arrangements are often ignored. Neither a wholly-medical nor a wholly social service model is by itself appropriate. Long-term care includes a multidimensional package of services which encompasses but is not limited to medical care, social service help, supported living arrangements, income assistance, transportation, etc. Current financing and delivery systems have resulted in a situation where many individuals are forced into medical institutions in order to receive care.

Lack of coordinated delivery systems
There are few coordinated delivery mechanisms for long-term care services in local communities reflecting the fragmentation in financing and administration.

To address this fragmentation and lack of a coordinating mechanism any intervention will require a strong central coordinating mechanism. This mechanism needs to identify services and providers and bring all of those affected by service decisions — case manager, client and relatives — into the decision process.

Lack of adequate case management mechanisms
At the present time there is no systematic method in operation nationwide for assessing individual needs, recommending placement alternatives, referring individuals and providing clients with a package of needed services. This is due in large part to the fragmented nature of funding and to a lack of adequate assessment instruments and techniques for determining service needs.

Inappropriate use of institutional care
Another problem with the current long-term care system is that many individuals are inappropriately placed in institutions.

Many national studies have revealed findings that indicate a significant portion of the institutionalized long-term care population could receive a lower level of institutional care or could be returned to the community. Estimates of inappropriate placement in skilled nursing facilities range from 10 to 25 percent and from 20 to 30 percent in intermediate care facilities.

The appropriateness of a particular setting will vary with the client's individual needs. There is no one criterion (diagnosis, income or age) that can be used to judge the need for one type of treatment or facility over another. Every aspect of the individual's life, including social supports, the role of the family, environment and independence need to be examined.

Insufficient home care resources in the community and the absence of a coordinated long-term system leave no alternative but institutional care.

Further, elderly persons are not represented proportionately in the mental health care delivery system. This reflects their reluctance to ask for help, which is probably strongly influenced by societal and cultural attitudes which lead the elderly to regard themselves as being underserved. It also reflects care givers' negative attitudes and lack of interest in the elderly. It often requires a strenuous outreach effort to locate older persons who have problems and to facilitate their contact with available caregivers and agencies.

Controlling the system

Coordinated management and improvement of institutional and noninstitutional long-term care services are essential if the needs of the elderly and developmentally disabled are to be met.

Control of the system needs to be shared by providers, consumers, State and Federal agencies. No one group should control the system. Particularly needed is increased consumer involvement in the planning, management, and evaluation of health care programs.

The future delivery of long-term care services needs to fit within a range of services to be provided by hospitals, nursing homes, home health care programs, community mental health centers, day care centers, and health maintenance organizations — all linked together by interlocking systems. This would require that long-term care services be managed efficiently and that patients/clients be appropriately placed within the system.

Quality control lacking in ambulatory care settings

A coordinated system of care is designed to integrate service delivery. This implies multiple sources of care and a mix of institutional and noninstitutional services. Ambulatory care settings do not typically provide the organizational and administrative support needed to sustain quality control. Institutional settings provide the resources to conduct quality control. Further, they provide built-in organizational incentives for remedial action that may be lacking in noninstitutional settings. The context of Community care places increased demands for integration of quality control with service delivery. Evaluation must be integrated with care delivery so that the processes and paperwork required are not burdensome but become part of care delivery tasks.

Quality control strategies have been most successful with patterns of care that are episodic and acute. The ratio of encounter in acute versus ambulatory care is approximately 10:1. The needs of the elderly, however, are typically chronic. These problems must be confronted by the type of the intervention used.

Quality control strategies have emerged from a medical care model. The needs of the elderly are broad and include social, physical, mental, emotional and financial dimensions. The medical model is inadequate to meet client needs or service responses. Strategies are needed that are multi-disciplinary.

Quality control in relation to long-term care is constrained by the lack of a unifying theory of quality control and the absence of integrated approaches. The key points, i.e., structure, process, outcomes and the dimensions of quality have been defined in terms of efficiency, effectiveness, accessibility, acceptability, provider competence and meeting the needs of the client.

A community approach that would coordinate or channel services to clients who need services provides challenges for introducing a quality control intervention.

It is agreed by most that the responsibility for quality assurance in long-term care belongs at the community level so that an integrated review of the total range of services can occur,

In summary, at a national conference on social welfare, participants delivered eleven principles of long-term social health care which help to identify the complexity of the issues and problems of providing health and social services for the elderly (DHEW, 1977). In essence the principles emphasize that:

- Stereotyped concepts limit long-term care to the services received by indigent aged persons preventing it from being an integral part of the health system
- Assisting individuals to cope with and maintain independent functioning appropriate to their capabilities
- Delivery of care is multidisciplinary and multi-agency
- All socioeconomic levels have needs for services
- Services must be community oriented, integrated, and planned and coordinated as a continuous process
- Quality of care must be defined by providing specific options and assurance given that there will be continuity of these services offered the entire population at risk

● Assessment of individual status and needs must be interrelated to assessment of community resources and patterns of care
● More consistent data are needed for the total population at risk
● Leadership is needed at all levels concerned with planning, data collection, evaluation and coordination.

EXAMPLES OF STRATEGIES USED TO SOLVE THE PROBLEMS

Long-term care channeling demonstration program at Federal level

Long-term care, especially with its current emphasis on nursing home services, is placing a major strain on personal resources and on Federal, State and local public finances. Future increases in the proportion of elderly in the population will further increase the demand for and associated costs of long-term care services. Spending on long-term care, which will have doubled between 1975 and 1980, will more than double between 1980 and 1985 under existing programs and current policies. Despite this projected increase in public and private spending, many people needing services may still not receive them.

Increasingly, the Congress, Federal officials, representatives of State and local government, service providers and consumers are in agreement that the large and growing resources devoted to long-term care are not being efficiently used. The following types of problems have been identified in current long-term care programs and policies:

● Publicly supported long-term care programs are fragmented, difficult to access, inequitable in their coverage, and do not capitalize on existing social support networks
● Federally subsidized long-term care programs foster an excessive reliance on costly medical and institution-based services
● There is an inadequate supply of accessible and affordable in-home and community-based services which might deter institutional placement or reduce the length of stay
● There are relatively few mechanisms at the local level for managing and coordinating the wide range of social, health-related, and medical services that are needed by many of the functionally impaired.

Over the past five years, some promising programs have emerged to address these perceived inadequacies. At the core of many of these programs has been a commitment to develop, at the local level, a capacity to organize and manage a range of in-home, community and institutional services on behalf of individuals who need long-term care.

The department of Health and Human Services (HHS) formerly the Department of Health, Education, and Welfare is exploring alternative conceptions of community long-term care agencies in a systematic fashion and in so doing to determine:

- Which approaches to organizing and delivering long-term care services have the greatest potential for achieving particular policy objectives
- What the barriers to the their implementation might be
- What their cost implications are.

HHS is initiating a National Long-Term Care Channeling Demonstration Program to develop, fund and evaluate channeling demonstration projects. These projects are designed to test the extent to which a local structure is able to manage, coordinate and arrange provision of in-home, community-based, and institutional long-term care services (with the introduction of additional service resources in a subset of projects) in order to assure that people who need long-term care receive the appropriate types and levels of services in the least restrictive setting and in the most cost-effective manner.

HHS has three key expectations with respect to the demonstration initiative:

1. To stimulate system level changes in the organization of the delivery system, the relationship among service providers, and in the way existing long-term care dollars are allocated
2. To create at the community level the structures that are necessary to coordinate, manage and arrange for the provision of appropriate and efficient long-term care services on behalf of the clients who need such services
3. To collect comparable information across the demonstration projects that will assist HHS in the development of a comprehensive long-term care policy including the Legislative and Administrative specifications required to implement policy objectives.

The principal target population for the Channeling Demonstration Program will be functionally impaired elderly.

Funds will be made available for State or local government agencies and existing or new non-profit agencies and organizations to participate as demonstration sponsors. It is expected that relevant State agencies will play a key role in the identification of potential project sites and will support the implementation of any project selected within the state.

Robert Wood Johnson Foundation Program

Also supporting channeling projects is the Robert Wood Johnson Foundation which has allocated up to $8 million to the Program for the Health-Impaired Elderly to be distributed to as many as eight states selected for participation.

Each participating state will develop in a defined area a community-based central unit for the coordination of services for the elderly. Community is defined as a geographic area in which reside a minimum of 20 000 persons 65 years of age or over. The community may be, especially in rural areas, an aggregate of towns and counties. An effort will be made to choose communities that together reflect the diversity of the country.

The specific objectives of the program are:

- To create an organization authorized by the major providers of services to develop and coordinate a community network of care for the elderly. The organization, referred to as the central coordinating unit, will operate under a formal agreement between the Area Agencies on Aging (AAA) and one or more major voluntary agencies
- To identify in the community served by the project the elderly in varying stages of dependency; to assess their needs; and to follow through with linkage to available resources
- To work toward the development of a broad range of interventions to allow flexibility and added responsiveness in meeting the needs of the health-impaired elderly, including persons receiving care in institutions
- To optimize current and available resources, and through coordination and integration, to serve an increasing number of the health impaired elderly
- To overcome current income and eligibility restraints on services
- To strengthen the natural support system.

The program seeks to foster the highest level of cooperation among concerned agencies at the state and local levels, and local voluntary agencies and groups.

Participating projects must include:

- Identification and assessment of the health-impaired elderly and their needs in the defined community
- Maintenance of an inventory of community-based services for the elderly
- Analysis and planning on a continuing basis
- Development of methodologies for the allocation of available resources, including establishment of a priority system operable after assessment of individual need

NEW DIRECTIONS IN THE CARE OF THE ELDERLY 17

- Development of a network of referral services that provides multiple points of access and includes personalized follow-up
- Development of a system of review and comment on provider contract for services
- Performance of systematic monitoring of services provided to the elderly
- Development of sources of support beyond the period of the project
- Assurance that all elderley will be eligible to share in the benefits of the project regardless of income.

TRIAGE

An example of a channeling project is TRIAGE, a demonstration model initiated in February 1974 to test the concept of a single-entry system for the provision of health and social services for the elderly (DHEW, 1979). Central to the model is the provision of comprehensive, humane, and appropriate long-term care, whether it be delivered in an institution and/or a home. Inherent in the model is an assessment process coupled with a coordination, monitoring, and evaluation function to ensure that elderly persons receive appropriate health and social services. Service is developed and organized around individual client need, rather than bending the client to existing 'reimbursement services'. One of the purposes of the project is to test the effectiveness and measure the costs of this system of delivering care to the elderly.

Both the demonstration and research aspects of the TRIAGE project were designed to yield experience and provide administrative and actuarial information about expanded services for the elderly

A significant finding to date is that TRIAGE has been able to provide a comprehensive array of both health and social services at a cost comparable to that spent on medical services alone at a national level. The service utilization and costs associated with the current demonstration raises questions as to whether, without staff determination of appropriateness, monitoring, follow-up and coordination of services, the same result can be achieved. The research findings will be helpful in determining where the information gained can be used, either for recommending new programs or modifications in existing programs.

Colorado Community Care Organization for the Aged and Disabled investigated whether Medicaid costs can be reduced and the quality of life improved through a comprehensive county-run system of in-home and community services as opposed to inappropriate institutional placement. The treatment of case management, consisting of client intake, screening and referral, client assessment, coordination of services, and an on-going evaluation of the appropriateness of care, was available to all Medicaid-eligible persons aged 60 and older in Boulder County, Colorado. Other counties in the state were to serve as the control group. It was hypothesized that the treatment does help keep people out of institutions and thereby saves public long-term care monies.

Massachusetts Department of Elder Affairs project attempted to demonstrate that a community-based home care program can provide a more cost-effective option for the care of the elderly. An assessment team assessed each Medicaid client and developed an 'optimal plan of care' to address the client's needs. Clients were randomly assigned to either the treatment (experimental) group or the control group. The treatment group received this 'optimal care', while the control group was dependent on the traditional service system. The relative cost-effectiveness of the treatment versus the traditional systems was evaluated. The conclusion was made that the data reveal no definite findings of positive impact on the treatment group with respect to any of the variables.

Monroe County Long-Term Care Program intends to demonstrate the cost-effectiveness of a coordinated approach to community services which maintains clients in their own homes as opposed to institutional care. A centralized case management system, which assesses all long-term care clients and certifies service provision, will attempt to allow more people to remain at home at a lower public cost. The case manager has an expanded (Medicaid) benefit package to draw upon when trying to maintain the individual at home. Rates of institutionalization and program costs will be examined. It was found that the 1978 Medicaid institutional admission rate in Monroe County declined 28 percent from the previous year, and that the Medicaid cost of home care is approximately one-half that of institutional care.

Mon Valley Health and Welfare Council demonstration developed a responsive, comprehensive and integrated long-term care delivery system to increase access, quality, and the overall cost-effectiveness of service delivery. Centralized case management, using a computerized management information system, attempted to facilitate the appropriate utilization and coordination of long-term care services for elderly clients. Cost-benefit and consumer satisfaction analyses of the treatment were performed. The final evaluation report of this project consisted of eight recommendations for an optimal delivery system in Mon Valley; issues of cost, effectiveness and utilization were not formally addressed.

Montefiore Hospital and Medical Center project measured the cost-effectiveness of day care as opposed to institutionalization. The public costs of an elderly day care client were compared to those of a person receiving institutional care in either a skilled nursing facility or intermediate care facility, and the life satisfaction and morale status of each group was recorded over time to allow cost-effectiveness analysis. A final conclusion was that the cost of in-home and comparable Intermediate Care Facility (ICF) care were approximately the same.

Philadelphia Geriatric Center demonstration examined whether an integrated group community services or a multipurpose center is more cost-effective and better meets the needs of clients and families. Rigorous case management, including information and referral, service coordination, advocacy, and on-going follow-through and follow-up (monitoring) services, tried to maintain the appropriateness of care for elderly clients living in the community. The treatment was evaluated in terms of whether it kept people out of nursing homes and saved money.

State of Washington Community-Based Care System assesses the impact and appropriateness of an integrated and centrally coordinated long-term care system. Multidisciplinary case management teams will assess client needs, link clients to appropriate service providers, and monitor service delivery at three different project sites. The characteristics of the three sites and the treatment effect will be evaluated for similarities and differences in terms of their cost-effectiveness, and then compared to the present system. This project is currently in operation; no interim findings are presently available.

Georgia Department of Medical Assistance Alternatives to Nursing Homes provides and tests the cost-effectiveness of alternatives to institutional care for persons who qualify for nursing home care. Three different treatments — adult foster homes, in-home services, and adult day rehabilitation — will be given to nursing home-eligible Medicaid clients. Each treatment's cost, utilization patterns, health impacts, and relative cost-effectiveness to one another will be analyzed.

Wisconsin Community Care Organization tests and demonstrates whether a comprehensive community-based system of coordinated home services can be developed which will prevent inappropriate institutionalization, improve the quality of life of the Medicaid elderly, and be less costly than institutional care. Three different demonstration sites will investigate whether case management, consisting of client assessment, development of a care plan, contracting for and coordinating appropriate services, and monitoring the appropriateness of the care plan, can help keep clients out of institutions, save money, and maintain client satisfaction. Their May, 1979 Interim

Report states that, to date, the cost of the experimental group is approximately $70 per month per client higher than the cost of institutional care, and the quality of life of the experimental group somewhat increased.

222 Experiments under the Social Security Act intended to discern whether homemaker and day care services should be covered under Medicare. Six different project sites — two day care, two homemaker, and two both day care and homemaker services — made these treatments available to Medicare clients in addition to regular Medicare benefits. The assignment to the treatment or control groups was random. Cost and utilization data were examined to ascertain the cost-effectiveness of these services as opposed to traditional Medicare long-term care benefits. The final report found that although those who received day care spent significantly fewer days in institutions than did the control group, the provision of those day care services cost almost twice as much. In addition, those who received only homemaker services had similar institutional experiences as did the control group while it cost 40 percent more to make such services available. For those clients who received both services, their institutionalization rates were again similar, and those services cost about 25 percent more than the traditional system.

One major conclusion to date is that most individuals requiring long-term care services need maintenance care for chronic illness rather than health or medical care. Thus, long-term care services should have a social and functional maintenance emphasis.

Research of the aging — *Redirecting the patient/client needs of the future*
Nurse researchers can make tremendous inroads in the area of long-term care. There are limitless opportunities for nurses through their research efforts (Abdellah, 1979).

Long-term studies needed in the biomedical area are:

1. Criteria for healthy and successful aging
2. Mutually interacting influences of aging and disease
3. Influence of cultural background on successful aging
4. Personal and economic costs of major diseases in old age
5. Prosthetic technology as an aid to the maintenance of an independent life.

Short-term investigations in the behavioral and social areas might include:

1. Social costs, system costs, and socioeconomic impact of an increased population of the old on communities, public and private services, and the old themselves
2. Advantages and disadvantages of flexible retirement policies to society as a whole and to the aged in particular
3. Occupational and social roles for older people
4. Adjustments to crises in the life cycle
5. Impact of income-maintenance programs

Long range projects that merit study are:

1. Relationships among family structure and support, life styles, and patterns of aging
2. Middle age as a transition to old age
3. Personality changes during life, from young adult to very old age
4. Improvement and maintenance of memory
5. Meaning and impact of the new age structure on American society.

The National Institute on Aging — Examples of major efforts in research

Genetics and aging
Life span is determined by the DNA (deoxyribonucleic acid) in genes; changes occur in the chromatin, which contains the genes. Such changes have recently been demonstrated. Researchers at the Gerontology Research Center (GRC) have found the DNA from chromatin in the cells of old animals is easier to split into pieces when it comes in contact with an enzyme (a kind of protein which speeds body processes) than DNA from chromatin in the cells of young animals. This would confirm that the structure of chromatin changes with age, strengthening the argument that aging is genetically determined.

An observation concerning changes associated with aging is that the rate of bodily repair deteriorates with age. Since the structure of DNA determines the structure of proteins in cells, the cell wall deteriorates if the DNA is damaged; such deterioration can be prevented if the damaged DNA can be repaired. Researchers at the University of California have found that the rate of repair DNA changes with age: damaged DNA from the cell of a young organism repaired far more readily than damaged DNA from the cell of an old organism. There is a relationship between the maximum longevity of a species and its ability to repair DNA. Species with longer life spans were found to have the ability to repair DNA more readily and more completely than species with shorter life spans (Eichhorn, 1979).

Genetic factors involved in intellectual levels in man and how these levels change with age are particularly significant issues. For instance, aged persons do less well than younger persons in registering, retrieving, and using information for problem-solving, and some of these age changes may have genetic components.

Other areas relevant to behaviour in late life include the study of those human diseases that are known to be inherited and that are characterized by premature aging such as Werner's syndrome, progeria, and Cockayne's syndrome. The role of genetic factors in senile dementias is also a particularly important area for research (DHEW, 1978).

Dementias of aging
Senility is probably a mixture of disease-derived changes coupled with less specific and poorly understood deteriorative changes associated with growing old. We now know that there are approximately one hundred, if not more, causes of 'senility', many of them reversible. They range from malnutrition to excessive medication, unrecognized congestive heart failure, walking pneumonia, to anemia. But there are presently severe irreversible organic brain diseases that develop among older people. One such condition is commonly called senile dementia or Alzheimer's disease and accounts for the presence of perhaps one-half of the 1.3 million persons in American nursing homes (DHEW, 1979). Alzheimer's disease and the dementias of aging are not the inevitable consequence of growing old; they represent pathologic disease states subject to investigation and treatment.

Approximately one million people over 65 suffer severe dementia with global intellectual deterioration and inability to carry out the normal tasks of daily living, while an additional two to three million are mildly or moderately affected. Chronic dementias account for about 50 percent of nursing home admissions at an estimated cost of $6 billion annually. Loss of productive members of society, disruption of families and loss of human dignity are among incalculable costs of chronic dementia. Demographic studies point to a rapidly escalating problem. By the year 2030 the population over 65 will have more than doubled and the annual cost of chronic care will be $30 billion, eight times the total amount now spent on all medical and mental health research.

Drugs and the elderly
An immediate contribution to the prevention of disabilities and institutionalization of the elderly is the support and conduct of

research in pharmacology and aging. Defining changes in physiology and learning and how they affect drug response in the elderly are new and important areas of pharmacologic research. The research has been carried out, in part, by identifying age differences in pharmacokinetics — a branch of pharmacology concerned with the rates of drug absorption, distribution, and elimination.

Age-related differences in body composition are reflected in differences in drug distribution. For example, two physiologic measurements of body composition which change with age are total body water and lean body mass: both are decreased in the elderly. In addition, body fat as a proportion of body weight decreases with age and, consequently, lean body mass as a percent of body weight decreases. The volume of plasma decreases slightly with age.

Between ages 20 and 80 there is, normally, an average decline of 35 percent in kidney function. Therefore, there is need for caution with drugs eliminated by the kidney since these drugs will accumulate in elderly individuals if appropriate adjustments in dosage interval and dosage level are not made.

Geriatric pharmacology will doubtless profit from the current interest in epidemiology and health care research. There is a need for additional objective information about drug use and adverse drug reactions in chronic care facilities (Vestal, 1979). Foerst conducted a study of drug prescribing patterns in skilled nursing facilities which documents the excessive use of drugs in the care of the elderly (Foerst, 1979).

Behavioral research
Intelligence and creativity. High intellectual abilities are observed at all ages, and age is not as highly correlated with intellectual ability as are experimental factors such as level of education. Large differences exist between individuals, with some persons showing marked declines in old age, but others showing little. One problem is to identify the factors that produce these differences: poor health, social isolation, economic disadvantage, limited education, or lowered motivation. Speed of response, for example, may be closely related to physiological processes and may accordingly decline with age, while verbal abilities, which improve with increased learning over a lifetime, may improve with age.

Neurological basis of behavior. Age-related changes in the structure and function of the nerve cell and of the nervous system are little understood, to say nothing of the relations between such changes and the psychological and social behavior of an aging individual.

The study of the brain and behavior is now in the forefront of scientific activity. Because of its special relevance to the field of aging, it is an area in which research support is particularly important. Behavioral, as well as medical, interventions directed at the maintenance of intellectual functioning and at the prevention of organic brain syndromes should receive high priority.

Sensory perception. Loss of hearing is a significant problem for older persons and is often associated with changes in personality and adaptation. Changes in hearing sensitivity may be due not only to physiological degeneration, but also to environmental influences, such as long exposure to noise (DHEW, 1978).

Uses of biofeedback with the elderly. The use of behavior therapy in the treatment of medical problems is not new. In behavior therapy, a specific problem that may involve several bodily functions is treated. Biofeedback is a kind of behavior therapy in which one specific bodily function is treated. It describes the process by which data obtained from a specific body function are given back to the subject through visual or auditory displays. Biofeedback has been used to control heart rate and to lower high blood pressure. Most of the studies of the applications of biofeedback to medicine are still at the laboratory stage. Two applications significant in treating medical problems of the elderly are now practical and have been successfully used with patients.

Patients with neurological disorders caused by stroke have been rehabilitated through the use of biofeedback. One of the most recent examples is in the treatment of foot drop, a condition in which the foot is extended because of muscle paralysis, following stroke. With these foot drop patients, biofeedback training in conjunction with physical therapy resulted in a degree of improvement at least twice as great as that obtained with physical therapy alone.

Another application of biofeedback that is now practical was developed at the NIH's Gerontology Research Center and is being used in treating incontinence. A significant number of older people are put into nursing homes because they are incontinent. Although urinary incontinence is more common, fecal incontinence is a significant problem and is socially very debilitating (Engel, 1979).

Nutrition and the elderly
Proper nutrition throughout life has been suggested as one of the best means of minimizing degenerative changes as well as increasing life span. Research in this area has been limited.

Little is known about the influence of nutrients taken in early life upon health in later life. Nor is much known about the health consequences of changes in food habits that may occur later in life. In order to study these areas, longitudinal studies are needed. Such studies help to define the degree of correlation that exists, over time, between individuals' health and their dietary intake. A longitudinal study, done in California over a 4-year period, found higher mortality among older subjects who had reported lower intakes of vitamin A and vitamin C.

There is need for research to establish cause-effect relationships between nutrient intake, clinical disorders, and biochemical measurements (such as vitamin levels in cells) in older people; frequently, a given clinical disorder, usually associated with nutrient deficiency, may be the result of the aging process rather than a lack of nutrients (Schlenker, 1979).

Studies of older women

● More longitudinal studies are needed of many aspects of women's lives, but such research needs to be anchored in the relevant social, economic and political events of the times
● Historical and anthropological research can provide both a cross-cultural perspective as well as valuable information about the plasticity of the human aging experience
● Network analyses, of the examination of the interpersonal connections between older women and their kin, friends, community and society, are needed to understand both the social lives of older women and the support available to them (DHEW, 1979).

INTERNATIONAL EFFORTS IN THE FIELD OF AGING

By the year 2000, the number of people in the world aged 60 and over will double to reach a figure of 580 million. Sixty percent of them will reside in developing countries.

While no boundaries apply to the equal rights of the world's elderly to physical, mental, and social well-being, scarce resources to meet these humanitarian needs must be based on scientifically sound and socially accepted principles.

United Nations and World Health Organization— Developments in aging

The World Health Assembly (WHA), the governing body of the World Health Organization (WHO). has worked for two years to develop strategies aimed toward attaining socially and economically productive lives for all the world's people. This was specifically expressed in resolution WHA 30.43 by which the Thirtieth World Health Assembly decided that the main social target of governments and the World Health Organization (WHO) in the coming decades should be the attainment, by all citizens of the world by the year 2000, of a level of health that will permit them to lead to a socially and ecnomically productive life.

The WHA considered that the report of the International Conference on Primary Health Care held at ALMA-ATA, U.S.S.R., September 1978 and document A32/8 of the WHA Executive Board entitled, 'Formulation Strategies for Health for All by the Year 2000'. The Declaration resulting from the ALMA-ATA conference reaffirmed WHO's definition of health namely that '... health is a state of complete physical, mental and social well-being... and is a fundamental right...' of all the people of the world.

Further, the WHA recognized that primary health care was the key to achieving health care for all. Thus, the theme of 'primary health for all by the year 2000' evolved as the central theme of this year's WHA.

Primary health care was defined at the ALMA-ATA Conference as a practical approach to making essential health care universally accessible to individuals and families in an acceptable and affordable way and with their full participation (WHO, 1978). It means more than the extension of basic health services and includes social and developmental dimensions.

At the thirty-third session (September-December 1978) the United Nations General Assembly adopted a resolution calling for a 1982 World Assembly on the Elderly, a forum to launch an international action program aimed at guaranteeing economic and social security to older persons through attracting world-wide attention to the serious problems besetting a growing portion of populations of the world, and through development of well-designed policies and programs for the aging.

In May 1979 the World Health Organization adopted a Resolution on Health Care of the Elderly which called for collaboration with the United Nations World Assembly of the Elderly (See A). The WHO Director-General delegated the Copenhagen Regional Office the responsibility for WHO's four-year Global Program on Care of the Aged and for preparing WHO's contribution to the 1982. U.N. World Assembly on the Elderly.

Examples of issues that will be addressed in these WHO and UN activities in aging that will involve the National Institute on Aging (NIA) relate to the provision of alternative systems of health care; Studies of the physiological and pathological differences in aging as for example, pharmacological studies of the absorption, effectiveness, and metabolism of drugs; retaining or changing attitudes and behavior through education and dissemination of information; and geriatric medical training through the incorporation of basic biomedical, clinical, and social sciences in medical school curricula.

The Institute's involvement in these activities is expected to expand, particularly with respect to WHO plans to co-sponsor a meeting of technical and scientific experts and national planners and policy makers on the subjects of the WHO Global Programme on the Elderly and the U.N. World Assembly on the Elderly.

The NIA will also reconvene the Directors of Institutes of Gerontology to coincide with the 1981 White House Conference on Aging.

Pan American Health Organization
The staff of the NIA Epidemiology, Demography, and Biometry program meets with senior staff members of the Pan American Health Organization to informally exchange ideas and consider the development of protocols of mutual interest as they relate to biomedical, clinical, and social research problems of the aging and the elderly. The wide array of differences in urbanization and socioeconomic status throughout Latin America would offer a potential for study, in addition to the availability of genetic and ethnic data and defined elderly populations for studies of dementia. In addition to collaboration with PAHO, the Epidemiology, Demography, and Biometry Program informally exchanges data and working materials with nations such as England, Scotland, Australia, Sweden, Japan, Switzerland, Israel, France, and West Germany.

U.S.S.R. — U.S. cooperation
In December 1978, the NIA Director and Scientific Director were invited to visit and meet with U.S.S.R. leaders in the field of gerontology. Their itinerary included visits to areas of the Soviet Union reporting extremely long-lived populations and geriatric facilities in Moscow, Kiev, Tbilisi, Sukhumi, and Leningrad.

Efforts are being made to strengthen collaborative relationships between the NIA and its U.S.S.R. counterpart, the Institute of Gerontology of the Academy of medical Sciences in Kiev, and to obtain information on the longevous populations. The Kiev Institute coordinates U.S.S.R.-wide efforts in gerontological research. Programmatically, its research interests are in the areas concerned with middle years, the antecedents to longevity, the extension of a productive work life, and longevous people. Future plans call for the establishment of laboratories of evolutionary gerontology, gerophysiology, communal hygiene, radiology, and biophysics and rehabilitation.

Romania — U.S. cooperation

Collaborative efforts have also been initiated by NIA and the world's first National Institute of Gerontology and Geriatrics in Romania to explore conducting possible workshops on immunology and cancer, exchange of scientists, and Romania's participation in the Fogarty International Center Postdoctoral Fellowship Program.

Immunology and aging

The NIA convened in May 1979 over 60 prominent immunologists from the United States, Italy, and the Netherlands to consider a wide range of topics relevant to the immune system which plays a significant role in the many diseases associated with aging and in the aging process itself. The immune system protects the body by allowing it to distinguish between its own normal tissues and invading viruses, bacteria and aberrant (cancer) cells.

The major focus of this conference addressed the fact that a poorly functioning immune system can be a major cause of disability, disease and death among the elderly.

Also pertaining to the subject of immunology and aging is the initiation by the NIA Molecular and Biochemical Aging Program of a collaborative effort with the Hospital Necker of Paris, France, to obtain Serum Thymic Factor for use in an NIA-supported contract on Thymic Hormones being performed at the University of Alabama in Birmingham. There Serum Thymic Factor is being used in short- and long-term restorative studies in order to ascertain whether or not immune function in aging mice can be augmented by the Factor.

International Conference on Psychobiology of Aging

In May 1979 scientists from more than 13 nations participated in the Conference on the Psychobiology of Aging, held in Walferdange, Luxembourg. The NIA co-sponsored this conference which is the first in a series dealing with various aspects of aging. This represented a unique effort in assembling European and American investigators to bear on the question of behavior and anatomical changes that occur as organisms advance from one end of the developmental spectrum to the other. The meeting resulted in a number of new collaborative research efforts and anticipated plans for a follow-up meeting in the future to discuss the state of the art of research and theory in aging.

Fogarty Senior International Fellowship Program

In 1978, this Program received an added appropriation of $200 000 to be used in coordination with the NIA to provide fellowships for midlevel and senior scientists to share their expertise and gain career-enhancing experience in some of the most advanced geriatric centers of the world.

EDUCATION FOR LONG-TERM CARE

Education for long-term care needs to include consumers as well as providers. It is the consumer who must support long-term care, understand its benefits for themselves and their families and urge its inclusion in the total health care system.

Increased Federal support is now available for the preparation of primary care and geriatric nurse practitioners. All levels of personnel need to be prepared including the nurse's aide and orderly.

Gerontological nurse practitioners as change agents

Primary health care giver
At the University of Colorado School of Nursing Continuing Education Services, a group of nursing and medical professionals proposed that the professional nurse be a 'primary' health care giver for many elderly clients (Heppler, 1976). Their recommendations were accepted and in 1976 were implemented by the School of Nursing Continuing Education Services. The program was specifically designed to meet the health needs of the elderly and built on the premise that the aging process, although accompanied by many chronic diseases, is not an illness but a normal process of living. Emphasis in the program is placed in age-related differences in the total care of the elderly recognizing the strong phychosocial factors that impinge on the person as he or she ages.

Family-centered (primary) care
The Administrator and Board of Trustees of Family Hospital, Milwaukee, Wisconsin made a commitment to the consumers of health services to provide the best patient care at the lowest cost. This was achieved over a three-year period by changing all direct patient care nursing visits into interrelating family-centered (primary) nursing system (Arnsdorf, 1977). The system of family-centered care provided more continuity of care, increased patient comfort level, more opportunity to meet teaching needs, more individualized care and more complete assessment of patient needs.

Geriatric nurse practitioner (GNP)
There are now a variety of educational programs that prepare nurses to assume the expanded role of GNP ranging from short-term programs to masters level preparation.

The Geriatric Nurse Practitioner Program Division of Continuing Education, Cornell University New York Hospital School of Nursing provides a one year continuing education program for RNs with at least two years of experience in nursing. Co-Investigators are Eleanor Lambertsen, Dean, School of Nursing and Dr Fletcher McDowell, Medical Director of Burke Rehabilitation Center, White Plains. Doris Schwartz and Dr Arthur Seligman serve as co-program directors.

The linkage with Burke Rehabilitation Center focuses on rehabilitation because of functional disability. This facility includes a 150 capacity day hospital and 175 bed inpatient facility.

The program includes an 18 weeks didactic teaching plus the assignment of a physician/nurse team to every four students. During the second semester students return to the sponsoring agency. The sponsoring agency pays 18 weeks salary plus expenses of the necessary medical backup during internship.

Another innovative program is the Geriatric Nurse Practitioner Program at the University of Rochester designed to prepare gerontological clinical nurse specialists at the masters level. The program is based on the functional concept of wellness — illness. The three clinical semesters (the first semester is a common core to all concentrations and includes research, social sciences, and physiology) starts with the essentially well elderly in the community, the subsequent semester is focused on the ill elderly at home and in institutions, and the last semester is a leadership opportunity to explore the clinical specialist role in a variety of settings and functions.

Clincial experience includes senior citizen and neighbourhood centers, nutrition sites, clients' homes, long-term and acute care institutions.

The nurse in an HMO

An example of this type of nurse is described by Wagner at the Harvard Community Health Plan where nurses provide direct care for individual patients and families (Wagner, 1974). They are considered vital members of the primary health team and render much of the primary care. The goal is to provide a single level of health care to all members. A strength of this HMO is its organized nursing service. A breadth of services are provided including home health services.

A related program is currently being sponsored by the Robert Wood Johnson Foundation in which the program will help cities provide medical care in neighbourhoods where currently there are not enough doctors (Johnson, 1975, 1977). Each site must offer to adults and children general medical care and preventive services. The intent of the program is to help a few cities demonstrate alternative ways to use better municipal resources in meeting the general care needs of residents in neighbourhoods. The Foundation is also supporting a related 'Rural Practice Project' designed to develop medical practice models that meet the health needs of the communities and must build these practices to overcome professional isolation. Nurses need to be fully involved in these projects as nurses too are affected by careers in rural practice.

Appendix to Chapter 1

THIRTY-SECOND WORLD HEALTH ASSEMBLY

Collaboration with The United Nations System — General Matters

Health Care of the Elderly

The Thirty-second World Health Assembly,

Having noted the resolution adopted by the Thirty-third Session of the United Nations General Assembly (Resolution 33/52), deciding to organize a World Assembly on the Elderly in 1982;

Recognizing the leadership role of WHO in the health care of the elderly, and in the hope that the United Nations will invite WHO to take a prominent role in organizing the Assembly;

Knowing that both the absolute number and proportion of older people are increasing in all regions of the world, while at the same time health and social support services are either lacking or deficient and need to be developed further;

Believing that by the year 2000 the populations of the developing nations and developed nations of the world will have increased significantly and thus will have to envisage critical problems in the promotion of health, economic and social policy;

Considering that attention must be given to prevention in the social, economic and health spheres, starting with young people, to develop lifelong patterns that will help avoid debilitating conditions of old age;

Considering that in addition to family care alternatives must go beyond institutional care, such as home care, day care and ambulatory care to greatly improve the quality of life of the elderly;

Noting also that the World Health Assembly on the Elderly will focus attention on the health, social and economic needs of the elderly;

1. *Requests* the Director-General to:

(1) continue to support the important efforts in this area already under way by WHO, and to mobilize the extra resources, both budgetary and extrabudgetary, which will be required;

(2) undertake activities in collaboration with the United Nations and other agencies for appropriate participation in the Assembly;

(3) consider the selection of 'Health of the Aged' as the theme for World Health Day, 1982;

(4) take appropriate measures to maximize the activity of the Global Programme, which is aimed at improving the health care and health status of the older populations of all nations;

(5) make use of present information systems to obtain and disseminate information on health problems and care of the aged;

(6) promote activities for determining effective approaches for providing health care to the elderly, including integration into primary health care;

(7) encourage comparative studies which provide a better understanding of the ways in which the elderly differ in physiological and pathological functions, as, for example, in absorption, effectiveness and metabolism or excretion of drugs;

(8) encourage studies of the life histories of healthy elderly to promote understanding of the factors able to prevent sickness and disability in later life;

(9) encourage participation by WHO in workshops and conferences composed of representatives of national government and international organizations for the purpose of discussing alternatives to institutional care for providing social security and minimum incomes, housing, health care, including maintenance of physical activity, meals, homemaker services, transportation and other needed services;

(10) transmit to the Secretary-General of the United Nations the text of the present resolution, with a view to ensuring that WHO assumes an appropriate role in the preparations for the World Assembly;

(11) report to the sixty-fifth session of the Executive Board and the Thirty-third World Health Assembly on the status of the preparations undertaken for the World Assembly;

2. *Urges* Member States to:

(1) undertake similar actions in their nations;

(2) explore alternative services and systems of health care for the elderly including arrangements for optimum coordination between them;

(3) promote activities and programmes that may help individuals to get prepared in time for later life;

(4) encourage efforts directed at retaining or changing attitudes and behaviour among some segments of the population toward the elderly, particularly education of families and communities with a view to accepting the elderly as an integrated part of the community;

(5) promote the development of informational materials including a glossary of terms about the elderly that can be widely disseminated;

(6) emphasize through local medical and health-related groups the importance of diagnosis of problems that if not treated can contribute to long-term debilitating problems in the elderly;

(7) take measures to have health professional schools include appropriate content on aging in basic clinical and social science courses that integrate knowledge about aging and the problems of the elderly, thus helping to assure an early commitment in the areas of prevention and gerontology.

REFERENCES

Abdellah F G 1979 PACE: An approach to improving the care of the elderly. American Journal of Nursing 79: 1109-1110

Abdellah F G, Levine E 1979 Better patient care through nursing research, 2nd edn. Macmillian, New York

Adams D L 1969 Analysis of a life satisfaction index. Journal of Gerontology 24: 470-474

Anderson N N, Patten S K, Greenberg J N 1979 A comparison of in-home and nursing home care for older persons in Minnesota. Hubert H Humphrey Institute of Public Affairs, University of Minnesota, Minneapolis

Arnsdorf M B 1977 Perceptions of primary nursing in a family-centered care setting. Nursing Administration Quarterly 1: 97-105

Bloom M, Blenkner M 1970 Assessing functioning of older persons living in the community. The Gerontologist Part 1: 31-37

Bradshaw J 1977 The concept of social need. In: Gilbert N, Specht H (eds) Planning for social welfare: Issues, models, and tasks. Prentice-Hall, Englewood Cliffs, New Jersey, p 290-296

Brietung J 1980 The geriatric care manual: Processes and procedures for nurses, health assistants, and home health aides. Tiresias Press, New York

Brickner P W 1978 Home health care for the aged: How to help older people stay in their own homes and out of institutions. Appleton-Century-Crofts, New York

Brodly E M, Kleban M H, Lawton M P, Silverman H A 1971 Excess disabilities of mentally impaired aged: Impact of individualized treatment. The Gerontologist 11: 124-133

Burnside I M (ed) 1976 Nursing in the aged. McGraw-Hill, New York

Butler 1975 Personal communication

Caro F G 1973 The personal care organization: An approach to the maintenance of the disabled in the community. Working paper, Levinson Gerontological Policy Institute, Brandeis University, Boston

Cohen 1977 Personal communication

Copeland J R M, Kelleher M J, Kellett J M, Gourlay A J, Barron G, Cowan D W, De Gruchy J (U.K. Team) Gurland B J, Sharpe L, Simon R, Suriansky J and Stiller P (U.S.A. Team) 1974 Diagnostic differences in psychogeriatric patients in London and New York: United Kingdom-United States diagnostic project. Canadian Psychiatric Association Journal 19: 267-271

Copeland J R M, Kelleher M J, Kellett J M, Gourlay A J (U.K. Team) Gurland B J, Fleiss J L, Sharpe L (U.S.A. Team) 1976 A Semi-structured clinical interview for the assessment of diagnosis and mental state in the elderly: The geriatric mental state schedule I development and reliability, Psychological medicine 6: 439-449

Department of Health, Education, and Welfare 1975 Long-term care facility improvement study. U.S. Government Printing Office, Washington, DC, 017-001-00397-2

Department of Health, Education, and Welfare, PHS, Division of Long Term Care, HRA 1977 The future of long-term care in the United States — The report of the task force. National Conference on Social Welfare, Washington, DC, U.S. Department of Commerce, NTIS, HRP-0016874

Heppler J 1976 Gerontological nurse practitioner: Change agents in the health care delivery systems for the aged. Journal of Gerontological Nursing 2: 38-40

Department of Health, Education, and Welfare, PHS, NIH 1978 Our future selves: A research plan toward understanding aging (Report of the panel on behavioral and social sciences research, national advisory countil on aging). U.S. Government Printing Office, Washington, DC, DHEW Publication No. (NIH) 78-1444, p 1-2, 5-7

Department of Health, Education, and Welfare 1978 Patient care management theory to practice. Health Care Financing Administration, Washington, DC

Department of Health, Education, and Welfare National Center for Health Services Research 1979 TRIAGE, INC. An alternative approach to care for the elderly 1974-1979. (Summary Report of Project Triage supported by Connecticut department on aging, Hartford, Connecticut and DHEW, NCHST Grant No. HS0256), Hyattsville, Maryland

Department of Health, Education, and Welfare. State agencies' mechanisms in handling patient relocations. Annotated bibliography transfer trauma in long-term care 1980. Health Care Financing Administration (Contract No. HCFA-79-HSQB-59/JR) Baltimore, Maryland

Department of Health, Education, and Welfare, PHS, NIH 1979 The older woman: Continuities and discontinuities (Report of the national institute on aging and the national institute of mental health workshop, September 14-16, 1978). NIH Publication No. 79-1897, U.S. Government Printing Office, Washington, DC, p 7-8

Department of Health, Education, and Welfare 1979 Long-term health care minimum data set. National Center for Health Statistics, Public Health Service, Hyattsville, Maryland

Donaldson S W, Wagner C C, Gresham G E 1973 A unified ADL evaluation form. Archives of Physical Medicine and Rehabilitation 54: 1975-1980

Eichhorn G L 1979 Aging: Genetics and the environment (National institute on aging science writer seminar series). DHEW, PHS, NIH Publication No. 79-1450, U.S. Government Printing Office, Washington, DC

Eliopoulos C 1979 Gerontological nursing. Harper Row, New York

Ellwood P M, Jr 1966 Quantitative measurement of patient care quality. Part 1 — Measures of care. Hospitals. Journal of the American Hospital Association 40: 42-45

Ellwood P M, Jr 1966 Quantitative measurement of patient care quality. Part 2 — A system for identifying meaningful factors. Hospitals. Journal of the American Hospital Association 40: 59-63

Engel B T 1979 Using biofeedback with the elderly (National institute on aging science writer seminar series). DHEW, PHS, NIH Publication No. 79-1404, U.S. Government Printing Office, Washington, DC

Fanshel S, Bush J W 1970 A health status index and its application to health services outcomes. Operations Research 18: 1021-1066

Foerst H V 1979 Drug prescribing patterns. American Journal of Nursing 79: 2002-2003

Ford A B, Katz S, Downs T D, Adams M 1971 Results of long-term home nursing: The influence of disibiliy. Journal of Chronic Diseases 24: 591-596

General Services Administration, National Archives and Records Service, Office of the Federal Register 1979 National long-term care channeling demonstration program, intent to initiate program. Federal Register 44: 75720-23

Goldfarb A I 1969 Predicting mortality in the institutionalized aged. Archives of General Psychiatry 21: 172-176

Grauer H, Birnbom F 1975 A geriatric functional rating scale to determine the need for institutional care. Journal of the American Geriatrics Society XXIII: 472-476

Gunter L, Estes C 1979 Education for gerontic nursing. Springer, New York

Gurel L, Linn M W, Linn B S 1972 Physical and mental impairment-of-function evaluation in the aged: The PAMIE scale. Journal of Gertontology 27: 83-90

Gurland B, Copeland J, Sharpe L, Kelleher M 1976 The geriatric mental status interview (GMS). International Journal of Aging and Human Development 7: 303-311

Gurland B, Kuriansky J, Sharpe L, Simon R, Stiller P, Birkett P 1977-78 The comprehensive assessment and referral evaluation (CARE) — Rationale, development and reliability. International Journal of Aging and Human Development 8: 9-42

Gurland B J, Fleiss J L, Goldberg K, Sharpe L (U.S. Team), Copeland J R M, Kelleher M J, Kellett J M 1976 A Semi-structured clinical interview for the assessment of diagnosis and mental state in the elderly: The geriatric mental state schedule II A factor analysis. Psychological Medicine 6: 451-459

Haber L D 1967 Identifying the disabled: Concepts and methods in measurement of disability. Social Security Bulletin, p 17-14

Hebrew Rehabilitation Center for the Aged, Social Gerontological Research Department, Sherwood S 1977 Selected listing of standardized scales, including scoring system and other pertinent data. Boston, Massachusetts

Iversen I A, Edwards N, Tjelta G 1967 A study of the inter-rater reliability of the Kenny self-care evaluation. Sister Kenny Institute (previously known as the American Rehabilitation Foundation) Minneapolis, Minnesota

Iversen I A, Silberberg N E, Stever R C, Schoening H A 1973 The revised Kenny self-care evaluation — A numerical measure of independence in activities of daily living. Publication Department 63, Sister Kenny Institute, Minneapolis, Minnesota

Jones E W, McNitt B J, McKnight E M 1973 Patient classification for long-term care: User's manual U.S. Department of Health, Education, and Welfare, PHS, NCHSR, Hyattsville, Maryland

Kahn R 1 1971 Psychological aspects of aging In: Clinical geriatrics. Lippincott, Philadelphia

Kahn R L, Goldfarb A I, Pollack M, Peck A 1960 Brief objective measures for the determination of mental status in the aged. American Journal of Psychiatry 117: 326-328

Kahn R L, Goldfarb A I, Pollack M, Gerber I E The relationship of mental and physical status in institutionalized aged persons. American Journal of Psychiatry 117: 120-124

Katz S, Downs T D, Cash H R, Grotz R C 1970 Progress in the development of the index of ADL. The Gerontologist 10: 20-30

Katz S, Ford A B, Chinn A B, Newill V A 1966 Part II, Long-term course of 159 patients. Medicine 45: 236-246

Katz S, Ford A B, Heiple K G, Newill V A 1964 Studies of illness in the aged: Recovery after fracture of the hip. Journal of Gerontology 19: 285-293

Katz S, Ford A B, Moskowitz R W, Jackson B, Jaffe M 1963 Studies of illness in the aged: The index of ADL, A standardized measure of biological and psychosocial function. Journal of the American Medical Association 185: 914:919

Katz S, Vignos P J, Moskowitz R W, Thompson H M, Svec K H 1968 Comprehensive outpatient care in rheumatoid arthritis. Journal of the American Medical Association 206: 1249-1254

Kelleher M, Copeland J, Gurland B, Sharpe L 1976 Assessment of the older psychiatric inpatient. International Journal of Aging and Human Development 7: 295-302

Koshel J J, Granger C V 1978 Rehabilitation terminology: Who is severely disabled? Rehabilitation Literature 39: 102-106

Kovar M G 1978 Elderly people: The population 65 years and over, Health, United States 1976-1977 DHEW Publication No. (HRA) 77-1232, Hyattsville, Maryland, ch 1

Kuriansky J B, Gurland B J, Fleiss J L, Cowan D 1976 The assessment of self-care capacity in geriatric psychiatric patients by objective and subjective methods. Journal of Clinical Psychology 32: 95-102

Kutner B, Fanshel D, Togo A M, Langner T S 1956 Five hundred over sixty. A community survey on aging. Russell Sage Foundation, New York

Lawton M P, Brody E M 1969 Assessment of older people: Self maintaining and instrumental activities of daily living. The Gerontologist 9: 179-186

Lawton M P 1971 The functional assessment of elderly people. Journal of the American Geriatrics Society XIX: 465-481

Lawton M P 1975 The Philadelphia geriatric center morale scale: A revision. Journal of Gerontology 30: 85-89

Leininger M M (ed) 1979 Transcultural nursing. Masson, New York

Linn M W 1975 A rapid disability rating scale. Journal of the American Geriatrics Society 15: 211-214

Linn M W, Gurel L 1969 Initial reactions to nursing home placement. Journal of the American Geriatrics Society 17: 219-223

Linn M W, Gurel L, Linn B S 1977 Patient outcome as a measure of quality of nursing home care. American Journal of Public Health 67: 337-344

Linn M W, Linn B S, Greenwald S R 1972 The alcoholic patient in the nursing home. Aging and Human Development 3: 273-277

Linn B S, Linn M W, Gurel L 1968 The cumulative illness rating scale. Journal of the American Geriatrics Society 16: 622-626

Lowenthal M F 1964 Lives in distress. Basic Books, New York

Mahoney F I, MaCallum J A, Wood O H, Barthel D W 1961 Rehabilitation of the chronically ill in the state of Maryland. Southern Medical Journal, Journal of the Southern Medical Association 54: 600-605

McKnight E M 1972 Nursing home research study. Quantitative measurement of nursing services. DHEW Publication No. (NIH) 72-223, Bethesda, Maryland

Meer B, Baker J A 1966 The Stockton geriatric rating scale. Journal of Gerontology 21: 392-403

Meer B, Krag C L 1964 Correlates of disability in a population of hospitalized geriatric patients. Journal of Gerontology 19: 440-446

Miller W R, Hurley S J, Wharton E 1976 External peer review of skilled nursing care in Minnesota. American Journal of Public Health 66: 278-283

Mitchell J B 1978 Patient outcomes in alternative long-term care settings. Medical Care 16: 439-452

Morris J N, Sherwood S 1975 A retesting and modification of the Philadelphia geriatric morale scale. Journal of Gerontology 30: 77-84

Murray R B, Zentner J P 1979 Nursing assessment and health promotion through the life span, 2nd edn. Prentice-Hall, New Jersey

Nagi S A 1976 An epidemiology of disability among adults in the United States. Health and Society, Milbank Memorial Quarterly Fall: 439-466

Neugarten B, Havighurst R, Tobin S 1961 The measurement of life satisfaction. Journal of Gerontology 16: 134-143

Pfeiffer E 1975 A short portable mental status questionnaire for the assessment of organic brain deficit in elderly patients. Journal of the American Geriatrics Society XXIII: 433-441

Pfeiffer E (ed) 1975 Multidimensional functional assessment: the OARS methodology, a manual. Center for the Study of Aging and Human Development Duke University, Durham, North Carolina

Plutchik R H, Lieberman C M, Baker M, Grossman J, Lehrman N 1979 Reliability and validity of a scale for assessing the functioning of geriatric patients. Journal of the American Geriatrics Society 18: 491-500

Reinhardt A M, Quinn M D (eds) 1979 Current practice in gerontological nursing, vol I. Mosby, St Louis

Robert Wood Johnson Foundation 1977 Municipal health services program. The Foundation, Princeton, New Jersey

Robert Wood Johnson Foundation 1975 The rural practice project. The Foundation, Princeton, New Jersey

Rosow I, Breslau N 1966 A Guttman health scale for the aged. Journal of Gerontology 21: Free Press, New York

Sarno J E, Sarno M T, Levita E 1973 The functional life scale. Archives of Physical Medicine and Rehabilitation 54: 214-220

Schlenker E D 1979 Effect of nutrition status on human life span. Nutrition and Aging (National institute on aging science writer seminar series), DHEW, PHS, NIH Publication No. 79-1409, U.S. Government Printing Office, Washington, DC

Shanas E 1968 Health and incapacity in later life. In: Shanas E, Townsend P, Wedderburn D, Friis H, Milhoj P, Stehouwer J (eds) Old people in three industrial societies. Lieber-Atherton, New York, p 18-48

Sherwood C C, Morris J N 1975 Strategies for research and innovation. In: Sherwood S (ed) Long-term care: A handbook for researchers, planners and providers, p 639-724

Sherwood S, Morris J N, Mor V, Gutkin C 1977 Compendium of measures for describing and assessing long term care populations. Hebrew Rehabilitation Center for the Aged, Boston, Massachusetts

Spitzer R L, Fleiss J L, Burdock E I, Hardesty A S 1964 The mental status schedule: Rationale, reliability and validity. Comprehensive Psychiatry 5: 381-395

Vestal R E 1979 Drugs and the elderly. (National institute of aging science writer seminar series), DHEW, PHS, NIH Publication No. 79-1449, U.S. Government Printing Office, Washington, DC

Wagner D 1974 Nursing in an HMO. American Journal of Nursing 74: 236-240

World Health Organization ALMA-ATA 1978 Primary health care: Report of the international conference on primary health care. ALMA-ATA U.S.S.R. World Health Organization, Geneva, Switzerland

2   Anne J. Davis

Ethical issues in gerontological nursing

Introduction
Ethics, as a discipline, deals with such concepts as rights, obligations, duties, autonomy, justice, beneficence and examines the ways in which we make our ethical decisions. Bioethics, or applied ethics, focuses on the ethical dilemmas in the health care arena and specifically deals with the interrelated issues of: 1) clinical decisions, 2) resource allocation, 3) research with human subjects, and 4) health policy. Bioethics does not provide us with easy answers but rather serves to structure the discourse on these issues.

Ethical reasoning
We, as individuals and as a society, have ordered sets of moral standards and rules of conduct so that when we refer to them and add factual knowledge of a given situation in which ethical choices exist, we can determine for that situation what we ought to do. A pluralistic society presents some built-in ethical stresses and strains between and among various individuals and groups since they may ethically reason using different ethical theories and thereby reach different conclusions. Additionally, discourse on ethical dilemmas can begin with different basic premises or philosophical presuppositions so that differences in basic definitions and values exist from the outset of the discourse. Whether to define and value the fetus as a person or not is such a case in point.

    Two normative ethical systems are widely discussed and defended in contemporary Western moral philosophy: utilitarianism and ethical formalism or deontology.

    Utilitarianism holds that an action is morally right either if a person's doing it brings about good consequences, or if the action is of a kind which, if everyone did it, would have good consequences. Utilitarianism says that an act is right when it is useful in bringing about a desirable or good end, an end that has instrinsic value. In this ethical theory, the right depends on the good. Something is right because it brings about good, and to be right, it *must* bring about good.

There are many complex questions in this ethical theory which remain beyond this discussion, such as how are we to determine the good in every case, and good for whom?

The other ethical system, called formalism or deontology, holds that an action is right if it accords with a moral rule. In this case moral rules are based on an ultimate principle of duty. So it is not the goodness or badness of the consequences of an action that makes it right or wrong here. In deontology, it is possible for an action to be morally right, even if it does not promote the greatest possible balance of good over evil for self, society, or the universe. In deciding what is the right action from this perspective, one's special status or position comes into play.

Some moral philosophers hold that the grounds for right conduct are both utilitarian and deontological, and that there is no single supreme principle from which, ultimately, the moral rightness or wrongness of every action can be derived. We are interested in both the means and end of our ethical behavior. According to this view, ethical pluralism, the moral reasons for or against some action lie in the consequences of those actions, while moral reasons governing other actions arise from their being of a kind required or prohibited by a rule of duty or obligation. Ethical pluralists argue that both sorts of reasons, in fact, can apply to one and the same action.

Cultural and historical value of longevity

Several important cultural and historical themes are present in our value of longevity. Throughout the development of Western civilization, complaints over the pains and disabilities of old age have coexisted with exortations to virtuous resignation and praise for old people who lead lives of strength and dignity. Generally speaking, older people receive more esteem in a society when they can continue to function in the roles of adult life.

Through the late Middle Ages both religious and humanistic ideals regarding the proper social role for the elderly mixed easily with one another. With the advent of Protestantism and especially Puritanism in the U.S.A., however, the social role of the elderly became identified as a continuous participation in the roles of adult life. Never entirely absent from Western cultural ideals, activism reasserted itself over more contemplative models of aging. Such contemplative models permitted people to serve as deposits of cultural wisdom thereby maintaining a valued social role.

Social structure has enormous impact on values. In the West, first England and then the U.S.A. and Canada, became industrialized within a capitalistic philosophy, the dominance of economic factors over all other social factors became a prime element in social definition including the role of the elderly. The dominant value of job-related social roles resulted to the extent that one's very identity became identified with one's work. Around 1900 when the average life span in many Western countries was approximately 47 years, this definition of personal worth had different social consequences than it does today. Today, we have systematically excluded the elderly and have in part ghettoized them. Although there has been some shift away from identity and worth tied to the work role, a less problematic old age will demand a change in social attitudes reflecting an appreciation of leisure and acceptance of personal goals which do not function to primarily maintain the economic order.

The larger social structure emphasizing the economic order assumes that freedom means mastery and independence. This belief makes it difficult to accept the dependency and losses which often accompany growing older (Christiansen, 1978).

Ethical analysis of selected problems of older adults
Autonomy
Automony, a form of personal liberty of action in which individuals determine their own course of action in accordance with a plan chosen by themselves, is a supreme value in Western philosophical tradition. Autonomous persons deliberate about and choose a plan and are capable of acting on the basis of these deliberations. A person's autonomy is his self-reliance, independence, and self-contained ability to decide. Autonomy implies being one's own person that is, deciding and acting without constraints either by another's action or by psychological, physical, or social limitations. It is one thing to be autonomous but quite another to be *respected* as an autonomous agent. When we respect autonomous agents, we recognize with due appreciation their own considered value judgments and outlooks even when we believe that their judgments are mistaken. Respecting others in this way acknowledges their right to their own views and the permissibility of their actions based on such beliefs. To grant them this right means that they are entitled to such autonomous determination without limitations on their liberty being imposed by others (Beauchamp & Childress, 1979).

Our general aversion to dependency and to the burdens it can create often leads to undue loss of dignity for older people. Ethics and bioethics attempt to ensure that dependency does not turn into humiliation since a correlation between being respected and aging with dignity has been established. Preempting the elderly's responsibility for their decisions is a serious infringement on their rights.

Concept of personhood
It may seem strange to speak of persons as ends although many Western philosophers have done so. As ends, persons are valuable in themselves and not valuable merely as means or for what they can do for another. Something has intrinsic value when it is valued as an end in itself and not as a means to some further end. The idea of intrinsic value applied to persons says that we ought to treat persons as valuable in themselves and this in turn is referred to in moral philosophy as respect for persons. But what do we mean in concrete terms by personhood? This question, and the answer we derive for it, has serious consequences for all vulnerable populations including the older adult and especially the infirm, institutionalized older adult. There are numerous ways to violate the autonomy, central to personhood of a person. Paternalism, the use of coercion to achieve a good that is not recognized as such by those individuals for whom the good is intended has been identified as one way in which health professionals violate autonomy of patients and clients (Beauchamp, 1977). Because coercing a person for his own good denies him a status as a person, we can and ought to strongly question its use. Many older adults are extremely vulnerable to paternalistic actions from those in, or perceived to be in, power or decision making roles.

Ethics and the care of the elderly

Despite the increased interest in aging on the part of researchers and clinicians over the past 20 years, little concern has focused on the ethical issues involved in social policy planning and health care delivery for this group. The remainder of this chapter attempts to identify the potential ethical issues involved in the decision-making regarding where and from whom an ill, elderly parent should receive care: at home or in an institution? This, can be defined as one of the key overriding ethical questions in gerontology.

There are three main ethical issues to be considered by families, health care professionals, and policy planners when thinking about the problem of home versus institutional care: 1) The lack of an adequate knowledge base for decision-making, 2) respect for persons, and 3) distributive justice.

Knowledge base
Despite the recent dramatic increase in the amount of literature published about older adults, there is a paucity of studies reflecting a balance between the social gerontological model and the medical model approach to aging. Much of the social gerontological literature seemed biased toward a rosy picture of aging as a growth process.

When viewed as a reaction to the earlier biological disintegration approach, this more positive orientation becomes understandable; however, by omission it underemphasizes the problems of aging such as loss of strength, cohorts, and chronic illness. The traumatic impact of institutionalization on the elderly individual has been well documented in the literature (Kayser-Jones, 1981; Townsend, 1971). Institutionalization results in decreases in physical and mental functioning and death. These consequences of institutionalization for the older adult must be weighted against the, as yet undetermined, impact of caregiving on other family members. Specific to the problem under discussion, predictors of family success at caregiving, familial coping styles, types of assistance obtained by families from non-traditional, non-institutional sources, decision-making about institutionalization, assessment of available services, and the emotional impact of transferring caregiving activities to an institution are areas which require more in-depth exploration.

With a better knowledge base about caregiving and institutionalization, decisions regarding where the ill parent should be cared for and who should assume the caregiving functions could be made more rationally, and more ethically. At present, these decisions are often made on an emotional level, with few avenues available for a cognitive appraisal of the situation and little support through the emotional trauma of the action.

Respect for persons

The second ethical issue related to the caregiving of an ill parent is that of 'respect of persons'. Mentioned earlier, this ethical principle is defined as 'active sympathy coupled with a sense of moral obligation, a duty to be concerned about the welfare of any and every person, for no reason other than that he is a person and thus has intrinsic worth' (Maclagan, 1960). This principle will be applied to several issues related to the phenomenon of offspring caring for sick elderly parents. Several questions are important to consider: Is there an obligation to provide care for a sick elderly person? What is the source of that obligation? Who is responsible for providing the care? Who has rights in decision-making? Under what circumstances can the familial obligation be ethically terminated?

Using the principle of respect for persons the conclusion is drawn that there is an obligation to care for a sick elderly person. As a person of intrinsic worth, he has a right to care. Traditionally, it was the children who gave care to the elderly person. At a time of less geographic and occupational mobility and higher early mortality rates, the extended family functioned well in the care-giving role. Fewer families were affected by prolonged chronic illness in elderly parents and community/neighborhood support was more common than today.

The assumption of caregiving responsibilities by family members is frequently done on emotional grounds which acts to create guilt in the family. Whether the offspring has a moral obligation to care for his elderly parents is a difficult question to answer. Does the care given to the child obligate the child to the parent's care? Has the obligation changed under the present societal conditions? Many families do not live near their parents since employment and career opportunities, or lack of them, frequently cause children to live at some distance from the parent.

A pervading attitude among citizens supports the belief that the state should assume at least part of the responsibility for the care of the older adult. However, despite these societal attitudes and changes, surveys indicate that many children do assume responsibility for the care of their parents (Shanas, 1967). This responsibility is often carried out at considerable cost to the caregiver and his or her family.

Distributive justice

Some ethicists believe that society has the responsibility of providing support and care to its elderly members. This is justified by the principle of distributive justice according to needs (Outka, 1974; Jonsen, 1976). This support can be offered in numerous ways. For those families who want to provide care for their parents, economic and support services such as income maintenance, health care, housekeeping, respite services, etc. should be provided for the parent and family. For the elderly without families, or for those older adults or families who do not wish or are not able to provide care for parents, adequate community services and insitutional alternatives should be accessible. Society should aim at the provision of a range of service options. These services should be evaluated according to the principle of respect for persons. Unfortunately, there is a tendency to view these issues as either/or questions. Usually, the question posed is worded as a forced choice: 'What should be the preferred channel for government support ... families or institutions?' Recognition of different needs of individuals and families is essential for the ethical treatment of the ill parent and his family.

Who has the right to decide on the kind of care obtained or given when a parent becomes ill and is no longer able to care for himself? It is necessary to consider several questions when addressing this issue. Is the parent capable of rational thought? What are the physical, emotional, social, and economic consequences of caregiving versus institutionalization on the parent and the other family members? Are decisions by others made for the protection of an elderly individual, at the expense of his autonomy, justified? In practice, the caregiving activities for the parent usually increase in small increments. Gradually, the nature and amount of assistance increases until it becomes a central focus in the caregiver's lifestyle. Time spent on caregiving activities must be taken away from some other aspect of life, and sometimes this affects the caregiver's abilities to meet the needs of other family members. Obviously, the caregiving situation can produce increased conflict and tension within the family. Conflicting rights of individuals — for example, the spouse's right to support from the caregiver, the child's right to time for discipline, attention and support, the entire family's need for respite from caregiving activities — must be considered in the decision-making about where a parent should receive care and from whom. The general attitude of the public as well as that of the health care professions tends to be that home is the best place for a chronically-ill, elderly parent. This attitude should be tempered by consideration of the physical, emotional, and social consequences of caregiving.

Ethical decision-making

Decision-making regarding home care or institutionalization will involve different people depending on the situation. It seems reasonable to say that if the ill, elderly parent is rational, chooses to maintain himself, and is not a danger to others, he should be allowed to care for himself. At the point where he requires the assistance of his offspring, the decision-making becomes a joint one between the parent and the child. When the right of the parent to care comes into conflict with the rights of other individual family members, and the cost to them is great (e.g. marital conflict, physical illness, etc.) it can be argued ethically that the family has the ethical right to terminate home care. The rights of each individual family member must be considered under the principle of respect for persons. Many families may feel an emotional commitment to continue providing home care despite a high 'cost' to family members but this should not be confused with their ethical responsibility to their parent. In a practical sense, this issue is difficult because of difficulty in quantifying 'cost'. Health care professionals can assist families in calculating the balance between conflicting rights of individuals, thus assisting in the decision-making process.

There is a danger of conflict of interest and unjustified removal of parental autonomy which must be considered. Although contrary to most of the literature, it is conceivable that an offspring would stand to gain by the forced institutionalization of a parent. In these cases, an ombudsman system could provide an impartial third party to protect the rights of, and articulate the needs of, the parent. Nurses are in a position to detect unjustified removal of autonomy, and to assist the elderly person in taking recourse.

Summary

In summary, three groups may be directly involved in the decision-making regarding home care versus institutionalization depending on the physical and mental functioning of the parent: the parent, the family, and the state. Health care professionals, including nurses, have some power of influence over these groups. Additionally, the power of 'definition of competence' or labeling is both legal and medical. An abuse of this power can remove the autonomy of the parent in an unjustified way. Nurses need to be cognizant of the possible conflict between helping others and preserving autonomy. Those who suffer from illness in old age are especially vulnerable to coercion by health care workers. The ethical system we use to ethically reason this dilemma will in part determine the outcome solution.

Several ethical issues may arise in the decision for home care or institutionalization: the lack of adequate knowledge in the area, the conflicting needs of individual family members (respect for persons), and the obligation of society to provide services for the elderly (distributive justice).

REFERENCES

Beauchamp T L 1977 Paternalism and biobehavioral control. The Monist 60: 62–80
Beauchamp T L, Childress J F 1979 Principles of biomedical ethics. Oxford University Press, New York
Christiansen D 1978 Implications in aging. In: Reich W (ed) Encyclopedia in bioethics, vol I. The Free Press, New York, p. 58–65
Jonsen A 1976 Principles for an ethics of health services. In: Neugarten B, Havighurst R (eds) Social policy, social ethics, and the aging society. US Government Printing Office, Washington, p 97–103
Kayser-Jones J 1981 Old, alone, and neglected: care of the aged in Scotland and the United States. University of California Press, Berkeley
Maclagan W G 1960 Respect for persons as a moral principle. Philosophy 35: 193–217
Outa G 1974 Social justice and equal access to health care. Journal of Religious Ethics 2: 11–32
Shanas E 1967 The health of older people: a social survey. Harvard University Press, Cambridge, Mass
Townsend C 1971 Old age: the last segregation. Grossman, New York

… Helen K. Evers

Tender loving care? — Patients and nurses in geriatric wards

Introduction
Introductory texts on geriatric medicine emphasise the importance of active intervention, rehabilitation and cure as being central to provision of health care services for the elderly. The modern approach to geriatric service reflects various concerns: the assumptions that the elderly prefer to be in their own homes and that it is cheaper for care to be provided at home; the rising numbers of elderly in the population, with increasing demand for acute health care services, particularly hospital services; the need for geriatrics to establish itself as a prestigious medical specialty and to attract more and 'better' professionals to it; and the tendency of medicine to concern itself with healing. Despite this emphasis in the professional literature on cure and rehabilitation, and despite the trend towards decreasing length of hospital stay and increasing throughput of patients per available geriatric bed, so-called long stay patients are a fact of life of geriatric units. For such patients, the professional literature briefly prescribes 'tender loving care', and the creation of an environment in the hospital where some level of quality of life, self-esteem, interest and activity is possible. Little is said about how this is to be achieved, and there is evidence that the problems of long stay, chronic patients are generally accorded lower priority in practice than those of acute patients.

This chapter aims to make a new contribution to considerations of the nature of the long stay care task in hospitals, and to explore possible avenues for innovations in organisation of this task, aimed towards maximising positive care outcomes for patients. The first section reviews some of the key features of current British policy on hospital care for the elderly, and some of the medical professions's recent statements about the aims of hospital geriatric services.

From the review of policy and professional perspectives, a number of explicit and implicit objectives of hospital geriatric care can be identified. Most of these have to do with patients who are in some measure remediable: little has been made explicit when it comes to care of long stay patients. But since there are no clear professional or administrative criteria concerning the distinction between remediable and long stay patients, it is reasonable to assume that the objectives of care provision for geriatric patients are meant to apply, although perhaps with differing emphases, to all geriatric hospital patients.

Next, from the present author's current research, an examination will be made of the extent to which these objectives are in practice embodied in patterns of care delivery in geriatric wards in hospitals, and under what circumstances this may occur. In particular the contrast between remediable and long stay patients will be illustrated, as well as contrasting approaches to long-term care. Differing patient career patterns were found to be associated with differing patient care outcomes. In the case of remediable patients, there was evidence that attempts to meet the policy-derived objectives for geriatric care were being made, and that many positive outcomes accrued for both patients and staff. In the case of long stay patients, attempts to meet the objectives were not readily apparent, and the routinised structure of social relationships, which underpinned creation of a blanket regime applied to all patients regardless of individual differences, prevailed to a greater or lesser extent. This is in accord with the findings of many studies of long stay care and custody institutions. But the present research facilitates a new appraisal of the problem and possible solutions, for geriatrics, because the patient's perspective has been taken as central. It now becomes possible to identify the conditions under which the objectives for geriatric care might be fulfilled, and positive care outcomes achieved for patients.

Moving on from this, the final section of the chapter will look at the possibilities for alternative approaches to the organization of long term hospital care, both at the level of policy and of practice.

Current government and medical policy: Hospital care for geriatric patients in Britain

Age Concern (1977) summarizes a range of data from various sources concerning the health of the elderly and their use of health services. The Department of Health and Social Services (DHSS) recommended in 1971 that there should be ten geriatric hospital beds per 1000 population over 65. In 1975, the average number was 8.66 per 1000. As the Age Concern document points out, there were wide regional variations. Geriatric beds account for 28.5 per cent of all hospital beds. Less than 3 per cent of hospital consultants worked in the medical specialty of geriatrics in 1975; and less than 13 per cent of nurses. Around 50 per cent of beds in all specialties are occupied by the over 65s. Approximately 95 per cent of the over 65s are living in their own homes, and about 3 per cent in hospitals (Jefferys, 1977).

Turning now to recent government discussion documents and policy statements regarding the elderly and their health care, a range of assumptions and themes emerge. Department of Health documents, e.g. *Priorities for Health and Personal Social Services* (1976), *The Way Forward* (1977) and *A Happier Old Age* (1978), all express concern with seeking to promote quality of life of the elderly, while at the same time maximising cost-effectiveness in provision of health care services. The Report of the Royal Commission on the NHS (1979) reaffirms this view. Cost-effectiveness has become a key issue given the rising number of very elderly in the population, and the projected fall over the next decade of the 'young' elderly, from amongst whom lay supporters and careers for the dependent very elderly may be expected to come (see, e.g. Chalmers, 1980). An assumption enshrined in current policy is that such 'official' health and social care support as may be required by old people is best provided for them in their own homes, both because that is what elderly people are said to prefer, and because 'community' support is alleged to be a cheaper alternative to institutional support. There is a dearth of empirical evidence on this topic. Wager (1972) suggested that the problems of costing alternative forms of service provision may be insurmountable. The Royal Commission on the NHS (1979) also recognizes this problem: 'There are ... a number of difficulties about comparing the costs of treating or caring for patients in hospitals and at home. The degree of dependency of patients may vary, the quality of treatment and care may be different and is difficult to measure, the outcome or effectiveness of the treatment is hard to assess, and treatment at home may impose heavy burdens on relatives and neighbours. More research is required into the relative costs and effectiveness...' (para. 6.26). Opit (1977) suggests that home care for very disabled elderly people may be no cheaper than institutional care. More recently, in an action research study of provision of intensive home help services to old people who might otherwise have been eligible for admission to old people's homes, Challis & Davies (1980) suggested that the cost of community support may be only marginally less than residential care at the present time. Attempts to cost alternative patterns of care tend in any case to be constrained within and reflect the framework of anomalies and inconsistencies in current patterns of service provision and division of labour in the care of the elderly. The programme of care for individual elderly people may be related as much or more to the perceptions and priorities of professional care providers than to the needs and wishes of elderly people themselves and their relatives (see Barker, 1980, for discussion of how 'official' support services tend to exclude and even undermine lay support systems).

Where, despite the official emphasis on community care, an old person becomes hospitalised, the policy documents commend an active approach to treatment, utilising the best of the acute health care services. *A Happier Old Age* (DHSS, 1978) asserts that: 'This can only be satisfactorily achieved in a general hospital, where the full range of diagnostic and therapeutic facilities are available, and ... there is adequate and suitable rehabilitation provision to assist recovery' (para. 7.4). *The Way Forward* (1977) acknowledging that increased in-patient facilities, to cope with the anticipated increase in demand for geriatric hospital services, are unlikely to be forthcoming in the foreseeable future, suggests employing more remedial therapists. The aim of this would be to raise patient throughput in geriatric units, thereby increasing the efficiency of bed utilisation.

DHSS policy and discussion documents on hospital care for the elderly devote more attention to acute care and rehabilitation than to long-term, or continuing care.

In its brief discussion, it is suggested that long term care should be provided in an environment which offers the opportunity for stimulating purposeful activity, and maximal functional independence within a home-like atmosphere. The DHSS (1971) observes that services for continuing care patients should, in the interests of both patients and staff, 'not be isolated from a therapeutic environment in which there is some output of recovered patients' (para. 6) although this does not necessarily need to be within the District General Hospital, they say. Thus it seems that the policy line on care of long stay patients is that this should be carried out within the same broad ethos as that for remediable, dischargeable patients.

Whether at home or in hospital, the elderly are assumed by the DHSS to have 'Distinctive medical, social and nursing needs (*A Happier Old Age*, 1978) as compared with other patient or client categories. To meet these distinctive needs, expert professional workers with special experience of the elderly are needed whose services are to be provided through the multidisciplinary health care team.

The professionals' view, as reflected in documents such as the British Medical Association report, *Care of the Elderly* (1976); the Royal College of Physicians' report (1977) and the British Geriatrics Society and Royal College of Nursing report (1975); all subscribe to a line of argument which parallels that to be found in DHSS documents: that care is best provided at home, but, where hospitalisation comes about, an active approach to treatment should be taken, calling upon the general facilities available in the acute care sector, and the specific skills and knowledge of the multidisciplinary team of professional workers experienced in care of the elderly. Where active treatment fails to restore the patient to some level of autonomous functioning, then long-term care may be necessary within the hospital sector. The professionals share the policy view that this should offer patients opportunities for purposeful activity, which is believed to create the conditions under which patients' dignity and self-esteem is best preserved or enhanced. Beyond this, professionals' policy statements have little to say about the aims and processes of care delivery for long-term geriatric patients.

Policy documents and the professional view implictly endorse an 'Active theory' (Havighurst 1963; Lemon et al, 1972) stance towards the ageing process. Activity theory, and the antecedent conceptualisation of ageing 'Disengagement theory' (Cumming & Henry, 1961) from the controversy about which Activity theory emerged, have been much criticised and poorly supported by empirical research. Yet their ideas have remained influential, particularly those of Activity theory. The Activity view of the ageing process regards 'successful' ageing as characterised by the replacement of those social roles which are lost with ageing, by new and purposive social roles, and through these, active social participation; both of which are mutually sustained by continuing personal autonomy.

The themes and assumptions running through current DHSS and professional policies regarding geriatric hospital care can be summarised in the form of four general objectives of care:

1. To make full use of diagnostic services, acute and rehabilitative health resources, as for any other category of patient, with a view to discharging geriatric patients from the hospital as rapidly as possible

2. While patients remain in hospital, to promote and encourage their physical and psychological independence

3. In order to sustain, restore or promote patient's self-esteem and reasonable quality of life, to create the conditions, while patients remain in hospital, where purposeful activity may take place.

4. Given that the elderly have, or are assumed to have, distinctive health care needs, to make available to them the skills of the multidisciplinary team of 'experts' in care of the elderly (The implications of this, and the practice of teamwork in geriatric wards, have been discussed in Evers, 1980).

Several points need to be stressed in relation to these four objectives. They focus to a far greater extent upon the potentially remediable than upon the irremediable or chronic. This is entirely consonant with the dominant approach towards health care in hospitals, which is based on the clinical-medical somatic model of illness and its treatment. That is, diagnosis of disease processes and application of efficacious treatment strategies with a view to reversal, arrest or amelioration of the disease processes. Geriatrics, like other medical specialties, has come to be centrally concerned with throughput. Demonstrable increases in patient throughput form an important part of the argument by geriatricians that the specialty should be regarded as of equivalent status to the longer established medical specialties. What, then, of objectives for long stay geriatric care in hospitals?

Irvine et al (1978) note that 'Long stay patients are not very numerous in proportion to the total numbers admitted to the geriatric unit, but... they occupy up to half the available beds' (p. 39). Yet geriatricians have little to say about long stay care. Ferguson Anderson (1976) remarks 'It is better... to avoid the use of the term long-stay... The words 'long-stay' imply to the patient and his relatives that there is no active treatment when in fact skilled medical and nursing attention, occupational therapy and physiotherapy, chiropody and perhaps speech therapy may be taking place' (p. 411). He proposes instead the term continuing care. This quotation suggests that like acute care, continuing care is characterised by 'active treatment', i.e. it is predicated on the clinical-medical model of health care: cure orientation. (In any case, to subscribe explicitly to the view that long-term care is qualitatively quite distinct from acute care could constitute a major problem for the argument that the specialty of geriatric medicine has an assured and secure future).

Why is it that there is so little guidance to be found in DHSS or medical-professional policy regarding the nature and objectives of long-term geriatric care? The work of MacIntyre (1977) suggests one possible reason. In an analysis of the development of British social and health care policy for the elderly between 1834 and 1976, MacIntyre notes that policies reflect differing balances between two opposing concerns. The 'humanitarian' view of the 'problem' of ageing emphasises the need for public policy to create the conditions for minimising the personal pain of growing old; whereas the 'organizational' view emphasises the need to minimise the cost to the productive sector of society of the 'problem' of the aged as a social group. The current policy emphasis in hospital care of geriatric patients, by stressing rehabilitation and discharge, and the desirability on both humanitarian and economic grounds of arranging the necessary follow-up care provision in the homes of the elderly, and relying importantly on the unpaid labour of their kin and neighbours, clearly serves 'organizational' interests. The 'humanitarian' need to provide long-term care for patients who become non-dischargeable from hospital is a clear embarrassment not only for the clinical-medical 'cure' model of health care, but also for 'organizational' objectives of social and health care policy. An open-ended commitment to providing institutional care for a rising number of dependent elderly sick people implies an open-ended drain on economic resources.

There is a related explanation for the observation that long stay geriatric care tends to be treated by professionals and policy makers as a residual, 'dustbin', category, remaining after provision for other categories of geriatric patient has been more positively defined. Namely, the historical development of health care and social services for the elderly has taken place in a piecemeal fashion. The current pattern of statutory service provision abounds with conceptual and empirical anomalies, as Grimley Evans (1977) among others, has pointed out. This fosters ambiguity concerning accountability for marginal cases such as the chronically dependent old person requiring long-term care, where it is not necessarily self-evident whether the prime need is for health or for social care services, for example. Provision of residential, social and health care support services is fragmented among three distinct organizations: the NHS, Social Services Departments, and Housing Departments, (the last two forming part of the local authority system) and is governed by a maze of different statutory instruments. Some illustrations of the outcomes of this situation can usefully be given.

There is evidence that there is no clear division, in terms of physical and psychological incapacity, between the categories of resident to be found in old people's homes and in long stay wards. Townsend (1973) reported an analysis of the relative incapacities of old people living in residential homes, in geriatric hospitals and in psychogeriatric hospitals. He concluded that there was considerable overlap between the three types of care environment with respect to the levels of dependency of the elderly people living in them. Booth (1980) found, in a survey of dependency among the residents of old people's homes in Sheffield, that two distinct groups emerged. First, those who were virtually independent physically and mentally, and could in Booth's view have survived very successfully in sheltered housing. Second, there were those who were almost totally dependent, and in some cases, incontinent. Booth considered that in terms of current criteria for admission to old people's homes, such people required care which could more appropriately be provided in hospital.

The confusion of purpose, and the fragmented institutional arrangements for long-term care of dependent elderly — a low status social group — renders it unsurprising that no caring professional concertedly seeks positive involvement with, and ownership of, this area of work, and explicit definition of what such work entails in terms of care objectives for patients.

In the light of anomalies in statutory service provision for the elderly generally, and for those entering long-term residential care in particular, and in the absence of any clear indications to the contrary, the working assumption to be made in the discussion below is that the policy and medical-professional derived objectives for hospital care of geriatric patients apply, with the exception of the first objective, to all categories of patient who come to be in geriatric units.

Having looked at the central themes within DHSS and medical policy regarding provision of hospital geriatric services, and identified four general objectives of hospital geriatric care, the next section will describe empirical research relating to this. By use of illustrative examples, the translation of the objectives into practice will be examined.

Research into work and its organization in geriatric wards
Little social research focussing specifically on hospital care of geriatric patients and its organization, is reported in the literature. A pioneer work in this field was Norton et al (1962). This concerned nursing care problems presented by the geriatric patient, including provision of appropriate clothing and equipment, and the diagnosis and management of patients at particular risk of developing pressure sores. Norton (1967) began to raise some of the issues associated with care of long stay patients in her survey of hospitals of the long stay patient. More recently, Baker (1978) has looked at nurses' attitudes to geriatric patients; Clarke (1978) looked at nurses' perceptions of their work in psychogeriatric wards; and Wells (1975, 1980) carried out a study of problems in geriatric nursing care, including not only some of those problems — e.g., of equipment and ward design — to which Norton (1962) had addressed herself, but also the fundamental question of what constitutes nursing work in geriatrics. Miller (1978) looked at care outcomes of differing work organization patterns for patients in psychogeriatric wards, drawing from the work of Jenkins et al (1977) for criterion measures of the level of patient 'engagement' or 'disengagement', i.e. alertness and involvement with environment. There have been various managerially oriented studies of nursing work and patient dependency in geriatric wards, aimed towards developing formulae for calculating 'appropriate' staffing levels, e.g. Adams & McIlwraith, 1963; Rhys-Hearn, 1979; Norwich, 1980. These studies suffer from the constraints of many such studies, namely, because of the goal of quantification, they concentrate on nursing care as it is currently delivered, and on that part of nursing

care which is concrete and observable, i.e. physical work with patients. Work focussed on psychosocial needs of patients is not easily amenable to observation and quantification, and thus tends to be omitted from the resultant normative prescriptions regarding staffing levels. Some of the other reported studies, particularly Miller (1978) and Wells (1975, 1980), reach conclusions which echo the early sociological studies of institutional care (Stanton & Schwartz, 1954; Goffman, 1961) and paint a depressing picture of routinised physical care provision, harrassed nurses battling against the clock, and depersonalisation of patients to the status of work objects, as described by Hughes (1956). Wells (1980) concluded that '... nursing work on the geriatric wards not focussed on patients' needs but on routines which might or might not be appropriate for each patient. Essentially, nursing care was depersonalised, and, because of this, was frequently thoughtless and sometimes unintentionally cruel. The work routines were based on minimal, universal needs ... Work was not organized in the sense that it was not assigned by individual patient or specified task... Work progressed by area of the ward and time of the day. ... The impression was of frantic, intense activity by nurses ... to complete the routine as quickly as possible. Individual patient preference or even necessary variation in care appeared to be obstructive to the goal, which was completion of the routine' (p. 92). She goes on to say how work organized entirely on the basis of routines results in a focus upon the nurse, and not upon the patient and her needs.

Many of the published studies referred to above, also some work in progress in Britain (e.g. Fielding, 1980), focus almost exclusively on staff perspectives of the problems of hospital care for geriatric patients. While many of these problems, as the work of Wells shows, are also rightly assumed to be problems for the patients too such as the depersonalised and rushed routine of nursing work, few studies have attempted to take explicit account of the patients' perspectives. Exceptions are Miller (1978) and Raphael & Manderville (1979). The latter elicited the opinions of a sample of geriatric patients concerning various aspects of their experiences of hospital care.

The research which forms the basis for this chapter was focussed on patterns of work organization in predominantly long stay geriatric wards, and patient care outcomes. The general aim was to describe and analyse the processes whereby work with patients came to be defined and accomplished, and the structure of social relationships among all the participants in ward work — including the patient and her or his relatives — within which the work process took place. Care outcomes were conceived in terms of crude indices of physical and psychological wellbeing, or, more precisely, 'illbeing', this being easier to define and measure. The notion of patient career formed the point of departure: that is, drawing from the concept of career as used by Pill (1979), the progression of patients, through time, space and social interaction, through the hospital system. Eight wards were studied, each from a different NHS hospital. Four of the wards were located in specialist geriatric hospitals in a large Midlands city and four in geriatric units within District General Hospitals in or near the same city. A sample of ten to 12 patients was chosen from each ward, and their careers and care outcomes were monitored by means of nonparticipant observation, analysis of written patient records and discussion with patients and staff. Data on patient careers, together with various quantitative data on staff levels and patient-nurse dependency were used to construct an analysis of ward organization.

By paying direct attention to the patient's experience of being in hospital, in terms of care processes and outcomes, this research offers the potential to move towards a new analysis of what might constitute appropriate strategies for care organization from the patients' as well as from the professionals' angle.

Patient care goals and career patterns

Four types of patient care goal were evident from different patients in the wards studied. These were: (i) short-term care, rapid cure and discharge; (ii) medium-term care, rehabilitation and eventual discharge; (iii) a 'good' death; and (iv) long-term care. Very often the 'rapid cure' goal, which applied to a minority of patients in the study wards, was explicitly acknowledged by staff and patients. In contrast, other types of goal, particularly the long-term care goal, were seldom explicitly defined, acknowledged or discussed. There was often consensus — explicit, or, more commonly, implicit — concerning patient care goals, and under conditions of consensus patient career creation took on the appearance of a rational, co-ordinated activity. Rational co-ordination appeared to be attained either through professional interaction having regard to an individual patient's needs as defined (usually) by the professionals; or, more typically, through the initiation of particular established routines for handling the various categories of patient; or by means of a mixture of both strategies. Dissention, when it emerged, usually did so either in the context of shifts from one point to another within a patient's career, or from one type of care goal, and associated career pattern, to another, for a particular patient. An example of a point of dissention arising within the career of a number of patients, was the decision to effect discharge from the hospital. Although the professionals concerned were often in overall agreement that the goal for a particular patient was rapid cure and discharge, there was sometimes dissention about the precise point at which discharge should be effected. This was most likely to happen where the case was not seen as a straightforward medical one, but where there were social and environmental issues too. The tendency was for doctors to work towards the earliest possible discharge, and for other health and social care workers to be more conservative. While the medical view usually won the day as expected, the result for the patient of such dissention was a certain amount of confusion and anxiety about what was to happen, when, and how it was to be accomplished.

Dissention arising over a change from one type of goal definition to another for a particular patient arose occasionally in connection with establishing the cut-off point between the goals rapid cure and discharge, and medium term rehabilitation and discharge; also between rehabilitation and long stay. In practice, such dissention was reflected in debates about how much remedial therapy patients received, and whether or not the therapists continued to assess patients' levels of independence in relation to activities of daily living, and if so, at what intervals. As with dissention about discharge, there were adverse consequences for the clarity of patient career management strategies. For staff, these were resolved usually by a tacit switch from one type of care routine package to another. There was attendant worry and confusion for patients. One patient for example said: 'I used to go to the physiotherapy on Thursdays — what's happened? Do they think I'm better? Or have they given up on me? Oh well, maybe they've just forgotten to come for me today...'

In most cases however, explicit or implicit consensus, rather than dissention over care goals for particular patients, prevailed. It might be expected that differing care goals would be associated with differing work strategies and patient careers, in the context of the policy and professional pronouncements discussed earlier, and the care objectives derived from these. It is now possible to use illustrative case studies as a basis for examining contrasts between types of patient career, and also whether the prescribed care objectives can be identified in practice. Two career types only will be examined here in order to develop the analysis: acute careers associated with the goal of rapid cure and discharge, and long-term careers.

The acute career
The case of Harry W. Harry W. was aged 95, and was admitted to the geriatric ward in a state of general collapse. He was diagnosed as suffering from anaemia — the cause to be discovered — and mild

congestive cardiac failure. Although mentally alert, on admission he was highly dependent physically, and also doubly incontinent. Prior to the gradual onset of his present illness, which had culminated in the collapse and admission to hospital, he had been in excellent health, and accustomed to looking after himself (he lived alone) and to getting out and about each day. Harry received intensive nursing care, and active medical intervention and investigation. Four days and seven units of blood after his admission, Harry was said by the doctors and ward sister to be much improved. Harry himself agreed that he felt better. The staff began to discuss with Harry the possibility of discharge within a few weeks. Harry was now encouraged to do a little more for himself each day and with help from the nurses, he was able to get to the toilet, and his incontinence ceased. The physiotherapist, in response to a referral from the ward sister, advised on walking aids as a temporary measure. The social worker was asked to investigate Harry's home circumstances, and what help he might need when discharged. The occupational therapist was asked to assess Harry's performance of activities of daily living: dressing and cooking in particular. After the acute stage of Harry's illness was resolved, during which time he was nursed primarily in bed, he was able to get up when he chose and rest when he felt tired. His progress was regularly assessed by the multidisciplinary care team: informally and almost daily on the ward, by means of discussion between the ward sister and other staff; and more formally on ward rounds and at multidisciplinary case conferences. The patient's own views on his progress and future were taken into account, and his career on the ward was individualised: his needs and personal wishes were assessed from day to day, primarily by the ward sister, and activities initiated — by Harry himself and by the staff — in the light of these. When Harry felt well enough, and staff were satisfied with his improved health and support services (a home help and meals on wheels) had been organized by the social worker, Harry W. went home. He had been in hospital for less than a month, and was highly satisfied in all respects. So also were the staff who had looked after him.

The case of Harry W. illustrates one translation of the policy and professional objectives for hospital geriatric care in practice. First, full use was made of diagnostic services and acute health care resources; second, as Harry's health improved, his independence was progressively encouraged and fostered until fully restored; third, Harry's days, after the acute phase, were usually busy, since he had a good deal of contact with therapy and other staff, also many visitors. In between, he was often glad of a quiet rest, since he became easily tired. Fourth, Harry had available to him a number of members of the multi-disciplinary team: doctors, nurses, physiotherapist, occupational therapist and social worker. Harry's care delivery was individualised, and, once his acute illness was resolving, he was actively involved in the creation of his own hospital career.

We can now move on to look at two examples of long-term careers, which differ in many respects from acute careers. It will in addition be shown how the typical long-term career of a patient in a geriatric ward does not bear much resemblance to that which is prescribed by the four policy-derived general objectives for care.

The long-term career
A. Minimal warehousing: The case of Florence B. Miller & Gwynne (1972) used the term warehousing to describe the application to patients of care routines which are predicated on implicit definition of patient need couched in terms of physical problems and dependency.

Florence B. was 91. She has been in hospital for about 15 years, since suffering a stroke. Six years prior to the research, it was written in her medical case notes that Florence B. was waiting for a place to become available in an old people's home. There was no subsequent mention of this possibility. Florence seemed well-orientated mentally. She was confined to a wheelchair, but was able to perform most of the basic functions of life unaided, apart from getting into and out of bed. She did not like to talk of her current and previous experiences of being in hospital. Indeed, Florence talked very little, and would almost never initiate a conversation herself. For Florence, every day was the same. Like all the other patients on the ward, she was woken very early. After breakfast in bed, she would have to wait until the nurses came round to her: sometimes two hours after breakfast. She was then helped out of bed, and only then was she able to get to the toilet, after which she spent the rest of the morning dressing, in clothes issued to her by the nurses. Sometimes she felt so exhausted, she wished she could have a day in bed. But this was never allowed. Florence never asked for help, because, she said, it had always been refused in the past. Having at last dressed herself, Florence would wheel herself to the day room, where she would spend the rest of the day. There she slept because she was exhausted by the effort of getting up. Her other activities included watching television, which on the whole she did not enjoy but could not escape from, reading the newspaper, and, occasionally, knitting. She had no visitors, and no contact with staff other than nurses, and her interaction with them was primarily concerned with particular tasks: being got out of, or put back to bed, receiving her medication and being given her food. She never left the ward: there were no outings, no remedial or diversional therapy sessions, nor was she ever explicitly reviewed by the nursing, medical or remedial staff. Florence's life in the ward was entirely the creation of an inexorable routine, which had even succeeded in precluding Florence's requests for help from the staff.

Thus, of the objectives for geriatric care, three out of four of which were assumed to be applicable to long stay patients, none was evident in the ward career of Florence B. Physical independence was enforced rather than encouraged or promoted (objective two), and psychological independence was not apparently considered at all. Opportunities for purposeful activity were almost totally absent (objective three). The multidisciplinary team was not in evidence (objective four). The care outcomes for Florence B. included various kinds of suffering, e.g. depression: 'I feel so exhausted today, I wish I were dead'; humiliation: 'Sometimes they leave me so long in the mornings before they get me out of bed, I have an accident. I dread this if Nurse D is on, she can be so cruel ... as if I did it on purpose'; boredom: 'It takes me such a time to dress, but then what does that matter ... there is nothing to do here, each day drags by and I'm thankful when it's time to go to bed again, though I dread the effort of undressing ...'.

B. Personalised warehousing: the case of Hetty C. Hetty C. was 98, and had been in hospital for seven years. She had been admitted from the old people's home where she had lived for 20 years for above-knee amputation of her second leg, her first leg having been amputated a number of years earlier. Hetty was mentally alert, and, once in her wheelchair, physically mobile. However, she needed some help with many of the ordinary day to day necessities of life. As with Florence B., the pattern of Hetty's day followed a regular routine. Early waking was the norm, and breakfast was served to Hetty in her night clothes as she sat in her wheelchair beside her bed. Soon after breakfast, the nurses would help Hetty with washing and dressing, in clothes of her choice. Hetty would spend the rest of the day either in the ward's day room, in the occupational therapists' Activities Room, or beside or on her bed. She was very sociable, and loved to chat with the nurses and some of the other patients. She often enjoyed diversional therapy, organized by the occupational therapy aides, and was free to choose whether or not she participated. She enjoyed reading the newspaper and magazines, and was interested in horse racing. The domestics regularly placed small bets for her.

Sometimes Hetty became tired and withdrawn: if she wanted peace and quiet, she was free to rest quietly on her bed during the day. If her withdrawn behaviour continued for any length of time, the ward sister would usually assign one of the nurses to spend some time with Hetty, to cheer her up and to discover if anything particular was the matter. Hetty was regularly in contact with the occupational therapists and domestics, also an occasional visitor, but primarily her interactions were with the nursing staff. Many of these interactions took place around social chat: they were not all focussed on the performance of specific nursing care tasks. Although Hetty C.'s life in the ward was largely a creation of the nursing routine, her career was personalised in the sense that she was able to express her individual preferences regarding aspects of her daily life, and in the creation of her career there was the flexibility within the routine for those preferences to find expression. This contrasts with the case of Florence B. for Hetty C., there were many positive outcomes of care: 'This is my home ... they are all so good to me here ... I enjoy a bit of a laugh with the girls' (the nurses and domestics).

The second, third and fourth objectives of geriatric care, which it was assumed would be relevant to the careers of long stay patients, find rather different expression in the case of Hetty C.'s personalised warehousing career than in Florence B.'s minimal warehousing career. Hetty's physical and psychological independence was encouraged and fostered but not enforced, as in the case of Florence. Even so, her life was highly routinised, the routine being the creation of the nurses. There were limited opportunities for activities which Hetty enjoyed. These activities had more of a diversional than a purposeful flavour. As for the fourth objective, it is true that Hetty sustained a wider range of regular interactions — with occupational therapists and aides, and domestics as well as nurses — than did Florence B., yet since she almost never had any contact with the doctor or other health care professionals, it can hardly be said that the services of the multidisciplinary team were provided for her.

To summarise thus far concerning the prescribed objectives for geriatric care, for Harry W., a fairly typical example of a 'rapid care' patient, there was evidence that the four general care objectives found expression in practice. Many positive care outcomes accrued for the patient. As for long stay patients, the situation looks rather different. The second objective, promoting and encouraging physical and psychological independence, was not attempted for Florence, and only partially evident for Hetty. So also it was for the third prescribed objective. Florence had almost no opportunities purposeful or diversional activities whereas Hetty had some. The fourth objective was not evident for either of these two patients. But it could be argued that, for long stay patients, it is entirely appropriate that the care be mediated almost exclusively through the nursing staff, since presumably medical intervention and remedial therapy will by this stage of the patient's career have been demonstrably inefficacious in terms of improving the patient's overall condition. Thus the prescribed objectives for geriatric care may need modifying to take account of this contingency. It has been argued elsewhere (Evers, 1980) that the mode of dissolution of the multidisciplinary team is crucial. Nurses should not become the prime carers for long stay patients by default, as a result of other professionals opting out. Rather, if they become the prime carers, it must be because they are the most appropriate professionals within the NHS to do this work (see Norton, 1965). This issue is discussed further on page   , in the context of considering a 'tender loving care' model for long-term geriatric patients.

The two long-term career patterns described above were fairly typical of long stay careers in all the eight study wards. Each ward tended to create long-term careers in one or other of these modes, but not both. On minimal warehousing wards, there was in addition some evidence of physical neglect, particularly of highly dependent demented patients. These were entirely creatures of the routine, and received attention during the getting up, feeding and putting to bed routines, but often looked unkempt and sometimes spent the whole day without attention to their toiletting and other basic physical needs.

Thus although neither career pattern fulfilled the objectives prescribed implicity by DHSS and professional policy, it can be suggested that the personalised warehousing career was to be preferred, for two reasons. First, it was closer to the prescribed objectives than the minimal warehousing career. Second, from research data, it appeared that so far as patient care outcomes went, personalised warehousing careers gave rise to less unintended suffering for patients. It also rendered work with patients less dissatisfying for nursing staff. On personalised warehousing wards, nurses made fewer spontaneous self-criticisms, e.g. regarding various tasks they would like to do with and for patients had they the time to do so, and appeared to find their work less professionally frustrating.

Organizational factors influencing the pattern of long stay careers

If we assume for the moment that personalised warehousing careers are to be preferred, although they do not match up to the prescribed model of care, we must now turn to a consideration of the contingencies which could account for the creation of personalised, rather than minimal, warehousing careers in different study wards.

The location of wards, either in District General Hospitals or in specialist geriatric units, bore no consistent relation to the type of stay patient careers to be found in different wards.

There was no discernible difference among the study wards with respect to nurse staffing levels. All wards regarded themselves as chronically understaffed, and all were heavily reliant on part-time staff, and untrained (albeit sometimes very experienced) nursing auxiliaries. There was also no discernible difference among wards regarding levels of patient-nurse dependency of long stay patients. Further, all wards suffered the constraints of less-than-ideal equipment and ward design, as well as problems, from time to time, with laundry and other 'hotel-keeping' services. Many of the staff of all the wards appeared very committed to their work, and there was no marked difference regarding training or competence of staff.

It appeared that the crucial differences between personalised and minimal warehousing wards concerned the ward sister's work scheduling strategy, and interrelated with this, the structure of social relations among the members of the multidisciplinary care team; most importantly, between ward sisters and consultant geriatricians.

First, let us consider sisters' work scheduling activities. In personalised warehousing wards, the sisters took account of patients' individuality in organizing work. They would regularly do a round of the patients, verbally review each patient and identify any particular needs, or tasks they defined as necessary. Thus within the general pattern of the routine, care was, to some extent, individualised. Patients' particular idiosyncracies, e.g., food preferences, sociability or sleeping patterns, were sometimes explicitly acknowledged, and often the routine was organized so patients' individuality might find expression.

In contrast, on minimal warehousing wards, the sisters almost never did a round of the patients, almost never reviewed patients — e.g., there were seldom any nursing report sessions — work was not explicitly defined nor allocated, neither were patients' preferences — e.g. choosing clothes, where they would sit in the day room — taken into account.

In the present research, the structure of social relations within which the ward sister schedules nursing work begins to emerge as a central factor in relation to the contrasting work scheduling activities of personalised warehousing and minimal warehousing ward sisters. In hospital care of geriatric patients, in common with hospital care generally, the dominant goal and modus operandi of the dominant professional group — the doctors — is that of discharging patients who, as a result of medical and other professional intervention, have been cured of their presenting illness, or at least have been stabilised or improved. All professional workers in hospitals, having been socialised into this cure and discharge oriented culture tend, like the doctors, to find their rewards in visibly contributing to the curing, restoring and discharging process. But geriatrics differs from many medical specialties: while it is true that increasing throughput of patients in geriatric units is the current trend, the long stay patient is a fact of life. The working relationship between doctors and nurses is crucial in relation to whether long stay *care* work is defined as a valid and valuable alternative to *cure* work, or whether it is to be seen merely as a result of a failure of the medical strategy. This proposition can now be elaborated.

Ward sisters who organized care at least partially on a patient-centred basis, and created personalised warehousing long stay careers like that of Hetty C., were to be found where care work was explicitly defined as valid and valuable by the doctors accountable for patients, *and* where verbal acknowledgement of this was embodied in the doctors' actual behaviour. Thus on personalised warehousing wards, the consultant geriatricians explicitly acknowledged the importance of providing long stay care in hospitals, and expressed the view that the nurses were the most appropriate people to be responsible for this care work.

The consultants' behaviour followed one of two patterns. In the first, the consultant would see long stay patients as regularly as any others, and pay the same regard to any medical problems they might present, always taking account of the ward sister's more intimate knowledge about the patient by consulting her and seeking her advice on medical intervention that he might contemplate. On matters other than medical, the ward sister had considerable autonomy to make decisions and to respond to perceived needs as she saw best.

The alternative behaviour pattern of consultants on personalised warehousing wards was that they reviewed long stay patients at regular but infrequent intervals, but would see any such patients at any time if asked by the ward sister or (occasionally) by the patients themselves, and would always be willing to respond to any requests from the nursing staff for advice. When seeing a long stay patient, consultants would give as thorough attention to presenting medical problems as for any other patient category. On personalised warehousing wards, consultants actively supported sisters who sought help from, for example, remedial therapists, in seeking to maintain patients' physical capacities.

In contrast, on wards where the sisters did not organize care on a patient-centred basis, and where minimal warehousing careers for long stay patients were the order of the day — e.g., the case of Florence B. — consultant geriatricians tended to define care work as less important than cure work in the hospital context. This view of care work was not only verbalised, but found expression in the consultants' work behaviour. Patients were described as 'hopeless cases' or 'bed blockers', for whom the hospital neither could nor should be doing anything. But since they were in hospital and could not be got rid of, then somebody had to look after them: the nursing staff. Consultants almost never saw long stay patients, and even if asked to do so would give them scant attention. For example, Mrs C., a mentally alert long stay patient, told Dr F., a consultant geriatrician, that she was suffering with a bad chest which was becoming worse, and sleeplessness. Dr F. told her he would do something about this, but neither did anything himself, nor initiated any other kind of response from another care worker, to Mrs C.'s expressed problem. Other health care workers, e.g., remedial therapists, were almost never to be seen with long stay patients on minimal warehousing wards.

Despite official and legal accountability of doctors for their patients, on all the study wards, the nursing staff informally became the prime responsible carers for long stay patients. But on minimal warehousing wards, nurses acquired their unlooked-for responsibility for care work, which had become defined as a second-best health care task, by default: the medical profession had opted out. The second-best care work had come to acquire a custodial flavour and ward sisters scheduled work almost solely by means of instigating established routines. In contrast, on personalised warehousing wards, the medical staff defined the nurses as the appropriate people to be responsible for doing a valid and important job. They had not opted out, but had explicitly allocated prime responsibility for care of long stay patients to the nursing staff, to whom they, the doctors, were available for medical consultation on demand. It was only on personalised warehousing wards that sisters scheduled work so as to take at least some account of patients as individuals.

Implications and future alternatives

The first part of this chapter has examined the objectives embodied in current DHSS and medical policies for geriatric care in hospitals in Britain. Research data has been used to show that, in the case of acute, rapidly remediable patients, the general objectives of care can be seen embodied in practice, and a number of positive patient care outcomes result. In the case of long stay patients, care objectives are not fully met. However, two distinct long term career patterns emerged — minimal warehousing and personalised warehousing — each of which was associated with a distinctive pattern of interprofessional relationships and informal accountability for care. Neither type of career approaches what might be considered as an optimum state of affairs, on humanitarian grounds, for long stay patients, yet a personalised warehousing approach appears preferable since it allows the possibility for some individualised patient care and management, and patient care outcomes which feature less unintended suffering. Thus the first aim of this final section is to examine more closely the conditions under which the probability of creation of personalised warehousing careers is likely to be increased. It will be argued that organization of long stay care of geriatric patients under the authority of the nursing profession, rather than under that of the medical profession, would contribute towards this general aim. However, this new mode of long stay care organization within the NHS represents a conservative model for change. A more radical approach to considering future alternatives for long stay care, under the auspices of the national state institutional arrangements for providing health, welfare and social support generally, could be taken. A general outline of the key issues can be sketched, including a reappraisal of the nature of the long term care task. A 'tender loving care' model can be outlined as a more acceptable basis for provision of long term care.

Maximising personalised warehousing within the NHS as a means of improving quality of long-term geriatric care

What appear to be the main features associated with the creation of minimal warehousing and personalised warehousing patient careers, and their care outcomes for patients, are listed in Table 3.1.

To reinforce the conditions under which the preferred model, personalised warehousing, predominates, it can be argued that changing features one and two would provide the organizational framework within which individualised long-term care can be provided by and under the management of professional nurses. That is, by conferring legal, administrative and professional authority on the nursing profession, the conditions are created whereby the care task, being organizationally segregated from the medically dominant cure and discharge approach, can be seen as valid, important and legitimate work to be done within the health care system. Creating the conditions for re-valuing of the long-term care task thus, would in turn serve to improve the status of those nurses taking on accountability for the task, and would also allow the possibility of identifying new criteria, qualitatively different from the traditional, medically-derived criteria such as patient throughput, for evaluating successful task performance. In parallel, there could be new possibilities for job satisfaction for nurses. This suggested formula for long stay hospital care is not, of course, new. Norton (1965) says of patients who become 'irremediable': 'This is true nursing, where ... medical science holds but a watching brief while Nursing really comes into its own'

Table 3.1 Features associated with minimal warehousing and personalised warehousing patient careers in geriatric wards

Feature	Minimal warehousing	Personalised warehousing
1. Formal organizational authority and responsibility for performance of care task	Doctor	Doctor
2. Legal responsibilitiy for performance of care task	Doctor	Doctor
3. Informal responsibility for performance of care task	Nurses by default	Nurses by delegation
4. Implicit definition of the care task	Failure of medical cure/discharge system	Valid in its own right
5. Ward sister's work scheduling strategy	Tendency for care to be produced by operation of inexorable routines	Tendency for care to be partially produced by routines, and partially managed on an individualised patient basis
6. Accessibility of other professional and lay heath workers to ward nursing staff	Virtually none	Some
Care outcomes for patients	Routinised, batch processing; higher incidence of unintended suffering	Routinised, batch processing; some individualisation; lower incidence of unintended suffering

(p. 57, 58). What is new is the suggestion made here for allocating legal accountability to the nursing profession for care of long stay geriatric patients within the NHS.

This formulation for the management of the long-term care task, aimed towards maximising the probability of the creation of personalised, rather than minimal warehousing careers, leaves many residual problems. First, it would constitute a challenge to the existing structure of power relations between medical and nursing professions, a relationship of gender as well as professional domination and subordination. While doctors might in principle be willing to reassign their 'dirty work' (Hughes, 1951) to the nurses, their 'ownership' of beds would, in parallel, be reduced. This could have adverse implications for the autonomy of geriatricians with respect to provision of hospital geriatric services. There is a further significant problem in suggesting that nurses rather than doctors become the prime accountable carers for long stay geriatric patients. Like doctors, nurses often find the major rewards of their work derive from their association with the miracle of healing (Hughes, 1956). The 'cinderella' specialties in nursing tend to mirror the 'cinderella' specialties in medicine: e.g., mental handicap, geriatrics. There is a danger that, while care of long stay patients is carried out within the NHS at all, despite the improvements anticipated through the organizational changes proposed above, that the ethos of cure would still impinge, and that care-work would be seen by professional nurses as less interesting and somewhat second-rate. This would be to the detriment of the impetus for the creation of personalised warehousing careers. Shore (1977), speaking of the American care system at an English conference on care of the elderly, observed that 'one of the reasons why we are having so many problems with long-term institutional care is that the context chosen as the criterion for modeling and for measurement is not only inappropriate, grossly inefficient and costly, but harmful to all as well. The medical model which has been used to describe the disease-oriented, acute, short-term hospital care system (emphasizing illness and cure) doesn't fit long-term care. Yet it is the absence of other models of care which contributes to our problems. I believe a different model is necessary...' (p. 122).

What are the possibilities for solving this problem? One possibility is to segregate long stay care from cure work, not only organizationally — by assigning accountability to the nursing profession — but also physically by locating this function in discrete, specialist NHS hospitals, away from the cure-dominated culture of the general hospital. Specialist geriatric units already exist, indeed DHSS policy (1976) stresses the desirability of this. While the culture of such hospitals should be subtly but profoundly changed by the shift in accountability from the medical to the nursing profession, this offers only a partial solution. If nurses continue to value cure-work the most highly, then Norton's (1967) warning is pertinent. Namely, that segregated long stay hospitals would come to be regarded as second class, '... implying that the patients are also second class and therefore requiring only a sub-standard nursing service' (p. 114). Meacher (1972) documents the dangers for patients of segregation, in connection with a study of homes for the elderly mentally infirm. And who is to reprieve the patient in the long stay hospital, legally 'owned' by the nurses, where a change in circumstances may warrant a patient moving to a cure or rehabilitation category, as may sometimes happen (Dartington et al, 1974)?

Brown (1973), the work of Hall (1975) and the lessons of reports of official enquiries into the management of hospitals (e.g., Report of enquiry into St Augustine's Hospital, 1976), and tragic evidence of the horrific side of institutional life (e.g., Robb, 1967) all point to the conclusion that it is vital for the boundaries of long stay institutions to be as open as possible. There should be maximal support to staff, and visibility of care work to outside individuals and organizations, if bad practice and a return to the bad old days of the workhouses is to be avoided and excellence in care provision promoted. Volunteers might have an important contribution to make here.

An approach to rendering care-work more acceptable to the nursing profession, as well as supporting constructive departure from the cure ethos, would be through the introduction of specialised, person-oriented rather than disease-oriented training in geriatrics. King et al (1971) in a study of institutions for care of handicapped children, showed how 'batch processing' routines were less likely to be found, and child-centred management practices more likely to be found, where unit heads had undergone child-care training, with the emphasis on the child rather than the disease or handicaps of children per se. In the U.K., the Joint Board of Clinical Nursing Studies (JBCNS) has supported provision of a post-basic course in geriatric nursing since 1974. (JBCNS Course 297) Few nurses have as yet undertaken such a course (JBCNS, 1980, reports that 303 nurses have completed the 24 week course). While the syllabus incorporates considerable attention to cure and rehabilitation work with the elderly sick, there is some evidence that the course offers the scope for the adoption of a person-centred approach to specialised training in geriatric nursing.

The possibility of developing specialised training, together with the creation of an organizational infrastructure which values and supports the performance of long-term care tasks by accountable professional nurses, in distinct NHS care units with 'open' boundaries seems, then, to offer a skeleton structure for a viable alternative to the present system. This alternative would create the conditions for building upon a personalised warehousing strategy for long stay care provision. Indeed, the DHSS itself is currently considering the possibility of setting up nursing homes for long stay geriatric hospitals within the NHS. (At present, although most nursing home managers must be registered by Area Health Authorities under the Nursing Homes Acts of 1975, the NHS itself does not provide such facilities).

To recap, then, it has been argued from research findings, that in order to maximise the chances for the creation of personalised warehousing rather than minimal warehousing careers for long stay geriatric patients, a new structure for care delivery within the NHS, with the nurse as prime accountable professional, is needed. However, this constitutes a conservative evolution. The possibility for other kinds of response to the challenge of long-term care delivery for the elderly sick must be considered. Modes of non-institutional care delivery are beyond the scope of this chapter, thus consideration will now be given to a possible development from the personalised warehousing long stay career.

The 'tender loving care' model of residential care
Personalised warehousing, the preferred of the two approaches to long-term care of patients in geriatric wards, can be criticised on the grounds that fails to confront the issues of subordination of patients to the professionals' definitions of their needs and the 'best' strategies for meeting these. Although personalised warehousing wards succeeded to some extent in individualising patient care, routinised work systems in a 'cure'-dominated health care ethos remained pervasive. Institutionalised processes for safeguarding patients' autonomy as human beings were not particularly evident. It is timely to reconsider how long-term care for geriatric patients is to be defined. No attempt at a comprehensive review of the relevant literature will be made here, but a few strategic definitions can be used to develop the concept of a 'tender loving care' model, and to analyse the conditions under which this might be expected to flourish. Kaufman (1980) notes the problems of defining long-term care irrespective of setting or client group. He quotes Sherwood's (1975) definition of a person in need of long-term care as being someone 'Who has reached, either suddenly or gradually, a state of collapse or deterioration in ... functioning which requires — for survival, slowing down the rate of deterioration, maintenance, or rehabilitation — the services of at least one other human being' (p. 8).

Shore (1977) defines long-term care for the elderly as 'Total care emphasising an appropriate balance betweeen social and health services. While it includes essential medical and nursing care, it must be recognised as separate from the hospital and medical model' (p. 124) Elliott (1975) says of geriatric care in hospitals 'A primary objective of any long-term institution must be to make the utmost of the potential of the resident'. The definitions of Shore and Elliott, while stated at a very general level, have nevertheless overtones of the personalised warehousing type of career. They pay no explicit heed to the status of the patient (and/or her relatives or advocates) as a participant in the production of care, and as a potential controller of some part of her own destiny. Provision of care for dependent people in such terms as these is in danger of becoming a take-over of the totality of the individual's lifespace. What is recognised in what is here conceived as a 'tender loving care' approach, is the patient's rights to exercise some, or perhaps a great deal, of autonomy and choice with respect to her own life. This is implicit in Sherwood's definition, quoted above. A 'tender loving care' model begins to move away from the pervasive routinised pattern of work organization which is a feature of personalised warehousing as well as minimal warehousing careers. Such an approach to care would emphasise the 'enabling' role of staff vis à vis patients' expression of individuality and scope for freedom of choice and independence within the limits of their physical and mental capacities. One view of the nature of the long-term care task for geriatric patients is that of the British Geriatrics Society and Royal College of Nursing (1975): 'Where ... (discharge from hospital) ... is not feasible the object is to *enable* the patient to live as full and worthwhile a life within the hospital as his infirmities allow and finally to die in dignity and comfort' (p. 11, emphasis added). Another source (King's Fund Centre, 1980) offers a definition of a residential service as a home-making service for people unable to sustain their own homes independently. The idea of the home-making function, and that of *enabling* patients to live their lives in as much accord with their wishes as is possible, forms the basis of the 'tender loving care' mode. The Personal Social Services Council (1977) quote their earlier (1975) observation, that 'The community has high expectations of public authorities, although these tend to be expressed only in reactions to those instances in which harm befalls people in care. As a result, a greater emphasis may be placed on the avoidance of risks than on the promotion of high standards of residential life, and may profoundly influence the context in which residential care is provided. In consequence, there is considerable tension between ensuring the safety yet promoting the freedom of people in care, between offering protection yet providing a convenient and reasonably low-cost environment, and between avoiding the visible instance of harm on the one hand and the promotion of a high quality of everyday life for residents on the other. Inevitably some risks do have to be taken' (para. 1.16). (This point has also been stressed by Ward, 1980; and Norman, 1980).

This statement, together with the definitions noted above, provide pointers towards care setting, tasks and skills for a 'tender loving care' model. The hospital ward offers limited potential for developing a home-like setting. Although medical and nursing tasks and skills have a part to play, other skills would be needed too, e.g. for remedial therapy, education, diversion and recreation. These might be provided by a range of professionals and lay workers or volunteers, or by training the prime carers in a wide range of skills.

If the 'tender loving care' model is to move beyond the personalised warehousing approach, it must probably be pursued outside of the NHS (although within the framework of state care provision rather than within the private sector). We must consider who, apart from nurses, the prime carers might be. Residential social workers are the most obvious alternative carers. Current training, leading to the qualifications Certificate in Social Services, or Certificate of Qualification in Social work, reflects in part a person-centred approach, which it has been argued is an important consideration. Taking on responsibility for long-term care of geriatric clients within a 'tender loving care' model can be viewed as an extension to the existing role of residential social workers in relation to the management of old people's homes. However, if the current anomalies in care provision for the elderly, including fragmentation of services among a number of different agencies, is not to be perpetuated, and if rationalised integration of service provision is to possible, changes in policy will be needed. (Current policies, and possible future directions, have been succinctly reviewed by the Personal Social Services Council, 1978).

Indeed, this would be essential if health care professionals' skills are to be efficiently and effectively provided in relation to patients resident in long term care institutions outside the NHS, but still within the general state-supported framework for care provision. (There is evidence from the U.S. experience that provision of residential care for the elderly in the private sector is fraught with problems. See for example Mendleson (1974) and Glasscote et al (1976).)

These, then, are some of the issues associated with the proposal for a 'tender loving care' approach to long-term residential care of the elderly sick. This model springs from a consideration of how the personalised warehousing model of care might be further developed to the benefit of long-term patients. However, in the interim, evidence from the research on which this paper is based, suggests that unnecessary suffering by patients is likely to be minimised if the conditions for creation of personalised warehousing can be fostered. These conditions turn upon the transfer of accountability for care from the medical profession to the nursing profession in the context of appropriate supporting organizational and policy changes, and training provisions. To effect such changes formally within the NHS would be impossible for one profession acting in isolation. Inter-professional collaboration in clarifying the goals of long-term care provision and evolving a new, more appropriate structure of social relations for long-term care provision within the NHS, will be needed.

Acknowledgements

The research upon which this paper is based was funded by a Social Science Research Council Project Grant. Some of the arguments developed here draw upon earlier papers (Evers, 1980; Evers, forthcoming). I am grateful to the patients and staff of the hospitals where this research was carried out for their kind co-operation. Thanks are due to my colleagues at Warwick University, particularly Margaret Stacey and Celia Davies, for their constructive comments on this work.

REFERENCES

Adams G F, McIlwraith P L 1963 Geriatric nursing. A study of the work of geriatric ward staff. Oxford University Press, London
Age Concern 1977 Profiles of the elderly: Their health and social services. Age Concern, London
Baker D 1978 Attitudes of nurses to care of the elderly in hospital. Unpublished Ph.D. Thesis, Manchester University
Barker J 1980 The relationship of 'informal' care to 'formal' social services: Who helps people deal with social and health problems if they arise in old age? In: Lonsdale S, Webb A L, Briggs T L (eds) Teamwork in the personal social services and health care. Croom Helm, London
Booth 1980 Measuring dependency. Community Care No. 300: 15-18
British Geriatrics Society Royal College of Nursing 1975 Improving geriatric care in hospital. Royal College of Nursing, London
British Medical Association (Board of Science and Education) 1976 Care of the elderly. Report of the working party on services for the elderly. British Medical Association, London
Brown G 1973 The mental hospital as an institution. Social Science and Medicine 7: 407-424
Challis D, Davies B 1980 A new approach to community care for the elderly. British Journal of Social Work 10: 1-18
Chalmers G L 1980 Caring for the elderly sick. Pitman Medical, Tunbridge Wells
Clarke M 1978 Getting through the work. In: Dingwall R, McIntosh J (eds) Readings in the sociology of nursing. Churchill Livingstone, Edinburgh
Cumming E, Henry W E 1961 Growing old: The process of disengagement. Basic Books, New York
Dartington T C C, Jones P J, Miller E J 1974 Geriatric hospital care. Unpublished report. Tavistock Institute of Human Relations, London
Department of Health and Social Security 1971 Hospital Geriatric Services DS 329/71
Department of Health and Social Security 1976 Priorities for health and personal social services in England. HMSO, London
Department of Health and Social Security 1977 Priorities in the health and social services — The way forward. HMSO, London
Department of Health and Social Security, Welsh Office 1978 A happier old age. HMSO, London
Elliott J 1975 Living in hospital: The social needs of people in long term care. King Edward's Hospital Funds for London

Evers H K 1980 Multidisciplinary teams in geriatric wards: Myth or reality? Paper read at Royal College of Nursing Research Society Annual Conference, March, published in Journal of Advanced Nursing May 1981
Evers H K The creation of patient careers in geriatric wards: Aspects of policy and practice. In: Social Science and Medicine (forthcoming)
Ferguson Anderson W 1976 Practical management of the elderly, 3rd edn. Basil Blackwell, Oxford
Fielding P 1980 Do nurses'attitudes matter? Paper read at Royal College of Nursing Research Society Annual Conference, March
Glasscote R M et al 1976 Old folks at homes. Joint Information Service of American Psychiatric Association and National Association for Mental Health, Washington, D.C.
Goffman E 1961 Asylums. Anchor Books, Doubleday, New York
Grimley Evans J 1977 Current issues in the United Kingdom. In: Exton-Smith A N, Grimley Evans J (eds) Care of the elderly. Academic Press, London
Hall D J 1975 Social relations and innovation: Play in children's wards. Unpublished Ph.D. Thesis, University College of Swansea
Havighurst R J 1963 Successful aging. In: Williams R, Tibbitts C, Donahue W (eds) Processes of aging. Atherton, New York
Hughes E C 1951 Studying the nurse's work. In: Hughes E C 1971 The sociological eye. Aldine-Atherton, Chicago
Hughes E C 1956 Social role and the division of labour. In: Hughes E C 1971 The sociological eye. Aldine-Atherton, Chicago
Irvine R E, Bagnell M K, Smith B J 1978 The older patient: A textbook of geriatrics, 3rd edn. Hodder and Stoughton, London
Jefferys M 1977 The elderly in the United Kingdom. In: Exton-Smith A N, Grimley Evans J (eds) Care of the elderly. Academic Press, London
Jenkins J, Felce D, Powell E, Lunt B 1977 Measuring client engagement in residential settings for the elderly. Research Report No. 120, Health Care Evaluation Research Team, Wessex Regional Health Authority, Winchester
Joint Board of Clinical Nursing Studies, undated Outline curriculum in the care of the elderly and geriatric nursing for registered and enrolled nurses: Course number 297 JBCNS, London
Joint Board of Clinical Nursing Studies 1980 Personal communication
Kaufman A 1980 Social policy and long term care of the aged. Social Work 25: 133–137
King R D, Raynes N V, Tizard J 1971 Patterns of residential care. Routledge and Kegan Paul, London
King's Fund Centre 1980 An ordinary life. Project Paper No. 24 King's Fund Centre, London
Lemon B W, Bengtson V L, Petersen J A, 1972 An exploration of the activity theory of aging: Activity types and life expectation amongst in-movers to a retirement community. Journal of Gerontology 27: 511–523
MacIntyre S 1977 Old age as a social problem. In: Dingwall R, Heulth C, Reid M, Stacey M (eds) Health care and health knowledge. Croom Helm, London
Meacher M 1972 Taken for a ride. Longman, London
Mendleson M A 1974 'Tender Loving Greed.' Alfred A Knops, New York
Miller A E 1978 Evaluation of the care provided for patients with dementia in six hospital wards. Unpublished M.Sc. Thesis, Manchester University
Miller E J, Gwynne G V 1972 A life apart: A pilot study of residential institutions for the physically handicapped and the young chronic sick. Tavistock, London
Norman A J 1980 Rights and risk. The National Corporation for the Care of Old People, London
Norton D 1965 Nursing in geriatrics. Gerontologia Clinica 7: 51–60
Norton D 1967 Hospitals of the lont-stay patient. Pergamon Press, London
Norton D, McLaren R, Exton-Smith A N 1962 An investigation of geriatric

nursing problems in hospital. The National Corporation for the Care of Old People, London
Norwich H S 1980 A study of nursing care in geriatric hospitals. Nursing Times 76: 292–295
Opit L J 1977 Domiciliary care for the elderly sick — economy or neglect? British Medical Journal 1: 30–33
Personal Social Services Council 1975 Living and working in residential homes. Personal Social Services Council, London
Personal Social Services Council 1977 Residential care reviewed. Personal Social Services Council, London
Personal Social Services Council 1978 Policy issues in residential care: A discussion document. Personal Social Services Council, London
Pill R 1979 Status and career. A sociological approach to the study of child patients. In: Hall D J, Stacey M (eds) Beyond separation: Further studies of children in hospital. Routledge and Kegan Paul, London
Raphael W, Mandeville J 1979 Old people in hospital. Pitman Medical, Tunbridge Wells, for King Edward's Hospital Fund for London
Report of the Royal Commission on the NHS 1979 HMSO, London
Rhys-Hearn C 1979 Comparison of Rhys-Hearn method of determining nursing staff requirements with the Aberdeen Formula. International Journal of Nursing Studies 16: 95–103
Robb B 1967 Sans everything. Nelson, London
Royal College of Physicians of London 1977 Report of the working party on the medical care of the elderly. Royal College of Physicians, London
Sherwood S 1975 Long-term care: issues, perspectives and directions. In: Sherwood S (ed) Long term care. Spectrum, New York
Shore H 1977 New approaches in the United States. In: Exton-Smith A N, Grimley Evans J (eds) Care of the elderly. Academic Press, London
South East Thames Regional Health Authority 1976 Report of the Committee of Enquiry, St Augustine's Hospital, Chartham, Canterbury SETRHA
Stanton A H, Schwarttz M S 1954 The mental hospital. Basic Books, New York
Townsend P 1973 The needs of the elderly and the planning of hospitals. In: Canvin R W, Pearson N G (eds) Needs of the elderly. Institute of Biometry and Community Medicine, University of Exeter
Wager R 1972 Care of the elderly. An exercise in cost-benefit analysis commissioned by Essex County Council. Institute of Municipal Treasurers and Accountants, London
Ward P 1980 Quality of life in residential care. Personal Social Services Council, London
Wells T J 1975 Towards understanding nurses' problems in the care of the hospitalised elderly. Unpublished Ph.D. Thesis, Manchester University
Wells T J 1980 Problems in geriatric nursing care. Churchill Livingstone, Edinburgh

Role stress reported by Directors of Nurses in skilled nursing homes

Many researchers have argued that nurses are members of a stressful occupation in that the positions they occupy and the roles they enact are frequently ambiguous, and are accompanied by role frustration and many types of role conflict (Stevens, 1976; Kinsella, 1976; Mauksch, 1972, 1957; Strauss et al, 1964; Taves et al, 1963). Some view the registered nurse (RN) working in the nursing home serving a majority of aged clients in a more problematic role than RNs in other health care settings. Speaking before a U.S. Senate Subcommittee on Aging, Shaughnessey, representing the American Nurses Association, and Knowles, the University of Florida School of Nursing, presented several reasons supporting this belief (U.S. Senate, 1975). They included the following. First, the average RN is ill-prepared to meet the needs of the elderly with long-term, complex medical problems for she has had little specialized training in caring for the chronically ill. Second, nursing homes have a poor public and professional image which frequently affects the RN's image of herself. Additionally, many homes have inadequate policies concerning patient care which hinders RNs in practicing safe nursing care according to accepted standards of practice. Furthermore, RNs lack the authority to carry out the kind of care that is required and they lack the stimulation and support of other nurses, physicians and allied health workers which are vital to an RN's professional growth. Finally, the design of long-term care facilities, and the delivery of services to residents are inadequately conceptualized and hinder the provision of quality care. The overall implication that RNs are under considerable stress in the nursing home and are dissatisfied with their work is supported by Hughes & Peters (1978), Barney (1974), Jaeger & Simmons (1970), and McCoy (1967).

Studies concerning the registered nurse in the nursing home are of interest due to the growing demand for RNs to work in this type of health care setting. Although a multitude of studies concerning RNs in other settings have been done, their findings are not fully applicable to understanding the nursing home nurse, for the nursing home differs from other health care organizations on a number of dimensions. In comparison to acute care hospitals, nursing homes generally have a less complex authority structure (Thirty, 1977; Kahl, 1976). Additionally, characteristics of the patients and their needs differ as does the composition of the patient care staff (Moss & Halamandaris, 1977). Furthermore, the reward structure for the nursing home professional nurse is severely restricted (Richard & Miedema, 1977). The questionable applicability of findings from studies of nurses in other settings and the paucity of studies concerning the nursing home nurse both point to the need to examine the professional nurse's role in the nursing home system.

This study concerned dimensions of role stress and job satisfaction reported by registered nurses working as Directors of Nurses (DNs) in skilled nursing homes serving the aged in America. Stress was viewed as a state or reaction of the DN to a stimulus in the environment. The focus was the DN's perception of the environment, rather than the objective environment. Three dimensions of stress (role ambiguity, role frustration, and role conflict), total role stress, and job satisfaction were examined. The study was guided by the Katz and Kahn (1978) social-psychological model of stress in the work role (ISR model) which was developed at the Michigan Institute for Social Research.

According to the ISR model, stress experienced at work is related to at least three sets of factors: characteristics of the objective environment, the individual worker and the interpersonal network in which the worker is involved. The stress sequence begins with objective characteristics concerning the organization, and the worker's position. It then moves successively to perceptions of these facts by the worker (e.g. stress), her immediate response (e.g. job satisfaction), and finally to her state of physical and mental health (Katz & Khan, 1978: 597). The stress sequence is modified by enduring characteristics of the worker and by the interpersonal context in which the work role is enacted.

Questions guiding this exploratory study occurred in three steps (for complete study, see Hughes, 1979). Initially, we asked what levels of role ambiguity, frustration, conflict, and total role stress are experienced by the DNs. Then we asked whether factors characteristic of the objective environment, the DN, or the DN's interpersonal network are associated with the different stress levels found across the nursing homes. Finally, we asked if the DN's perceived stress is related to reported job satisfaction.

Variables examined
Characteristics of the psychological and objective environment of the DN, characteristics of the DN and one characteristic of the DN's interpersonal network were examined.

Variables that reflect the DN's psychological environment

Three dimensions of role stress (ambiguity, frustration and conflict) and total role stress, all characteristics of the DN psychological environment, were the primary variables examined. Initially, they provided the basis for describing the level of stress perceived by the DN. Then, following the ISR causal model, characteristics of the objective environment, the DN, and the DN's interpersonal network were examined for relationships with the stress dimensions and total role stress. Finally, the stress measures were treated as independent variables and examined for their associations with DN job satisfaction.

Role ambiguity refers to a situation in which information received by the person is less than that required for adequate role performance (Kahn et al, 1964). Information may be lacking concerning rights and responsibilities of the occupied position, the specific activities that will fulfill the responsibilities, and/or the nature of rewards and punishments. The role ambiguity index was derived by summing the DN's responses to seven items. The higher the score, the greater the ambiguity. Two questions concerned the adequacy of role expectations and evaluation of role performance sent to the DN by other staff. Five of the questions focused on how clearly the DN understood various dimensions of her role (e.g. limits of her authority).

Role frustration refers to the inability of the DN to fulfill perceived role expectations because the resources are inadequate. This index was developed by adding the DN responses to eight questions. The higher the score, the greater the frustration the DN perceived. One item concerned the extent to which the DN felt other staff expected her to accomplish more than what was realistic. The other seven reflected her degree of frustration due to lack of supplies, shortage of qualified staff, inadequate data on medical needs of residents, lack of information concerning ways to meet residents' needs, frequent turnover in personnel, design of nursing home, and rules and regulations concerning the operation of the nursing home. The response categories ranged from never to very frequently.

Role conflict refers to the simultaneous occurrence of two (or more) role expectations such that, even if the DN had infinite resources at her disposal, compliance with one expectation makes compliance with the other difficult, or impossible. Briefly, this index was derived by combining a home consensus index for DN role expectations, and conflict scores reflecting the number of different groups (administrator, charge nurses, nurse aides and residents) that the DN perceived herself disagreeing with in regards to expected role behaviour in three hypothetical situations. For each situation, the maximum number of groups the DN could disagree with was four.

The higher the score, the greater the potential conflict. Situation I concerned criteria that the DN should use in helping her determine the types of health care to provide to residents. Situation II concerned a physician's slow response to a resident who appeared to need immediate medical attention, while Situation III concerned a conflict between a resident's rights, group rights and state laws regulating safety within the nursing home.

Total role stress is the summation of the three indexes — role ambiguity, role frustration and role conflict. The higher the score, the greater the perceived stress.

Variables representing the objective organization
Characteristics regarding three elements of the objective environment were examined for associations with the role stress measures and DN job satisfaction. These elements and their characteristics were: 1) the nursing home (personnel resources, staff stability measures and cost of care); 2) the DN's role-set within the nursing home (staff consensus on DN responsibilities and DN conformity to expectations); and 3) the DN position (salary).

Personnel resources are measures reflecting the proportion of licensed nursing staff available to carry out the goals of the nursing home. Three measures were derived: RN/resident ratio, licensed nurse (registered nurse and practical nurse)/resident ratio, and the RN/nursing staff ratio.

Staff stability measures refer to the turnover of staff occupying different positions in the home. Staff turnover is viewed by many as one of the most frustrating problems which confront nursing home RNs (Hughes & Peters, 1978).

A crude separation index was calculated for three groups (administrators, management personnel including the administrator, and nursing service personnel):

$$\text{CSI} = \frac{\text{Number of separations}}{\text{Average number of members}} \times 100$$

The higher the index, the greater the turnover.

Cost of care was used as a crude measure of adequacy of resources available to staff in the nursing home. This measure was derived by taking the average of the fees charged for basic care in a semi-private and private room. Extra costs such as medications were not included.

Variables characteristic of the DNs role-set, another element of the

DN's objective environment, were staff consensus on expected DN role responsibilities and DN conformity to role expectations.

Staff consensus on DN role responsibilities refers to the degree of agreement among the respondents on dimensions of expectations held for the DN. Consensus was measured on six activity dimensions derived through factor analysis of a 55 item role conception inventory (Hughes, 1979). The activity dimensions presented in descending order of importance were: 1) direct resident care activities, 2) nursing department administration activities, 3) professional nurse consultant activities, 4) activities directed by others, 5) communication facilitator activities and 6) activities related to the assessment and planning of care.

A microscopic consensus measure for each of the six dimensions above was based on the variance of the respondents' factor score for the single factor plus the sum of the squared difference between the DN factor score and three other position groups in the home — administrator, nursing service staff, and other staff. A total nursing home consensus index obtained by weighting each dimension consensus measure by the amount of total variance it accounted for and summing across the six dimensions. A high score indicated low consensus and vice-versa.

Role conformity refers to role behavior which fulfills the expectation(s) to which it is referred (Gross et al, 1958). The conformity score was derived by examining the correlations between staff members' expectations and their observations concerning whether or not the DN conformed to the expectations. Eighteen items, three representing each activity dimension delineated by the factor analysis of role expectations, were examined with the Pearson product-moment correlation test. The DN conformity measure represented the percentage of these items having a significant correlation ($\leqslant 1\cdot 0$). The higher the score, the greater the DN conformity to staff expectations.

DN salary refers to the monthly salary earned by the DN. This was the only variable examined which reflected the DN position, the third element of the objective environment.

Variables related to attributes of the DN

Four variables that reflected characteristics of the DN were examined for associations with perceived role stress and reported job satisfaction. The *DN employment measures* refer to the length of experience the DN had in nursing, in the nursing home examined in any position, and in the DN position.

DN professional level refers to the interest expressed by the DN in professional nursing activities within and outside the nursing home.

The index was derived by summing the responses to five questions which reflected the type of basic nurses training received, application for certification by the American Nurses Association, attendance at continuing education programs, memberships in professional associations, and reading of professional nursing literature. The higher the score, the more interest the DN showed in professional activities.

Variable related to the DN's interpersonal network
One variable which reflected the DN's interpersonal network was examined for associations with the DN's perceived role stress and job satisfaction. The *DN potential social support indicator* refers to the presence of positive regard for the DN by her role-set members. That is, to what extent did they respect and like her. It was assumed that there is a linkage between the degree of positive regard held for an individual and the amount of emotional aid that is available to this person. Furthermore, it was assumed that the presence of emotional aid will lessen the negative impact of a stress stimulus on the worker. This measure was derived by summing the responses of role-set members for two items and taking the mean score for the nursing home. The first question asked the respondent to identify on a five point scale the degree of respect held for the DN. The second asked how well the respondent liked the DN on an eight point scale. The higher the social support indicator, the less potential support available to the DN.

Variable related to DN's response to perceptions of the environment
One variable, job satisfaction, reflected an affective response of the DN to her perceived environment. Following the ISR stress model, it was treated as a dependent variable and examined for relationships with the stress measures and characteristics of the objective environment, the DN and the DN's interpersonal network.

Job satisfaction, a multi-dimensional concept, refers to the degree of gratification experienced by an individual occupying a specified position (Robinson, 1969). A composite job satisfaction score was derived by summing the responses to seven dimensions of work: pay, job security, kind of working place, chance to use my skills and abilities, kinds of people I work with, freedom to plan my own work, and chance to learn or try out new things. The five response categories ranged from definitely not satisfied to very satisfied. The higher the score, the less the job satisfaction.

Sample and method

Registered nurses occupying the Director of Nurses position and selected staff from 11 skilled nursing homes were studied. Data were collected through semi-structured interviews with the 11 DNs and 11 nursing home administrators, and through the administration of a structured questionnaire to all 146 respondents.

Nursing homes included in the study were selected by purposive sampling. All were located in Kansas, America, had a stable resident population and were medium sized (94-117 beds). With one exception, all were proprietary, for profit, homes and were licensed as skilled nursing homes.

A multiple systems model described by Gross et al (1958) was used to determine the study participants. The DN was selected as the focal position. The other positions examined were limited to staff members in the DN's role-set working in the home on a regular basis. They included the administrator, department heads, and nursing supervisors and nurse aides/orderlies representing the three traditional work shifts.

The DNs ranged from 31 to 58 years in age. The median age was 44·5 years. Most received their basic nurses training in 1960 or before from a diploma school of nursing in the U.S.A. The three youngest nurses received an Associate Arts or Bachelor of Science degree in nursing from a collegiate program in the 1970s. The DN's employment in nursing positions of any type ranged from $2\frac{3}{4}$ years to 25 years. The median was $13\frac{1}{2}$ years. Their employment history in the nursing home examined ranged from $\frac{1}{3}$ year to $9\frac{1}{3}$ years. The median years of nursing home employment was $3\frac{2}{3}$ years. Length of time spent in the Director of Nurses' position ranged from $\frac{1}{4}$ to $4\frac{1}{4}$ years. The median was $2\frac{1}{2}$ years. Their monthly salary as DN ranged from $811 – $1175, the median was $900. There was not a direct relationship between years of experience in the nursing home and salary.

In addition to the general demographic information summarized above, the DNs described their role in the home. Additionally, they reported on factors they viewed as influencing their work behaviour, and on dimensions of role stress, job satisfaction, and relationships with staff in their role-set. Administrators provided data concerning characteristics of the nursing home and personnel. All respondents completed a role conception inventory concerning activities they expected the DN to perform and attributes they expected the DN to have. They also reported on DN role behavior and on dimensions of their relationships with the DN.

Data was analyzed at three distinct levels: the individual DN, the nursing home, and the DN in relationship with specified members of her role-set. Since the study was considered exploratory in nature, formal hypotheses were not stated. Following the measurement of role stress and its three dimensions (ambiguity, frustration, and conflict), correlates of role stress were examined. Although correlation studies do not permit inferences of causation, correlation is necessary to establish a causal relationship between two variables.

The correlation analysis was guided by the ISR stress model. Initially, DN role stress and each of the three dimensions were examined for associations with characteristics of the objective environment, the individual DN, and her interpersonal network. Then, the role stress measures were examined for relationships with DN job satisfaction. Finally, associations between characteristics representing the objective environment, the individual DN and her interpersonal network and DN job satisfaction were examined.

We expected characteristics of the objective environment to be related to the stress measures. Furthermore, we expected the DNs perceived role stress to be correlated with DN job satisfaction. We also speculated that the potential social support available to the DN would be negatively correlated with perceived role stress and positively correlated with job satisfaction. Thus, we expected to find significant associations between the social support measure and the role stress measures and with DN job satisfaction.

Findings and discussion

Role stresses experienced by the DNs

Data concerning the intensity and level of role ambiguity, frustration, conflict and total role stress reported by the DNs are presented in Table 4.1. For each measure the higher the score, the greater the

Table 4.1 Role ambiguity, frustration, conflict and total role stress measures reported by DNs by nursing home (The greater the score, the greater the perceived stress. Scores rounded to two decimal places. H = high stress level, L = low stress level. The stress indexes were dichotomized into high and low stress level groups.)

Home	Ambiguity	Amb. level	Frustration	Frust. level	Conflict	Conf. level	Total stress	Stress level
1	17·43	H	26	H	6·42	H	49·85	H
2	13·33	L	18	L	6·75	H	38·08	L
3	15·16	H	23	L	3·58	L	41·74	L
4	13·91	L	26	H	6·54	H	46·45	H
5	9·29	L	25	H	4·29	L	38·58	L
6	13·94	L	24	L	5·96	L	43·90	L
7	19·00	H	25	H	7·98	H	51·98	H
8	—	—	28	H	—	—	—	—
9	18·56	H	25	H	7·70	H	51·26	H
10	13·37	L	20	L	5·25	L	38·62	L
11	11·68	L	28	H	10·17	H	49·80	H
$\bar{X}$	14·57		24·36		6·46		45·03	
S.D.	3·06		3·07		1·90		5·56	

ROLE STRESS IN SKILLED NURSING HOMES 83

degree of stress. Spearman correlation coefficients between role ambiguity, frustration and conflict were low (·05, P ≤ ·45) to moderate (·45, P ≤ ·09) in strength. Thus, it was concluded that different dimensions of stress were being measured.

The three dimensions of stress and total stress reported by the DNs varied from one home to another (Table 4.1). Four patterns of role stress derived from stress level measures were identified. DNs in homes 1, 7, and 9 reported high stress levels on all four measures, while DNs in homes 6 and 10 reported low levels of stress on all four. DNs in homes 4 and 11 reported low levels of role ambiguity, but high levels of role frustration, role conflict and total role stress. In homes 2, 3, and 5, low levels of stress were reported by DNs on three of the four stress level measures. Although the high stress measure differed for each of these homes, all reported a total stress level.

Using Fisher's exact probability test, the phi correlation statistic and the Spearman rho correlation test, factors characteristic of the objective environment (nursing home and role-set), the DN, and the DN's interpersonal network that might account for the differences were examined. The results are summarized in Tables 4.2 and 4.3.

Table 4.2 Selected variables correlated with high and low levels of role ambiguity, frustration, conflict, and total role stress: the phi statistic. (The indexes for role ambiguity, frustration, conflict and total role stress presented in table 4.1 were dichotomized into high and low stress level groups.)

	Role ambiguity level		Role frustration level		Role conflict level		Role stress level	
	P[1]	Phi	P	Phi	P	Phi	P	Phi
RN/resident ratio[2]	—	—	·50 (6)	·33	—	—	·20 (6)	·71
Prof. ns./ Resident ratio[2]	—	—	·50 (6)	·33	—	—	·20 (6)	·71
RN/ns. service ratio[2]	—	—	·50 (6)	·33	—	—	·20 (6)	·71
Turnover administrator[2]	·55 (10)	·17	·35 (11)	·31	·45 (10)	·25	·26 (10)	·41
Turnover management personnel[2]	·33 (10)	·36	·11 (11)	·57	·17 (10)	·53	·08 (10)	·65 —[4]
Turnover ns. service personnel[2]	·37 (7)	·42	·50 (8)	·26	·37 (7)	·42	·37 (7)	·42
DN professional level[3]	—	—	·47 (11)	·21	·33 (10)	·36	·08 (10)	·65 —[5]

[1] P = probability
[2] Variables representing the objective environment
[3] Variable representing attribute of the DN
[4] — = relationship in expected direction
[5] — = relationship opposite to direction expected

84 CARE OF THE AGING

Table 4.3 selected variables correlated with role ambiguity, frustration, conflict and total role stress: Spearman correlation coefficients[1]

Variable	Role ambiguity		Role frustration		Role conflict		Role stress	
	r	P	r	P	r	P	r	P
Consensus[4]	−·33 (10)[2]	·17	—	—	—	—	·18 (10)	·31
Conformity[4]	−·24 (10)	·16	—	—	—	—	−·38 (10)	·06 —
Cost of care[4]	—	—	·22 (11)	·26	—	—	·23 (10)	·26
Experience as DN[5]	−·45 (11)	0.8 —[3]	−·37 (11)	·13	−·19 (10)	·29	−·47 (10)	·07
Experience in nursing home	−·47 (11)	·07 —	−·22 (11)	·26	−·11 (10)	·38	−·38 (10)	·12
Experience as RN[5]	−·55 (11)	·04 —	−·49 (11)	·06 —	−·59 (10)	·03 —	−·68 (10)	·01 —
Potential social support	−·18 (10)	·31	−·67 (10)	·02 —	−·58 (10)	·03 —	−·62 (10)	·02 —

[1] r = correlation coefficient, P = probability level
[2] Number in ( ) = number of cases
[3] — = relationship in expected direction
[4] Variables representing the objective environment
[5] Variables representing attributes of the DN
[6] Variable representing the DN's interpersonal network

Correlates of role stress

Four measures, one characteristic of the nursing home (turnover of management), two of the DN (experience as RN and DN professional level), and one of the DN's interpersonal network (potential social support indicator), showed significant correlations of moderate strength with DN total role stress (r = ·62 or greater, Tables 4.2 and 4.3). Two measures, one characteristic of the role-set (DN conformity), and one an attribute of the DN (experience as DN), showed a low, but significant correlation, with total DN role stress (r = ·39 to ·47, Table 4.3).

A majority of the variables characteristic of the objective environment (nursing home and role-set) were not correlated with total role stress. They included cost of care, the three personnel resource measures, turnover of administrators, turnover of nursing staff personnel, and staff consensus on DN expectations. By contrast, three of the four variables characterizing the DN showed significant correlations with total role stress perceived by the DN. The only exception was DN experience in the nursing home examined, and it showed a trend in the expected direction. These findings suggest that individual characteristics rather than environmental characteristics are the primary factors involved in the perception of role stress. A significant correlation between the potential social support indicator and total role stress suggests that the presence of social support lessens the intensity of stress.

DNs in homes with a high turnover of management personnel reported a high level of total role stress (phi = ·65, P ⩽ ·08, Table 4.2). Role frustration and role conflict appeared to be the primary dimensions accounting for the significant relationship. The absence of a significant relationship between turnover of administrator and total stress suggests that relationships with all management level personnel and not just the administrator are important in influencing the level of stress perceived by the DN. This finding is congruent with the DN's stated responsibility of coordinating nursing department activities with activities conducted by other nursing home departments. It was surprising that turnover of nursing service personnel was not related to the stress measures for a majority of the DNs reported that nursing staff turnover was one of their most frustrating problems. The limited data available for testing this relationship (N = 7) may have contributed to this negative finding.

Reported DN conformity to role expectations, a characteristic of the role-set, showed a low, but a significant correlation with total role stress (r = –·38, P ⩽ ·06, Table 3). As reported DN conformity to staff expectations increased, the DNs' reported role stress decreased. The significant correlation was a result of the combined effects of all three dimensions. None of the three by themselves showed a significant correlation with DN conformity.

Regarding the DN attributes, two of the three nursing experience measures were significantly correlated with total role stress: experience as RN (r = –·68, P ⩽ ·01) and experience as DN (r = –·47, P ⩽ · 07, Table 4.3). The third experience in the nursing home examined, showed a trend in the expected direction (r = –·38, P ⩽ · 12, Table 4.3). As the experience level increased, total DN stress decreased.

Significant correlations ranging from (r = –·45 to ·55) were observed between each of the three DN experience measures and role ambiguity (Table 4.3). As experience increased, role ambiguity decreased. These findings along with findings that variables characteristic of nursing home and role set were not correlated with role ambiguity suggest that aspects of the DN herself may be the key factor in the perception of role ambiguity. Perhaps role ambiguity is related to the DN's self confidence in carrying out her role responsibilities.

Experience as RN was the only DN experience variable that was significantly correlated with role frustration (r = –·49, P ⩽ ·0.6) and role conflict (r = –·, P ⩽ ·, Table 4.3). For both, as experience increased the role stress dimension decreased. The first finding suggested that the development of nursing competencies acquired through the practice of nursing are more important in determining the level of role frustration experienced than familiarity with the nursing home and DN position. Perhaps the more experienced nurses have developed ways to improvise when resources are inadequate in the environment and, thus, perceive less frustration. The second finding suggests that the more experienced nurse is able to project an image of competence in her position which results in fewer staff questioning her behavior.

The DN professional level was significantly associated with total role stress (phi = ·65, P ⩽ ·08, Table 4.2). Low DN professionalism was associated with high role stress. We had assumed that the direction of the correlation would be in the opposite direction reasoning that the high professional nurse would have higher standards and would experience greater role frustration and role conflict than low professional nurses. The unexpected finding suggests that high profession DNs, as compared to low profession DNs, may have greater skills, confidence and/or support in carrying out the role responsibilities associated with their positions.

The final variable that showed a significant correlation with total role stress was the potential social support indicator which represented the DN's interpersonal network. The lower the potential support available to the DN, the greater the role stress reported by the DN (r = –·62, P ⩽ ·02, Table 4.3). The presence of social support appeared to lessen the stress experienced.

Two of the three dimensions of stress (role frustration and role conflict) appeared to account for the correlation between the social support indicator and total stress. As the potential social support increased, DN perceived role frustration decreased (r = –·67, P ⩽ ·02) and DN role conflict decreased (r = –·58, P ⩽ ·03, Table 4.3). These findings and the fact that a significant correlation was not found between the social support indicators and role ambiguity support a notion of Kahn & Quinn (1970). They state that for group support to mediate the effects of stress, a cooperative solution to the stress must exist. Role ambiguity as measured in this study is a problem for the DN only and is not shared by others in the nursing home. By contrast, role frustration and role conflict as measured in this study can be shared with others in the home.

DN Job satisfaction
The DNs reported being satisfied to very satisfied with six of the seven work dimensions examined: job security, kind of working place,

chance to use skills and abilities, kind of people in work setting, freedom to plan work, and a chance to learn or try out new things. A majority of the DNs (7) reported ambivalent feelings about their salary. The chance to use skills and abilities was viewed most important by the DNs, while pay and job security were viewed as least important.

The composite job satisfaction score based on the above seven dimensions ranged from 9–17, the mean composite score was 12.36, the standard deviation 2.62. Noting that the degree of job satisfaction as measured by the composite score varied across the homes, we tested for a relationship between job satisfaction and each of the role stress measures using the Spearman rho correlation test. The results are presented in Table 4.4.

Correlates of job satisfaction
Total role stress and its three dimensions were not significantly correlated with DN job satisfaction. This suggests that intervening variables are operating.

Table 4.4 Selected variables correlated with the composite DN job satisfaction score: Spearman Rho Correlation Coefficients

Variable	N[1]	r[2]	P[3]
Turnover management personnel	11	·26	·21
RN/resident ratio	6	·81	·03
RN + LPN/resident ratio	6	·07	·44
RN/ns. service ratio	6	·81	·03
Consensus on expectations	10	·55	·05
Conformity, DN expectations	11	·47	·07
DN role ambiguity	10	−·25	·23
DN role frustration	11	−·30	·17
DN role conflict	10	·39	·12
DN role stress	10	−·16	·32
Experience as DN	10	·39	·12
Experience in nursing home	11	·53	·05
Experience as RN	11	·17	·29
DN salary	11	·64	·02
Potential social support	11	−·40	·12

[1] N = Number of cases
[2] r = Correlation coefficient
[3] P = Probability level
[4] — = Relationship in expected direction

A majority of variables examined that characterized the nursing home, the role-set and the DN position were significantly correlated with the composite job satisfaction measure (Table 4.4). These variables presented in descending order of their importance are RN/resident ratio ($r = \cdot 81$, $P \leqslant \cdot 03$), RN/nursing staff ratio ($r = \cdot 81$, $P \leqslant \cdot 03$), DN salary ($r = \cdot 64$, $P \leqslant \cdot 02$). Staff consensus on DN expectations ($r = \cdot 55$, $P \leqslant \cdot 05$), and DN conformity to staff expectations ($r = \cdot 47$, $P \leqslant \cdot 07$). As the ratio of RNs to residents and nursing staff increased, as DN salary increased, as staff consensus on DN expectations increased, and as DN conformity to staff expectations increased, reported DN job satisfaction increased.

DN experience in the nursing home was the only DN characteristic that showed a significant relationship to job satisfaction ($r = \cdot 53$, $P \leqslant \cdot 05$). As experience in the nursing home increased, job satisfaction increased. Potential social support was not related to job satisfaction.

Summary and conclusions
To summarize, the purpose of this exploratory study was to identify stress experienced by registered nurses working in the Director of Nurses' position in skilled nursing homes. Three dimensions of stress (role ambiguity, role frustration, and role conflict) and total role stress were examined. The DNs reported experiencing varying levels of each stress dimension and total role stress. Using the ISR stress model as a guide, three sets of variables were examined for associations with the stress dimensions and total stress. The variable sets examined were characteristics of the objective environment (the nursing home, DN role-set, and DN position), the individual DN, and the DN's interpersonal network in the nursing home.

A majority of the DN characteristics (DN nursing experience measures and DN professional level) showed a moderate correlation with total role stress. Differences in the presence and strength of correlations were found across the stress measures. All DN nursing experience measures were correlated with role ambiguity, but only the DN's experience in nursing was correlated with role frustration and role conflict. As the DN's experience increased, role stress decreased. It was suggested that intervening variables such as the DN's self-confidence in carrying out her responsibilities or coping mechanisms developed through experience were operating.

For the most part, characteristics of the objective environment were not correlated with role stress. Turnover of management personnel which showed a moderate correlation with total stress was the one exception. DNs in homes in which there was a high turnover of management personnel reported a high level of total stress.

The potential social support indicator, a characteristic of the DN's interpersonal network, had a moderate correlation with total stress and two of its dimensions: frustration and conflict. It was not correlated with role ambiguity. As the presence of social support increased, reported frustration, conflict, and total stress decreased. The findings support the belief that the presence of social support serves to mediate the impact of stressors in the environment.

The three stress dimensions, total role stress, the potential social support indicator and a majority of the DN characteristics were not correlated with DN job satisfaction. The DN's experience in the nursing home was the exception; it had a moderate correlation with job satisfaction. As experience in the nursing home increased, job satisfaction increased. In contrast to the DN characteristics, a majority of the objective environment characteristics (personnel resources, salary, staff consensus on expectations for DN performance, and DN conformity to staff expectations) had moderate to high correlations with job satisfaction. As the RN resources, the salary, staff consensus on expectations for DN role performance, and DN conformity to staff expectations increased, reported job satisfaction increased.

In comparison to role stress, correlates of job satisfaction differed. Characteristics of the objective environment were related to job satisfaction, while characteristics of the individual DN were associated with role stress. Potential social support was not related to DN job satisfaction, but it was to role stress and two of its dimensions.

Given the fact that the sample of DNs was small, and the analysis restricted to a bivariate correlation analysis, the implications of the study are limited. Nevertheless, the findings supported some notions expressed in the stress literature and raised questions concerning the causes of stress and its impact that merit more extensive investigations using multivariate analysis procedures.

As reported in previous studies (see Katz & Kahn, 1978), stress is multidimensional. Although variables correlated with each of the stress dimensions varied, characteristics of the individual rather than the objective environment appeared critical to the development of stress. This supports the notion that it is an individual's perception of an event rather than the event itself which results in stress. However, more information is needed to understand the relationship of perception to the development of stress. What factors are operating to change a worker's perception — self-confidence in carrying out role responsibilities, coping mechanisms for resolving problematic issues, or other psychological or social-psychological characteristics?

Job satisfaction was not correlated to role stress or any of its dimensions. Nor was it related to a majority of the individual characteristics of the DN or her potential social support. Rather, characteristics of the objective environment were the crucial variables in this study related to DN job satisfaction. Such findings leave one questioning the causal sequence suggested in the ISR stress model. The model suggests that job satisfaction, an affective response to stress, is affected by the environment, the worker and the worker's interpersonal context. Questions worthy of investigation include the following. Are there situations in which role stress and job satisfaction are correlated? If so, under what conditions? If stress does not affect job satisfaction, what response does it invoke in the worker?

In addition to addressing the above questions, researchers need to move beyond the scope of this study and examine the impact of stress and its dimensions on role behavior. For example, within the context of the nursing home, there is a need to examine how stress affects the nurse's ability to plan and implement nursing care. Is it possible that there is a relationship between a nurse's coping mechanisms for managing stress and the low quality patient care that is frequently attributed to nursing homes? Current knowledge does not allow us to answer this question.

Acknowledgement

This work was supported in part by the Midwest Council for Social Research in Aging.

REFERENCES

Barney J L 1974 Nursing directors in nursing homes. Nursing Outlook 22: 436–440
Gross E 1970 Work, organization and stress. In: Levine S, Scotch N (eds) Social stress. Aldine, Chicago, p 54–110
Gross N, Ward M, McEachern A 1958 Explorations in role analysis. Wiley, New York
Hughes D 1979 Role expectations and role performances of nurses in the nursing home: the case of the R.N. as director of nurses. Unpublished doctoral dissertation. Kansas State University, Manhattan, Kansas
Hughes D, Peters G 1978 Organizational position and perceptions of problems in a nursing home. Journal of Gerontology 33: 279–287
Jaeger D, Dimmons L W 1970 The aged ill — coping with problems in geriatric care. Appleton-Century-Crofts, New York
Kahl A 1976 Nursing homes. Occupational Outlook Quarterly 20: 26–29
Kahn R, Quinn R P 1970 Role stress: a framework for analysis. In: McLean A (ed) Mental health and work organizations. Rand McNally, Chicago, p 50–115
Kahn R L, Wolfe D M, Quinn R P, Snock J D, Rosenthal R A 1964 Organizational stress: studies in role conflict and ambiguity. Wiley, New York
Katz D, Kahn R L 1978 The social psychology of organizations, 2nd edn. Wiley, New York
Kinsella C 1976 Nursing service administration: the state of the art. American Nurses' Foundation Nursing Research Report 11
McCoy L 1967 Study shows cause of staffing problems. Modern Nursing Home Administrator 21: 71–77

Mauksch H O 1957 Nursing dilemmas in the organization of patient care. Nursing Outlook 5: 31–33

Mauksch H O 1972 Nursing: churning for change? In: Freeman H E, Levine S, Reeder L G (eds) Handbook of medical sociology. Prentice-Hall, Englewood Cliffs, New Jersey, p 206–230

Moss F, Halamandaris V J 1977 Too old too sick too bad nursing homes in America. Aspen Systems Corporation, Germantown, Maryland

Richard E C, Miedema L 1977 The nurse practitioner in the nursing home. Journal of Nursing Administration (March): 11–13

Robinson J 1969 Occupational norms and differences in job satisfaction: a summary of research evidence. In: Robinson J, Athanasiou R, Head K (eds) Measures of occupational attitudes and occupational characteristics. Survey Research Center, Institute for Social Research, University of Michigan, Ann Arbor, p 25–78

Stevens B J 1976 Education in nursing administration: where are we and where should we be? American Nurses' Foundation Nursing Research Report 11 (3): 14–17

Strauss A, Schatzman L, Bucher R, Ehrlich D, Sabshin M 1964 Psychiatric ideologies and institutions. Free Press of Glencoe, London

Taves M J, Gorwin R G, Haas J E 1963 Role conceptions and vocational success and satisfaction. Research Monograph No. 112, Bureau of Business Research, Ohio State University

Thiry R D 1977 Dissertation summary — relationship of communication satisfaction to need fulfillment among Kansas nurses. The Kansas Nurse 52: 8–9

United States Senate, Special Committee on Aging, Subcommittee on Long-Term Care 1975 Nurses in nursing homes: the heavy burden (the reliance on untrained and unlicensed personnel). Nursing Home Care in the United States: Failures in Public Policy Supporting Paper No. 4 94th Congress, 1st Session

5

Val M. Hardy

Modifying attitudes toward geriatric nursing in Australia

The ageing population and societal attitudes
The current proportion of those over 65 years in Australia is 9 per cent of the total population; the 1981 census is predicted to reveal an increase to 11 per cent, and estimates to the year 2000 are for 14 per cent. This will create a disproportionate demand for funding of health and welfare services to meet the needs of the elderly, because the growth rate of the aged population will be in excess of the growth rate of the work force.

The consequential increasing demand for nursing support in caring for the ageing because of the increased expectation of life of those who reach 60 years, has been further accelerated in many Western societies, by the collapse of the extended family. In Australia, increasing urbanisation and smaller houses, increased numbers of women in the work force, and the geographical mobility of families to obtain employment has resulted in the elderly receiving less and less help from their families than in the past. In parallel the image and esteem of the elderly has been depressed by the attitudes of a youth-oriented society that has all too frequently stereotyped the elderly as being unproductive, uncreative, sexually disinterested or impotent, and mentally stagnant; and has frequently labelled any defects, neatly but cruelly, as 'senile'. The tragedy is that in some long-term care facilities, hospitals, and other health care agencies, this image has overflowed into the nursing care, creating mental blocks that have excluded even the slightest possibility of maintaining or improving the total quality of life of those admitted to such residences or hospitals.

Because of our social structure and social attitudes deprivation of any sort of the elderly has therefore not been so much a possibility as it has been a frightening probability. Fortunately the biological and social problems that beset us all with the passing of time beyond our years of full-time gainful monetary employment are now better understood, and hopefully the day may soon arrive when the elderly should not, in any setting in which they reside, have to accept deprivation as an inevitable progression in our society. It is slowly being accepted that passive leisure is not enough for the majority at any age, and that idleness is the death of a living person. Conversely, activity is life and the means of binding an individual to reality and his fellow man.

The response to these social and health needs has been a broadening of, and increase in, services available to support the elderly in the community, and an increase in the provision of homes and hospitals for extended care. This burgeoning of extended care services, has brought about an increasing demand for nursing resources, both within the community and in residential or hospital facilities.

Professional attitudes
In the 1970s the science of gerontology and practice of geriatric medicine have been vigorously activated by the dynamics of societal change, and the reverberations have certainly been felt by nurses working in the field of extended care services for the aged. Acceleration in the input from the allied health professionals of physiotherapy, occupational therapy and social work, and the emerging multi-disciplinary concept has also changed and sometimes even threatened the role and status of the nurse, who for so many years was the only professional involved and concerned with caring for the aged on a daily continuing basis. Nurses now need to be educated to perceive and accept new concepts of broader programmes of care, and to increase their knowledge of the biological and sociological changes that confront the ageing person, so that they may be more effective in whatever setting they provide care and support for the elderly, and more confident about their role and contribution to team care programme planning. However, the profession itself has been slow to respond to the need for such programmes. At this time in Australia there has been no concerted thrust at a national level, and very little within each of the six states of Australia, to elevate the status and quality of geriatric nursing education so that nurses can be prepared to meet the increasing demands for more, and improved, care programmes. In most states students in basic general nursing courses are not required to undertake a component of clinical experience in this field, and the inclusion of the theory of the ageing process is minimal or even non-existent.

Kayser & Minnigerode (1975) studied nursing students' interest in working with aged patients by administering a Tuckman-Lorge attitude questionnaire to baccalaureate nursing students, and the findings concluded that students showed minimal interest in working in nursing homes; it was found that they preferred to work with children and adult patients. Those whose responses indicated stereotype attitudes about the aged, and those who had previously worked in a nursing home or convalescent hospital, showed the greatest interest in working with elderly patients. This suggests that those who rejected stereotype misconceptions about the aged, preferred not to work in settings that they believed fostered an institutionalising environment. The authors suggest that schools of nursing include gerontology in their curricula and that nursing students be provided with clinical experience in institutions for the aged to acquaint them with, and to encourage interest in, this increasingly important field of specialisation.

Other studies demonstrate that when there is negativity about the ageing process displayed in the attitude of any of the care givers in long term nursing facilities, this may influence the institutionalising effects on patients, and contribute to their social and physical deterioration and dependency. Campbell (1971), using a modified Tuckman-Lorge attitude questionnaire, reported positive correlation between the number of misconceptions about the aged and expressed interest in working with them among registered nurses, licensed practical nurses, and nursing assistants. Although registered nurses stereotyped the aged less frequently than the other groups, they expressed the least interest in working with them. It would seem that the work performance of those who did work with the elderly could be affected by their attitudes and expectations about the behaviour of elderly people. It was suggested in this study that while physical disabilities could be a cause of dependence, inactivity and isolation in patients, if on all occasions such problems were attributed to physical disabilities, an environment might be created in which patients were expected to behave in a particular manner. Seemingly this would not inspire staff to attempt rehabilitation.

Studies by Wolk & Wolk (1971) showed, by use of a free response questionnaire, that there was a demonstrable degree of stereotype negativity displayed by professional workers' attitudes toward the aged. Although nurses were found to be the most positive in their attitudes, it was thought to be significant that their work involved physical contact as well as verbal communication. It was suggested that the physical needs of the patient and the satisfaction of these needs by the nurse, may create and permit greater dependency feelings for the nurse. The nurse, in kind, may respond more positively if she enjoys the role of a parent-surrogate. Hence, it could be assumed that the more positive attitude of nurses may not necessarily be due to the fact that nurses view old age more appropriately than other professionals.

Yurick et al (1980) described studies demonstrating that clients in nursing homes preferred nurses who had more favourable attitudes, and who held rigid expectations of the behaviour of clients. Conversely, nurses had been observed to prefer clients who themselves displayed positive attitudes and behaviours, or who were appreciative and made less excessive demands than those with limited self-care ability, incontinence, or who failed to co-operate.

Wells (1980) conducted a study in a geriatric unit in a teaching hospital, using an open-ended questionnaire, about problems commonly encountered in geriatric nursing. Respondents were also asked specific knowledge questions about the giving of geriatric nursing care. The sample included both trained and untrained nursing staff. Trained nursing staff were also requested to complete a modified Kogan old people scale questionnaire to form, to analyse their general attitudes towards old people. Seemingly, the quality of the answers from the sample of both groups of nurses was cause for concern, and the implications from the results of this study have been interpreted as an indication of the pressing need for educational programmes for staff working in the geriatric wards of the particular teaching hospital studied.

Similar studies measuring nurses' attitudes toward old people or geriatric nursing have not been reported in Australia, and because of the variability of methodology and design in American studies (Wells, 1980), it cannot be assumed that any particular study would have direct positive application to Australia. However, difficulties of recruiting registered nurses to this field, and the limited emphasis given to gerontology and contemporary geriatric nursing both in educational curricula and in practice, would tend to indicate that similar negative attitudes toward old people and to geriatric nursing would certainly be prevalent among nurses in this country.

Government funding of health services is currently considered to be in a 'no growth' period, and therefore most nursing research and pilot operational projects must be planned within existing budgetary allocations for both staff and other resources. Compounding the problem is the fact that few basic general nursing courses are funded through the Ministry of Education, therefore both nursing education and research must compete fiercely for funding with all other aspects of the health budget of the nation. This is one of the main reasons that geriatric nursing research in Australia has been sparse and slow to develop; and as a consequence there is a dearth of local documented data available to assist those who wish to change preconceived prejudices about extended care nursing services for the aged. Those who seek to change the image of nurses as others see them through the window, or indeed to change the image of those who see themselves in a traditional unchangeable mirror, must pioneer and initiate such changes at the grass roots level of nursing care.

The stage and pace of evolution of geriatric nursing education and practice in Australia, is therefore largely dependant upon the initiative of nurses in the practical field, supported by management of the individual institutions providing care for the aged. This tenuous arrangement depends inevitably on the capacity and quality of such centres to provide an educational environment, to prepare innovative programmes, and to implement and evaluate such programmes. Consequently only a few in several states have been able and prepared to establish formalised post-basic courses in geriatric nursing.

Facilitating change

The following describes the experience of nursing management in an extended care centre for the elderly, where changes were considered desirable to facilitate alternative options of care for the 400 long term and 56 short term residents. The home is sited in a provincial city of 54 000 people, and has a regional referral centre responsibility for a population of 138 200 distributed over an area of approximately 21 460 km^2. The number of persons over 65 years in the region is currently 16 000 (11.6 per cent) of the population. This extended care centre could be described as comparable to others in the nation that are known to foster a progressive gerontological approach, and where all professional staff are encouraged to implement innovative care programmes. However, like most, there are many instances where one can observe the effects of transplanting an individual from the community into an environment that unwittingly acts as a culture medium for uniformity of identity, with consequent psychosocial denigration and a withdrawal from individual expression to one of passive behaviour.

Most of us in nursing in all settings are at times culpable of yielding to the temptation of stereotyping those in our care; this we do by disease (the appendicectomy); by the Doctor (Mr Jones' patient); by bed number (the man in bed 12); by behaviour (good or demanding); by age (kid, Gran); and by disability (high functioning or low functioning). This stereotyping can also lead us into errors of misconception and misinterpretation on which we proceed to base our decisions. It also influences our choice of communications, and hence our relationships with those in our care are affected. Elderly persons come to us often already feeling rejected or betrayed by families and society, and, in some nursing care homes for the aged, then find themselves in an environment of ambivalence or prejudice; hence they may finally submit to the pressures of the environment, passively withdraw, and in so doing, surrender control of their lives. The true and personal story written by Ellen Newton (1979) places descriptive critical evidence of this kind before us, and her graphic account indicates the strength of character and self-discipline that she required to remain a 'person' in the many extended care nursing homes where she was a resident.

Registered nurses, in large geriatric centres, may suffer the greatest pressure and stress in their attempt to avoid or reject stereotype attitudes, because their role is largely one of nursing unit management and supervision of state enrolled nurses (second level of nurse in Australia); and the priority required to be given to their major function usually restricts their ability to give significant direct personal care to patients. The enrolled nurse, on the other hand, may well become task oriented and develop stereotype attitudes, because the system of nursing management in the unit allows her little scope beyond 'getting the work done'. Tender loving care is interpreted as keeping patients hygienically clean, well fed, preventing decubitus ulcers and being kind and cheery to patients; and many patients survive very well on such care and appear seemingly contented. But one should ask the questions: 'Are they really contented or just resigned to their fate?' and 'Is the level of life the best we can offer?'.

Accepting the premise that nursing attitudes toward the ageing process is a major influencing factor in determining programmes of care, and that individual nurses' attitudes are expressed through their behaviour, the concern of nursing management in this particular institution was not primarily one of quantifying workload and calculating staffing levels, or attempting to justify additional staff for current patterns of care. Rather, it was one of stimulating a change of attitude toward systems of nursing care. The hypothesis was, that if staff were more positively 'problem oriented' in their planning of individual patient care, the assignment of workload by tasks would be less significant. If tasks became less significant, it was felt that routines would be less rigid, and the physical and social environment and staff resources could be used more flexibly within the framework of the patients' day. With existing patterns of care it was possible to evaluate nursing only in terms of the accepted concurrent audit systems. While valuable information can, and should, be obtained this way, one needs also to ask whether the level and variability of a patient's dependency, and the humanistic aspects of care are of greater personal importance to the elderly person than the speed and efficiency with which nursing care is performed and documented.

Nursing care plans

To focus the attention of staff on problems, needs, action and overall goals for individual patients, the inital assignment in mid-1977 was the development of a problem-centred nursing care plan. The design of the nursing care plan was undertaken by the staff of four wards, supported in meetings and workshops by staff from the nursing administration and the nursing education departments. The final draft was approved by the Nursing Care Procedure Committee, and by the end of 1978 nursing staff were assessing patients' problems and documenting a plan of action in all fifteen wards.

However, it should be emphasised that the introduction of nursing care plans did not, in the majority of wards, bring about many changes in nursing management. Traditional assignments of work load continued, and hence any beginnings of developing and co-ordinating a program of comprehensive (holistic) care were continually frustrated by rigid organisational methods and seemingly insufficient staff resources. The execution of care continued to be accomplished by intentionally collaborative, but frequently independent, functioning of nursing staff and other professionals. The environment had not changed, and flexibility, to permit preferred preferences of patients' behaviour, was still minimal. The less enthusiastic charge nurse, initiated and reviewed the plans with a passive and often negative approach, and, as a consequence, other nursing staff working in the unit frequently disregarded the content of the care plan. Nevertheless, it was a break away from the generalised custodial (protective/preventive) nursing care system. The passive acceptance by staff, of irreversible mental or physical impairment being the normal outcome of the degenerative process and pathology of the elderly, was at least partly shattered.

More significantly it became evident that if nurses were to be motivated to focus on positive behaviour directed toward achieving quality of life, and not just prolonging life for those in their care, it was vital that a formalised educational programme should be established at the centre.

Nursing education

Basic general nursing education in Australia has focused its thrust during the last decade on increasing the nurse's scientific and technical care knowledge to complement similar progress in medicine. The plethora of specialised care units has developed as fast as the needs of the ageing population, but while the former has attracted every source of expertise available, the latter has almost been ignored in both medical and nursing educational programmes. Hence, there is a dearth of gerontological professional expertise. The first Chair of Gerontology in Australia was not established until 1976, and this was associated with Melbourne University. Two others, in New South Wales, have now commenced.

The nurse engaged in geriatric care is, and will continue to be, faced with many conflicts and attitudinal barriers which, unless resolved, will block the progress and utilisation of each individual's potential professional ability. Inherent in the future is the need for geriatric nursing to have a solid educational base so that a flow of innovative management and client care programmes will result. The breaking down of negative attitudinal mores, and the vital support needed to enable staff to accept change, will largely be achieved through education that is consciously planned to involve students in clinical experiences that allow them to evaluate the effectiveness of less traditional patterns of care, and to observe personally the outcome of such care. The assumption is that the attitude of registered nurses toward the aged will be more positive if they are directly involved in helping the elderly with their physical and environmental problems. This has certainly been confirmed at this geriatric centre, by the positive response of students to the clinical experience arranged as a component of the geriatric nursing course.

Post-basic course for registered nurses

The Committee of Management of the geriatric centre supported the concept of a twenty-six week post-basic certificated course for registered nurses, and this commenced in May 1979 following approval from the State statutory nursing registration body. A maximum of twelve students are admitted to each course, with no more than half the placements being allocated to students currently employed at the centre. The other students are selected from applicants who are employed in various geriatric centres throughout Australia, or who wish to have an initial experience in this field of nursing.

The aims and objects of the course are:

To provide further education for registered nurses working in the specialised field of geriatric nursing, so that they are able to improve their professional performance and their job satisfaction

To encourage registered nurses to practise in all areas of the field of geriatric nursing

To understand the effects of physical and mental changes that occur with the progression of age, and as these affect different individuals

To stimulate an interest in improving methods of patient care of the elderly and in evaluating problems specially related to such care

To develop a positive supportive approach toward rehabilitation and independence of the elderly, and to give support to the dying

To appreciate all levels of dependency of the aged for which community and professional services must be provided and co-ordinated.

Primary nursing care. The feature of the course is the clinical experience programme which allows students to practise primary nursing care, and to judge it as a viable alternative nursing care system to more traditional task oriented systems. Although primary nursing care systems were initiated in acute care settings it would seem that their relevance to extended care is even greater. Short hospital stay and changing staff within nursing units as experienced in many general acute hospitals, are not, to the same degree, barriers to comprehensive co-ordinated care in the extended setting, and the opportunity for continuing care and evaluating patients' response to that care is considerable. The use of students also allows time for nursing management to test the system, before plunging into a total pragmatic situation which may be difficult to reverse or modify.

Students are assigned three patients, and the philosophy and objectives of the primary nursing modality as described by Marram et al (1979) is accepted as the guideline for the students. For the first course it was vital that charge nurses were involved in the planning of the students' clinical experience and understood the principles of primary nursing care; hence to facilitate consistency in method and monitoring, the students on the first course were allocated to four selected long term care units, and two short term restorative care units. Both students and charge nurses had to perceive that there was a need to strengthen the planning and implementation of individualised patient care, and that primary nursing may offer an alternative to traditional systems in use. Behaviour patterns and attitudes of other staff on the nursing units had to be considered and organisational implications reviewed. Senior nursing staff needed to give encouragement and reinforce the efforts of the staff of the nursing education department and the nursing units, so that motivation was maintained.

Through the vehicle of primary nursing care it soon became evident that students were developing an awareness of the frequently suppressed physical and mental capacity of patients; they became sensitive but discriminatory about the individual's needs to maintain or restore independence, and as a consequence they developed their skills in communicating through their close personal relationships with their patients. They had time to sit and listen to patients, and time to make a nursing assessment of each person as an individual.

The subsequent professional performance evaluation and assessment interview conducted with registered nurses who have had the opportunity, through primary nursing experience on this course, to assess, plan and personally experience the outcome of their nursing, has shown that they have developed more positive attitudes about planning restorative care or maintaining independence of the patients. Because their own attitudes are less ambivalent, they are able to stimulate and support enrolled nurses to be less routine oriented. They have also shown enthusiasm for attempting new concepts, introducing choices and options in the patient's day, and they readily accept evaluation of their performance as professional growth.

Without the enriching experience of being so closely involved with every aspect of the elderly person's life in the nursing units, the theoretical content and conceptual theories presented on the course would have less impact; and when faced with the realities of practice in extended care facilities for the aged, which often function with many constraints related to staff resources, geographical environment and equipment, the knowledge and interest gained as a student may well dissipate with the weight of workload. Knowledge must be supported by enthusiasm, creativity and determination, if it is to survive extraneous frustrating influences, and an educational experience is less than worthwhile if it does not stimulate and improve the confidence of a student to perform well against odds in the practical field.

With the completion of two courses there was a core of registered nurses on the staff of the geriatric centre, seeking support and co-operation to introduce less traditional systems of management in the nursing units to improve the patients' life style. They were seeking opportunities to show by their behaviour that their attitudes toward the concept of planning and achieving individualised care of the elderly was strongly positive. However, to achieve demonstrable change, all levels of nursing staff would need to be encouraged and guided, and all health professionals would in some way need to be involved. Thus the time was right to explore the possibilities of implementing an effective multi-disciplinary approach in the long-term care nursing units.

Attitudes of multi-disciplinary groups

Gerontological medicine now preaches, although practises to a lesser extent, the multi-disciplinary concept; and the nurse must now, or in the near future, adjust to this new professional relationship. However, past experience in geriatric nursing have left their imprint on many nurses, because all too frequently they received very little support from others, and as a result, emotional and irrational prejudices may have developed. The extent to which the nurse is able to resolve any conflicts arising during the process of adaptation to change, will depend on her personal reaction to others in the team.

The upsurge of allied health professionals contributing to restorative and rehabilitative patient care in short term care facilities has left some nurses feeling vulnerable, particularly when participating in general professional discussions. On the other hand, those in long term care units have frequently expressed the need for greater multi-disciplinary support to assist them in coping with the depressing workload that they have all too often been left to manage alone. Working with others in a multi-disciplinary team, requires the nurse to be aware of her own feelings and attitudes toward others in the health team. The nurse needs to be aware that her positive or negative attitudes are expressed in her behaviour, and this may influence her relationship with other professionals and, hence, influence the effectiveness of the practical functioning of the team and weaken the viability of the team concept.

Medical and Nursing Directors need to be aware of this dilemma, and it requires them to instigate supportive measures to facilitate the breaking down of barriers. One such method is to bring the various groups together in a common forum so that there is a base for planning and reviewing all projects that each group may otherwise institute alone. The first assumption being that the more one knows about others' activities, the less suspicious, apprehensive or aggressive one will feel toward them. The second assumption being, that out of this understanding will come the impetus to co-operate generally in common areas of responsibility, and to assist each other with common operational problems or projects.

Multi-disciplinary committee

The formulation of a planning and review committee for patient care can do much to achieve this co-operation, and the following example describes such a venture established at the centre in 1980.

The general aim is to implement, monitor, and continually review all professional systems of patient care so that standards can be established that are valuable and realistic. The organisational structure to achieve this is as follows:

Administrator: Chairman
Medical Director
Director of Nursing

Principal Nurse Educator
Charge Nurses of patient care study units
Chief Physiotherapist
Chief Occupational therapist
State Enrolled Nurse

The Nursing Administrator — Patient Services co-ordinates all study projects and arranges meetings. Working parties are structured according to the particular current studies or projects being undertaken. These are led by a member of the committee with appropriate staff co-opted.

The initial study approved by the Committee aimed to investigate the two major patient disabilities that were seen to cause most difficulties for all multi-disciplinary staff in planning patients' care programmes. These were problems of altered mental state with disturbed behaviour, and maintaining continence; these often pose multiple difficulties for an individual patient, and were seen to have varying effects on the dependency level of the person. Both problems are likely to create barriers to social acceptance, both physically and mentally. The study objectives were then determined:

1. to estimate the extent of the population in the geriatric centre identified as having these functional disabilities

2. to measure the dependency of the population with such functional disabilities

3. to make a definitive assessment of these functional disabilities by the use of appropriate validated tools of assessment.

Accepting the hypothesis that such disabilities and the consequent effect on a patient's dependency, could be directly or indirectly influenced by the effectiveness of existing care programmes, it was further decided:

4. to endeavour to improve the dependency of the selected population by implementing a specific change/or changes to the individual's pattern of care, and/or the environment in which they live. For this a multi-disciplinary approach was essential.

185 patients (in six nursing units) of the total of 400 long-term care patients were assessed by the following several parameters to establish a composite file of information relevant to the particular disabilities of patients, and how these affected their level of function and degree of dependency. These collective parameters were then used for subsequent comparative measurements of progress.

1. *Patient-nurse dependency study.* Hearn (1974), describes a patient-nurse dependency study as a tool to examine and measure requirements for nursing staff time in terms of workload generated by patients' needs, interpreted according to the policies, standards, resources and restrictions of the particular environment. From a review of literature of various nurse-dependency studies used in general hospitals, it is evident that in developing an appropriate tool the emphasis is generally placed on measuring clearly defined direct basic and technical nursing care activities. While many of these activities are appropriate and equally important to geriatric nursing, other factors such as patients' disturbed behaviour patterns, sensory disabilities and requirements for psychological support or activity stimulation, make high demands on the nurses' time. It was therefore decided that an appropriate dependency form would be designed to categorize the identifiable needs for nursing care of the elderly in the centre. The dependency score form included the following major areas of nursing care requirements, under which specific items of activity were listed:

1. Identification data
2. Assessment of normal social functions — supportive care given in previous 24 hours
3. Assessment of physical problems — care and preventative measures in previous 24 hours
4. Assessment of elimination functions — problems and care in previous 24 hours
5. Assessment of technical nursing care — requirements during previous 24 hours
6. Monitoring of vital signs — requirements during previous 24 hours
7. Supportive care and surveillance related to — sensory disabilities (speech, hearing, sight, perceptual), behaviour patterns (disoriented, confused, restless, aggressive, demanding), and psychological needs
8. Activity stimulation — therapeutic or maintenance.

To assess the relative weighting for each listed item of care random multiple time checks were undertaken, and/or check comparisons made against previously documented dependency studies. A weighting factor determined by a subjective value judgement was added for the items listed under the areas seven and eight. Patients were then categorized within a rating scale of 1-5. It should be emphasised that this study was undertaken as a broad screening tool to identify disabilities and the associated dependency levels of patients; it was not done to determine specific staffing requirements for the current estimate of nursing workload. However, it is intended to continue to develop and refine this tool, for the ultimate purpose of estimating variations in nursing care workload. From the population of 185, figures were extracted to identify those with a single incontinence problem, or incontinence linked with behaviour and/or sensory problems. 121 patients were so identified. A random sample of 52 patients from six nursing units was chosen for further study.

2. *Incontinence survey.* The existing pattern and degree of incontinence was observed and charted for each 24 hours in one week using a chart similar to that used for a study in homes in the West Riding of Yorkshire as described by Browne (1978). A habit training programme for management of incontinence was then conducted for the following four weeks.

3. *Medical Assessment.* All patients in the study received a general medical examination so that diagnoses and related documentation was complete. To assess mental function and physical functional capacity the Medical Director instructed and supervised a registered nurse, who had completed the post-basic geriatric nursing course, to complete the following questionnaires:

Barthel Index of Independence: to score the ability of a patient with neuromuscular or musculoskeletal disorder to care for himself (Mahoney & Barthel, 1965)

Katz and Akpom Index of Independence in Activities of Daily Living: an assessment that reflects profiles of behavioural levels of six sociobiological functions (Katz & Akpom, 1976)

Kahn Mental Status Questionnaire (modified): an objective measure for determination of mental status in the aged (Kahn et al, 1960).

A special patient project file of all base line data was then raised by the Medical Records Administrator for ease of monitoring the progress and analysis of the study.

Activation therapy programme

It was now time to consider the major objective: 'To endeavour to improve the dependency of the population by implementing change/or changes to the individual's pattern of care, and/or environment in which they live'.

The assumption was that behaviour and mental awareness can be affected by such factors as a decrease in routinisation of basic care, and an increase in responsiveness to individual needs, by providing stimulating activity and allowing patients to exercise a right of individual choice. The techniqes used varied depending on the ability of patients to respond, and included grooming sessions aimed at creating greater self awareness and improved body image, reality orientation, physical and mental exercise, relaxation music therapy and cooking. Activities external to the nursing unit included picnics, bus trips through the streets of the city, and entertainment by films or concert artists. Activities were both on a one-to-one basis and in selected groups according to the particular need of the patient. While such types of activities were already frequently arranged for many of the patients in the centre, many of those with disturbed behaviour patterns or who were incontinent were excluded because of their need for individual support supervision, or because they were seen to be socially unacceptable. For some patients, a considerable period of time had passed since their previous outing away from the nursing unit.

Relatives were informed of this programme by the Charge Nurse of the nursing unit, and they were given a small hand-out incorporating the above information. They were invited and encouraged to join the activities at any time. They were informed that it was hoped that the results would assist in future planning to meet patients' care needs.

The Chief Occupational Therapist and the Chief Physiotherapist were the motivators and mentors of this activity programme, but the nursing staff were to be totally involved. To allow the nursing unit staff more time and freedom to participate, the programme was conducted over a five week period when registered nurses who were students in the post-basic course, and occupational and physiotherapy students, could be allocated to the nursing units selected for the study. The experience in activation therapy was also expected to be an important and valuable educational experience for the students. It was suggested to the nurses involved that they wear civilian clothes, so that they would feel less inhibited by their nursing identity, and this might also be of importance in accepting a change of activity by some patients.

Although planned specific programmes of activity was the main approach, nurses were also expected to use reality orientation methods as described by Hahn (1980) at every opportunity, to increase the individual's awareness of person, place, time and situation. The post-basic course students were requested to document their observation of each patient's reaction, and to assess and document any change observed in the physical or mental state of the patient.

Weekly multi-disciplinary team meetings were held on each of the nursing units in the study, so that problems of organisation and staff relationships could be aired, and progress and care plans of individual patients could be discussed. All members of the team were encouraged to participate actively in the review process. Most of these meetings were attended by the Medical and Nursing Directors. Their role was to be supportive to staff, and to initiate quickly any administrative organisational requests.

This project has been presented to illustrate that breaking down attitudinal barriers in the practical field can be achieved by practical projects, and by a multi-disciplinary team approach which requires the personal involvement of staff with staff, as well as with patients. Although it is beyond the scope and purpose of this account to give a detailed description and clinical analysis of the outcome as assessed in terms of improved patient dependency, the degree of success in achieving this in terms of attitudes to individualised care planning by a multi-disciplinary group, may be interpreted from the questionnaire submitted to thirty six members of staff at the conclusion of the project.

All professionals involved with the patient care project were given the same questionnaire; and 100 per cent returned the questionnaire. It was structured as a close-ended questionnaire offering three to five choice answers for each item. Where appropriate the further alternative response of 'other' was offered. Free response additional comments were invited at the end of the questionnaire.

The activation therapy questionnaire

Three questions sought knowledge about, and personal reaction to, the philosophy of activation therapy; the results are summarised in Table 5.1. Four questions sought attitude response to the multi-disciplinary team care concept; the results are summarised in Table 5.2. As shown in the tables, a high proportion of all staff responded 'positively' to questions in these sections of the questionnaire. Registered nurses

Table 5.1 Response to activation therapy questionnaire: knowledge and personal reaction to the philosophy of activation therapy (Code: S = strongly; g = generally)

Category of staff	Response expressed in percentages				
	Positive		Negative		Uncertain Non-specific Not answered
	s	g	g	s	
Reg nurses (ward staff)	50	44			6
Reg. nurses (students)	33	64			3
Enrolled nurses	3	87			10
Medical officers	22	56			22
Occupational therapy students	45	44			11
Physiotherapy students and assistance	8	75			17
Total	26.9	61.6			11.5

Table 5.2 Response to activation therapy questionnaire: attitudes toward the multi-disciplinary team care concept (Code: S = strongly; g = generally)

	Response expressed in percentages				
Category of staff	Positive		Negative		Uncertain
	s	g	g	s	Non-specific Not answered
Reg. Nurses (ward staff)	62	30			8
Reg. Nurses (students)	53	35	5	2	5
Enrolled Nurses	27	60	5		8
Medical Officers	42	42			16
Occupational therapists (students)	50	33	8		8
Physiotherapy students and assistants	31	44		6	19
Total	44.2	40.5	3.0	0.4	11.8

(both staff and students) and occupational therapy students recorded the highest proportion of 'strongly positive' attitudes. Because of their close personal relationships with patients throughout the project, this was to be expected. Enrolled nurses recorded the lowest proportion of 'strongly positive' attitudes. This group indicated in their free response comments that they did not know enough about the programme before it started; this has been accepted as a valid criticism, and could be the cause of their response level. Physiotherapy students were less involved with the programme than others, and this could explain their low 'strongly positive' response to the questions.

One question asked respondents to identify and rank the areas that caused them the most difficulty during the programme. Registered nurses (both staff and students) ranked in exactly the same order of difficulty:

1. assessing patients for a plan of care
2. documenting patients' progress
3. multi-disciplinary group meetings
4. working with other professionals
5. getting to know other professionals.

All other professionals also ranked the 'assessment of patients' to be the most difficult. Occupational therapy and physiotherapy students ranked 'working with other professionals' to be the second highest difficulty for them, and enrolled nurses ranked 'getting to know other professionals' as causing them a high level of difficulty. It is significant that 'assessing patients for a plan of care' was the area of greatest difficulty for all; and it could be assumed that this reinforces the belief that both experience and education are necessary to enable staff to feel confident about planning and achieving appropriate individualised care of the elderly.

One question sought attitude response toward group professional relationships, and the benefit of any particular group to the individual staff member. All groups ranked the occupational therapists and student registered nurses in the first or second position. Enrolled nurses were ranked by all groups in either second or third positions. The remaining groups of registered nurses (staff), medical officers and physiotherapists received scattered rankings from second to fifth position. The significance of this result was the recognised contribution, by others, of enrolled nurses who have the most direct patient care contact, and this was signified by the rankings.

The remaining questions sought quantitative information about improvement of patients, and are not pertinent to this particular report.

The problems, as described by Treece & Treece (1977), which arise because of the interpretation of questions by respondents, and in formulating results of this type of questionnaire, are acknowledged. However, it was considered to be a direct simple method of obtaining information from staff to supplement other specific clinical findings related to patients. It was also important to take into account the relatively early stage of development of operational research into the practice of geriatric nursing and multi-disciplinary concepts in this country, and that emotional reaction to any misinterpreted apparent criticism is yet to be overcome. Therefore, there was no justification for being insensitive to the possible threat to the self-esteem of staff, by subjecting them to a barrage of probing or complex research techniques. The implementation of any specific elements of this project on a continuing basis, for the ultimate benefit of all patients in the geriatric centre, will rest with the enthusiasm of the staff who have been involved in this project, and their colleagues who, it is to be hoped, will be stimulated by them. It is therefore important that the value of their contribution is acknowledged, shown to be appreciated, and preserved. The summary of the findings of the questionnaire are submitted therefore, with the knowledge of the limitations and possible bias of the tool used.

General discussion of the project study
For a project of this scope involving professional groups with different knowledge and different expectations of their particular input and power to achieve a common objective, it is essential that management

appreciates the complexity of the degree of autonomy and interdependence required of each group. Thus a leadership structure supportive of conditions that will stimulate initiative, while being actively responsive to monitoring and co-ordinating the whole, is essential. Innovative programmes inevitably also require co-operation of the general support services of the institution, and the overall climate of the total structure of the organisation needs to be such, that it is capable of responding to demands made on it if established practices need to be changed.

It is necessary for management and group leaders to be aware that a challenge to existing systems can result in anxiety and defensive responses. Staff need opportunity to express their concerns and uncertainty, and to work their way through conflict between the 'established' systems and suggested change. If individuals, who do feel threatened and defensive and unable to negotiate their relationship within the multi-disciplinary group, are not given opportunities to do this, they may suffer considerable conflict which they are unable to resolve easily. It may be that some nurses feel that their previous professional contribution was not of an acceptable standard or quality. If this is apparent, their morale must be reinforced by encouragement and positive objective statements, about both past and present work performance. The Director of Nursing needs to be particularly alert to such situations.

This pilot operational research study was essentially concerned with the implementation of change, rather than with the production of scientific theories. The general aim was to produce organised multi-disciplinary activity, and to reach the best possible decision with regard to individual patient care, within the various constraints of any particular situation. The concept of an inter-disciplinary team has been accepted in theory in long term care settings for some time, but it is not always easily recognisable in the practical daily activities at the service level. Some of the barriers that mitigate against successful collaboration are such realities as : limited time to talk; non-acceptance of flexibility and overlap between disciplines because it might imply usurpation of another role; and lack of understanding, that although each discipline's perception of a problem may be different, concurrent co-ordinated action will often achieve the appropriate results where individual action fails. Because of these barriers there is frequently misunderstanding, or little understanding, of the plan of action for each group with regard to patients. There is overlap and sometimes duplication of services that leads to confusion by the patients and/or their relatives. Conversely, resources are not always utilised because of lack of knowledge about the scope of a particular professional group.

It is believed that the experience of this project has enhanced the understanding of all disciplines; the team discussions during the project became notably more relaxed, and anxieties and tensions were absorbed by the sharing of common experiences which cut across traditional roles, resulting in a more cohesive group that should be able purposefully to continue to plan improved patterns of care for all patients in the centre. This project has shown that the matrix of professional groups in an extended care centre for the aged, should, and can, be used to mobilise interaction and co-operation in the planning of particular patterns of care for patients. Recognition of both autonomy and the interdependence of each group's contribution is essential and also possible, and the benefits of a positive approach to comprehensive patient care are considerable.

The ongoing tasks of the project team are: to seek ways and means of changing the attitudes of those in the community and in other professional health fields who, through limited understanding, negatively stereotype elderly persons admitted to long term care facilities, hospitals and other health agencies; and, to motivate and assist the staff of this geriatric centre to increase their positive attitudes, and hence their overt behaviour, by implementing cohesive patterns of care. The message for nursing staff is one of recognising that they can function with effect and benefit in a multi-disciplinary team. More importantly, as they are the pivotal influence in any long term care setting, they must accept the co-ordinating function of a multi-disciplinary care approach. The nurse, because of her role and capacity to give constant holistic care at any time of the day, is the only generalist, and this allows her the fortunate opportunity to both co-ordinate and share experiences with all members of the team. If nurses do not accept this responsibility, and develop their understanding and capacity to work with other professionals, there is every likelihood that the patient will continue to receive fragmented care.

Conclusion

Attitudinal barriers to the concept of contemporary geriatric nursing are many in Australia, and there are no quick solutions or smooth rides to achieve either short or long term goals. Nevertheless, the problems cannot be ignored. A national survey of nursing personnel (Commonwealth Department & Health, 1978) estimated that the staffing establishment (expressed as full-time equivalents) for government, private and deficit financed nursing homes was 7003 registered nurses and 4290 nursing aides (enrolled nurses); representing 13.47 per cent registered nurses and 20.98 per cent nursing aides of the total establishments for all types of health care institutions. Another survey conducted by a State statutory nursing authority (Facts, 1980) reported that 25.7 per cent of all nurses renewing practicing certificates indicated that geriatric nursing was their field of employment. As the demographic forecasts for the elderly population become a reality, we can only assume that the proportion of nurses working in the field of geriatric nursing will need to increase; and our problems are likely to also increase, unless we face the issues now.

Nurses in the geriatric field in long term care facilities and community services are enveloped by historical ambivalence toward the elderly frail, arising from both external societal and internal professional beliefs and myths. Without adequate knowledge of the biological and sociological changes which occur with an increasing life span, and the knowledge and ability to maximize the potential of each aged person in their care, the effectiveness of nurses' genuine caring behaviour may dissipate, if they become immersed in a series of routinised procedures designed to get each aged person through each day as quickly and efficiently as possible. Changes to traditional patterns of nursing care may be viewed as just adding to the workload, with little chance of achieving or improving the quality of life of patients; others may express the view that patients are well cared for, contented with their level of function and activity, and it is therefore inappropriate to disrupt their regular routines. Such reactions typify the negativity which still abounds in many long term care homes for the aged. Many defend their routine approach, by claiming that patients are dressed and out of bed daily, and patients do participate in activities. However, contemporary geriatric nursing in its widest sense is more meaningful than this, and there is a pressing need for all nurses to be educated to understand the broader aspects; and it is essential that those practising in the field are knowledgeable about the specifics. The demands on nurses working in the field, as in the transition from traditional to contemporary approaches to gerontology and geriatric nursing occurs during this next decade, may cause stress and anxiety to some staff. Directors of Nursing particularly need to recognise this, and they must be both agents of adaptation and facilitators of change. Administrative systems and techniques must be developed to permit and encourage staff to cast aside historical prejudices. Educational programmes must be established to enable staff to gain knowledge, so that they may respond to the changing needs of the patient population.

Finally, the sheer weight of numbers means that nurses will continue as they have in the past, either to impede or advance progress in the field of long term care of the elderly. It is vitally important to the profession that they accept and demonstrate accountability for their actions; only then will they be able to kill the myths of tradition, and change the iconic representations of the past — only then will they have broken down or modified the many attitudinal barriers.

REFERENCES

Brown B 1978 Management for continence. Age Concern, England, p 47
Campbell M E 1971 Study of the attitudes of nursing personnel toward the geriatric patient. Nursing Research Journal 20 (20): 147-151
Facts 1980 Nurses and nursing in Victoria. Victorian Nursing Council, Melbourne, p 22
Hahn K 1980 Using 24-hour reality orientation. Journal of Gerontological Nursing 6 (3): 130-134
Hearn Rhys C 1974 Evaluation of patients' nursing needs: prediction of staffing. Nursing Times occasional papers, September 19, 26: 69-72; October 3, 10: 77-84
Kahn R L, Goldfarb A I, Pollack M, Peck A 1960 Brief objective measures for the determination of mental status in the aged. American Journal of Psychiatry (October) 117: 326
Katz S, Akpom C A 1976 A measure of primary sociobiological functions. International Journal of Health Services 6 (3): 493-506
Kayser J S, Minnigerode F A 1975 Increasing nursing students' interest in working with aged patients. Nursing Research Journal 24 (1): 23-26
Mahoney F I, Barthel D W 1965 Functional evaluation: the Barthel index. Maryland State Medical Journal, rehabilitation section (February): 61-65
Marram G, Barrett M W, Bevis E O 1979 Primary nursing, a model for individualized care, 2nd edn. C V Mosby, St Louis, p 47-82
Newton E 1979 This bed my centre. McPhee Gribble Publishers, Melbourne
Nursing Personnel 1979 A national survey: report of the committee on nursing personnel survey. Commonwealth Department of Health, Canberra vol 1, p 28-64
Wells T J 1980 Problems in geriatric nursing care. Churchill Livingstone, Edinburgh, p 29-49
Wolk R L, Wolk R B 1981 Professional workers' attitudes toward the aged. Journal of the American Geriatrics Society 19 (7): 624-639
Yurick A G, Robb S S, Spier B E Ebert N J 1980 The aged person and the nursing process. Appleton Century Crofts, New York, p 101
Treece & Treece (1977)

6   *Margaret F. Hudson*

The older adult, primary care and the geriatric nurse practitioner

Introduction

A promising new development in health care in the U.S.A. is the emergence of the geriatric nurse practitioner (GNP). This new role is especially exciting because it blends the old — nursing — and the new — gerontology, geriatrics, the nurse practitioner role and primary care.

Definitions of the terms older adult, primary care and GNP might be helpful. In the U.S.A., the older adult has typically been defined, for legal and sociological reasons, as an individual 65 years of age or older. Some experts in gerontology are currently choosing to refer to the 'young old', 65-75 years, and to the 'old-old', 75 years plus. Recently the mandatory retirement age has been changed from 65 to 70 years. In time this legal 'definition' of old age will probably also alter the social definition. Whatever his age, the older adult is any individual who is in the latter part of the life span and thus has special needs and problems — the impact of accumulating aging changes and illnesses unique to later life, concurrent multiple health care problems, multiple losses, atypical responses to disease and therapy, stresses of chronic disease and aging, and the effects of being old in America.

Primary care is a new term for, and more comprehensive approach to, an old concept in health care. General medical practitioners and public health nurses have practiced aspects of primary care for years. 'Primary care is a range of services delivered for the most part in ambulatory settings to meet the majority of needs for personal health care. It focuses upon the assessment of health status, the prevention of diseases and maintenance of health. Management is provided for minor illnesses, slowly progressive chronic diseases and non-specific symptomatic complaints with referral for specialty care as needed' (University of North Carolina School of Nursing, 1979). On the whole older adults require more primary care than any other age group with the possible exception of infants and very young children.

The GNP is an experienced registered nurse whose skills have been expanded with additional formal training and education in the diagnosis and management of minor acute and stable chronic medical conditions, and in gerontology/geriatrics. The additional knowledge and skills enable this nurse to assume the responsibilities of meeting many of the primary care needs of older adults.

Older adults in the U.S.A.

In recent years, the older adult segment of the U.S. population has rapidly increased, both in numbers and as a percentage of the total population. In 1977 there were 23.5 million persons 65 years and older, comprising 11.1 per cent of the general population, as compared to 3.1 million (4.1 per cent) in 1900 and 16.5 million (9.2 per cent) in 1960 (U.S. Department of Health, Education and Welfare — US-DHEW — 1977). As these figures demonstrate, America's older adult population is growing more rapidly than the nation's total population, and this trend is expected to continue into the 21st century, with significant impacts on American society and its health care system.

Other significant shifts have occurred within the older adult population. One out of three is now 75 years or older, and one out of 16 is 85 years or older. The proportion of elders 65-74 years old is getting smaller and the proportion 75 years and older is getting larger (a 10-fold increase since 1900). The fastest growing age group is comprised of those elders 85 years and older, a 17-fold increase since 1900 (US-DHEW, 1977). Thus America's older adult population is not only increasing in size, it is also 'growing older'. These shifts hold major significance for health care. The prevalence of disease and multiple health problems increases more rapidly after age 75. With the 'growth and aging' of the older adult population, the need for effective and efficient health care and social services also increases, as does the need for research, health maintenance, and disease prevention and control.

Other important factors must be kept in mind regarding America's older adults. Their mortality rate declined from 1960 to 1975 by 13 per cent (US-DHEW, 1977). Most of the decrease in mortality in older adulthood is accounted for by significant decreases in two of the three leading causes of death — heart disease and cerebrovascular disease. The death rate for cancer, the second leading cause of death, has gradually increased. The death rate has continued to be considerably higher for older men than for older women (and this difference is increasing) and higher for non-whites than for whites. Since women now outlive men by an average of eight years, they comprise a disproportionate segment of the older adult population and consequently face additional problems, such as living alone, often on inadequate incomes.

Older adults are a very heterogeneous group, for with aging comes greater uniqueness as each individual lives through more numerous and diverse life experiences. However, as a group, America's older adults experience certain similar problems. They are more likely than younger people to suffer multiple health care problems and chronic diseases, often with resultant disability. Many older adults experience problems related to housing. With limited income and in the face of inflation, they may be forced to move into substandard housing in areas of urban blight or rural neglect. If fortunate enough to be able to stay in their long-term home, they may find themselves unable physically or financially to manage the necessary upkeep. Their physical safety within the home may be endangered by stairs, rugs and heating appliances. Physical changes with aging and being alone makes them especially vulnerable to crime, which is on the increase. Problems with transportation make it difficult for them to obtain needed commodities and to utilize community resources.

In the U.S.A., financial problems are more likely to arise in older adulthood than at any other time of life, especially among women and minorities. With retirement many elders experience a decrease in income from between one-half to one-quarter of their average pre-retirement level. In the mid-1970s there was an increase in both the number and proportion of poor older adults. Our elders were the fastest growing poverty group, and many experts believe much of this was new poverty, poverty occurring after becoming old. During this time 33 per cent of all older adults (51 per cent of elderly women living alone and 75 per cent of elderly blacks living alone) had incomes at or below the poverty level (Butler, 1975). Since the mid-1970s the average income of our elders has improved slightly. A variety of factors have helped. Recent cohorts of older adults are better educated, held a higher proportion of white collar jobs, and have contributed to social security for more years. Support programs such as Supplemental Security Income, Medicare, food stamps and housing subsidies, and improved social security benefits (husband's full benefits to widows and the cost-of-living escalator clauses) have also helped. Although improvement has occurred, inadequate finances are still a major problem for a significant portion of our older adult population, and this situation may worsen if inflation continues and if the social security program fails.

Some final issues relevant to the older adult and their health care needs are 'ageism' and cultural/ethnic diversity. 'Ageism', as defined by Dr Robert Butler, is 'a deep and profound prejudice against the elderly. It is a process of systematic stereotyping of and discrimination against people because they are old, just as racism and sexism accomplish this with skin color and gender. Old people are categorized as senile, rigid in thought and manner, old-fashioned in morality and skills .... Ageism allows the younger generation to see older people as different from themselves; thus they subtly cease to identify with their elders as human beings.'

Ageism is prevalent in the U.S.A. (for it is found to some degree in all of us) and is one of the major blocks to effective health care of our elders. Typically it shows itself in subtle, covert ways: health care and social service agencies with inadequate and distant parking facilities; doors difficult to handle if one is weak, has a cane, walker or wheelchair; traffic lights that change too quickly for the older pedestrian; buses with steep steps; doctors' offices that require hours of waiting; receptionists and practitioners who call clients by their first names without permission; health care providers who expect elderly clients to keep up with the provider's pace, etc. Dr Jacquelyne J. Jackson has challenged us to be aware of our elderly who are in double, triple or quadruple jeopardy — old, poor, female and minority — because of the combinations of ageism, sexism and racism. Another subtle form of ageism and racism is still apparent in the fact that many health care educational programs have minimal or no required content in gerontology, geriatrics, culture and ethnicity.

Future cohorts of older adults are predicted to be better educated, healthier and more politically active than most present cohorts. These differences may well alter the problems, needs, concerns and resources of these future cohorts. Even now current and future cohorts of older adults are making their impact felt on the health care system by demanding greater expertise and more appropriate care. For example, the Grey Panthers organization has been a major supporter of older adults and their concerns.

All of the issues mentioned above must be acknowledged and responded to appropriately if health care providers are to be responsive to our older adult clients and their special needs.

Primary care in the U.S.A.
The health care system as it has developed during the past three decades does not respond well to the everyday health needs of people, especially older adults. It is expensive, highly specialized, inflexible and demographically mal-distributed. Hospitals are complex and bureaucratic, and the nursing home industry has become a big business. Older adults have increasingly come to fear and suspect doctors, hospitals and nursing homes, as they perceive these sources failing to meet their health care needs effectively.

Primary care as a rediscovered and improved approach to health care services is especially appropriate for the needs of America's older adults. The goal of primary care, and of most elders, is maximal functioning of the individual with emphasis on the quality of life. Primary care with its focus on meeting the general health needs of the individual, can be the client's entrance into the health care system. Its services should be affordable, flexible, available twenty-four hours per day and provided by a consistent clinician. Consideration should be given to location since transportation is a major problem in many areas. When possible, home visits should be part of such service, and maximal utilization of area resources by clients should be encouraged.

These characteristics are important for the older adult client. A familiar local clinic and provider are needed as one gets older and finds change more difficult and large hospitals overwhelming, inflexible and confusing. The elder is much more likely to come to a small local clinic, and to a known and trusted provider. This enables health care problems to be dealt with earlier and more completely, and improves client compliance. Home visits also help meet elders' needs in safe, comfortable ways. Being alone and sick at night is terrifying, especially for the elderly, and being able to have your health care provider available by phone at any hour is most reassuring. Location and affordability are especially crucial to our elders for whom transportation and inadequate or fixed incomes are frequent problems.

Primary care services should also be the point where holistic baseline assessments are done, where health care problems are defined and solved, where clients' common acute and chronic illnesses are diagnosed and treated, and where co-ordinative, comprehensive approaches are arranged to make secondary and tertiary medical care services available when needed. This approach enables the health care to be more effective and economic with greater continuity and less fragmentation of care. These characteristics are especially important to older adult clients for whom comprehensive assessment and care are essential because of the prevalence of multiple health care problems. Health maintenance measures and treatment of acute illnesses can often keep or return an elder to the mainstream of life. A serious acute illness can begin a negative cycle (snowball effect) that throws the elder's chronic illnesses and previous balance out of control. In this event, rapid access to care, continuity of care, and often referral, are essential.

Primary care's emphasis on health education, to promote clients' understanding of their therapy and responsibility for their own health care, is appropriate in light of the elderly client's usual desire for continuing maximum independence and self-control. Such health education — for coping with life's crises, home management of illness, coping with illness in ways to produce growth, and for mobilizing personal resources for life and death — also blends the services of primary care nicely with the needs of elderly clients. Take, for example, the needs of the elderly woman on a fixed income who can't afford to keep her husband in the nursing home and support herself. Does she divorce him so he can be eligible for public support and live with the resultant guilt, or what? Primary care services can help her face this dilemma, explore alternatives, utilize available resources and support her during this crisis.

Currently primary care services are located in rural satellite clinics, hospital clinics, doctor's offices, public health department, nursing homes and home health agencies. These services are provided by a variety of health care practitioners — doctors, nurses, physical therapists, nurse practitioners and physician's assistants. The roles and functions of these various primary care practitioners are diverse and yet similar, often overlapping and complementing each other. Primary care services need the expertise and collaboration of each of these practitioners.

The geriatric nurse practitioner

The GNP is one role in which primary care, gerontology/geriatrics and nursing are blended. The GNP is ideal for primary care. This nurse has the skills necessary to deal with the whole client. Her clinical assessment goes beyond the medical history and physical exam to include consideration of psychosocial factors ranging from mental status to life style to environment. She (in this chapter, 'she' is used for the nurse and 'he' for the client only for purposes of clarity; obviously clients include women, and men are also in the role of GNP) can listen, interview, observe and care .She also builds relationships with clients, educates, does anticipatory guidance and manages common acute and stable chronic health care problems. The GNP's role has evolved from three major factors: women's and nursing's historical role in care of the elderly, the shortage of doctors in underserved areas, and the growing awareness in America and the health care system of the numbers and needs of our elderly.

In the U.S.A., gerontology as a field of research began in the 1920s. In the 1930s, as infectious disease decreased and chronic illness increased, more emphasis on aging occurred, with Society Security beginning in 1935. The 1940s saw the occurrence of conferences on aging, with formation of the American Geriatric Society in 1942 and the Gerontology Society in 1945. The 1950s and 60s saw increased research and publication on aging, and the first international conference on gerontology. The White House Conference on Aging was held in 1971, and the National Institute of Aging was established in 1974.

Gerontological nursing gradually evolved, first by default and later by design. In 1935 with money available from the Social Security Act, many aged poor went to live in boarding homes which were run by the first 'geriatric nurses'. For years nurses, mainly licensed practical nurses, cared for the elderly, especially the frail elderly, in rest homes, nursing homes or as private duty nurses while the elderly and their special needs were largely ignored by the mainstream of the medical and nursing professions. In the 1950s some nursing leaders began to focus attention on the needs of our older adults. Slowly, more and more nurses began to enter this area. By 1962 the American Nurses' Association (ANA) began a geriatric nursing conference group, by 1966 there was a division on geriatric nursing practice, and in 1973 standards were established for geriatric nursing. Gerontological/geriatric nursing is the most recent specialty in nursing, and as such, it has only recently been accepted as a valid specialty for professional nurses. Dr Virginia Stone, Irene Burnside and others have done much to give credibility to this area. Dr Stone also led the first Masters of Science program in gerontological nursing at Duke University. Now there are several such programs in the U.S.A. Unfortunately the inclusion of gerontology in basic nursing education has not been consistent or complete, with most nurses getting this content at a graduate level either in Masters of Science in Nursing or Continuing Education programs. In 1978 ANA House of Delegates passed resolutions which supported universal inclusion of gerontological nursing content in curricula of basic nursing education, as well as graduate and continuing education programs in gerontological nursing.

Continuing education programs were the first educational programs producing GNPs. Many began with grants from the U.S. Department of Health, Education and Welfare. During the late 1960s and early 1970s nurse practitioner programs began in Colorado (pediatric nurse practitioners) and North Carolina (family nurse practitioners), partly in response to the realization that nurses had been under-utilized in providing health care, and they could provide quality health care at lower costs. With time these educational offerings in primary care and gerontology/geriatrics merged into long-term continuing education programs which educated and certified professional nurses as GNPs. Now a few universities are enabling nurses to get their Masters degree and their nurse practitioner certification within the same educational program.

The education of GNPs varies from program to program, but due to

ANA's guidelines for GNP curriculae, required content is fairly uniform and includes the following areas: the aging process, special communication issues (interviewing, history taking, dealing with sensory deficits and counseling), community health care delivery systems, developmental tasks of older adulthood, gerontological health problems (diagnosis, management and referral), psychosocial issues of older adulthood, role change of the GNP, pharmacology, assessment procedures and methods (American Nurses' Association, 1974). Most GNP programs are one year in length and include didactic content and a preceptorship for clinical experience in the new role. Upon successful completion of the program the nurse is certified as a GNP. In North Carolina she must then apply to the joint subcommittee (members from the boards of nursing and medicine) for approval to practice. When this approval is granted, it enables the GNP to practice with designated approved physician(s) and in a specified site(s).

The ANA helped to solidify gerontological nursing as a legitimate specialty by publishing in 1973 its *Standards of Geriatric Nursing Practice*. These standards focus on and define quality of practice, and they are guidelines for all gerontological/geriatric nurses in all settings. The standards include appreciation of the heritage, values and wisdom of older persons; resolution of conflicting attitudes regarding aging, death and dependency; maintaining life with dignity and comfort until death ensues; observing and interpreting minimal and gross signs and symptoms associated with both normal aging and pathologic changes, and instituting appropriate nursing measures; differentiating between pathologic social behavior and the usual lifestyle of each aged individual; supporting and promoting normal physiologic functioning of the older person; protecting aged persons from injury, infection, and excessive stress and supporting them through the multiplicity of stressful experiences to which they are subjected; employing a variety of methods to promote effective communication and social interaction of aged persons with individuals, family and other groups; designing, changing or adapting the physical and psychosocial environment to meet the older adult's needs; assisting older persons to obtain and utilize devices which help them attain a higher level of function and ensuring that these devices are kept in good working order by the appropriate persons or agencies (American Nurses' Association, 1973).

The GNP is a licensed professional nurse and certified practitioner who is responsible for providing primary health care by forming contractual relationships with clients. She exercises independent decision-making and judgments within the limits of her education, knowledge and skills. Her clients can be individuals, families, groups or communities. Her nursing expertise and additional practitioner knowledge and skills complement and enhance each other, and allow her to be more effective and flexible in serving older adults who typically have multiple health care needs and problems. The GNP's role includes direct client care, supervision of nursing personnel and collaboration with physicians and other health team members. The GNP is able to perform nursing functions with greater depth and broader applicability. She does holistic health status assessments; makes nursing diagnoses and sets realistic goals with clients; plans and implements nursing interventions and evaluates results of care given; assists older adults and their families in managing psychological, social and economic concerns affecting their health; educates and counsels older adults and their families regarding aging, health, illness and resources; meets the health care needs of elders in co-operation with physicians and other health team members; utilizes personal and community resources appropriate to client's needs; functions as a client advocate for older adults; provides emotional support to clients during illness; coordinates health care resources; refers clients as needed for their health care needs; and helps create a therapeutic milieu for older adult clients. The GNP is also able to perform selected medical functions under supervision of an identified physician — preceptor and within established protocols. These functions include obtaining medical histories; performing physical exams; diagnosing and managing, consulting or referring clients with common acute and chronic illnesses; prescribing and managing clients on selected medications; giving direct health care and providing health care follow-up.

The GNP functions in many settings and sites: in nursing homes, hospitals, clinics, home health agencies, public health departments and in independent practice, alone or with a physician colleague. GNPs are especially needed in nursing homes, where quality nursing care and physician coverage have traditionally been lacking. Here the GNP can function to upgrade the level of primary care and nursing care available, maintain ongoing staff education, be readily available to assess residents' health care needs and be a liaison between the elderly resident and staff and the physician. In hospitals, clinics, home health agencies and public health departments, the GNP can provide primary care and in-depth nursing care for older adult clients, often in the client's own home via home visits. These home visits are crucial in geriatrics if maximal independence and health care are to be achieved, for this approach allows assessment of the client's environment and real life situation. In independent practice the GNP has an ideal opportunity to develop primary care responsive to older clients' needs, to be an aging advocate and to guide clients to various community resources.

Health assessment

In any setting two priority functions of the GNP include performing an on-going holistic and comprehensive health assessment of the older adult client, and assisting the client to achieve and maintain his maximal level of health and independent functioning. The nurse's own attitudes about aging, disability, dependency and death are crucial for biases and ignorance can only produce erroneous assessment and care. Priority is given to accurate and complete assessment, and to accurate and individualized problem definition, for if these two are achieved for the individual client, realistic goals, and meaningful and acceptable interventions are more likely to be implemented.

In a holistic health assessment the nurse should first assess the elder's current physical and psychosocial developmental status. These data must then be applied as guidelines so that pertinent priority data in all other areas (sociodemographic, nutritional, occupational/ meaningful productive activity, past and current medical problems, environment, medications, health habits) can be collected. Only in total data analysis can the assessment be adapted to the older adult. This analysis helps to differentiate normal from abnormal, functional from pathologic and realistic from unrealistic. For analysis, the key questions are: 1) what are the relationships among these data? and 2) what do these relationships indicate regarding what this client is able/unable to do (functional assessment) in maintaining his own homeostasis? For example, if the client is mildly depressed, how does this affect his ability to recognize and utilize his internal and external resources? If the client's family does not understand and appreciate aging, and constantly go at their own fast pace, how does this affect the elder's independence, safety and self-esteem? In light of the other physical and medical history data, is the S_4 heart sound functional or an indication of disease? If the client has always valued autonomy, productivity and independence, how do these values interface with his declining physical strength and his changing behavior with his family? Again if another client has always been passive with authority figures, is that why she won't tell her dentist her dentures rub and hurt, resulting in her not wearing them and her inadequate nutrition? Could a client do her own shopping at the grocery store down the hill if she didn't have to walk uphill carrying groceries? Understanding of the client as a unique individual and careful analyses of the data are crucial to finding solutions which are acceptable, meaningful, realistic and effective.

Holistic assessment is important for all clients, but it is crucial in dealing with the multiplicity of health care problems found in the elderly. In addition, there are special considerations in each data area for older adult clients. Complete discussion of appropriate considerations is impossible within one chapter, but selected examples should suffice.

Physical assessment
Each body system should be evaluated for normal aging changes versus pathology. The nurse should seek data about strength of stimuli needed to elicit a response, i.e. with heat, cold, smell, touch; visual acuity, peripheral vision, color vision, whether glasses correct vision; normal pace; degree of decrease of reflex and conscious reaction time; heart's response to stress, causes of tachycardia for client; mental status; orthostatic hypotension; hearing acuity, auditory stimuli missed, client's response to decreased hearing; balance, muscle strength and joint mobility; bowel elimination and hygiene, self-treatment of constipation; peripheral circulation and impairment of it by client; usual Bp range; usual temperature; baseline blood sugar, serum creatinine, electrolytes, and albumin; how readily client tires and causes of tiring; urinary elimination and hygiene, nocturia, urgency, and frequency of voiding; usual fluid intake per day; condition of skin, any suspicious changes or lesions; rest and activity balance, any exhaustion and its cause; sexual activity, any unmet needs; client's recognition of an adaptation to own physical aging changes; review of systems for signs and symptoms.

Psychosocial
The nurse should be alert for indications regarding client's feelings about himself, aging, health and illness in general, own health, health care providers and death, and evaluate the effects of these feelings on his health care behaviors; client's priority goals and expectations of future, client's feelings about achieving these, help needed/wanted; his views of his life to date — integrity v. despair, current life — best/worse about it, three happiest and saddest events, accomplishment and failures; his strengths and limitations; his view of his past and current roles, recent changes/losses, those he values most; his perception of social norms in his area, effects on him; his feelings of confidence, hope; site of client's locus of responsibility/decision-making/control — is it where he wants it; significant problems he has faced, ways he dealt with them; his coping strategies and defense

mechanisms; losses he has suffered, dates, concurrency, his view of these losses, his stage in the grief process, consequences of each loss, his adaption to each, substitutes found for these losses, by whom, client's response to these; components of his support systems, their effectiveness, losses or changes in these or his reference group; people comprising his family and significant others, relationship to client, location, health status, ways they interact with client and he with them; decision-making processes in family; feelings of family members and significant others regarding client, aging, illness and dependency; things family does for and with client, client's responses and feelings, client's expectations of family and significant others, are these realistic; most important people in client's life, does he have at least one confidant, client's feelings of importance and being cared about; client's financial situation, income, expenditures, balance, handled by whom and why, major financial worries; senior citizen benefits entitled to, whether receiving these; possible sources if help needed; client's formal/informal educational level; religion, meaning to him.

Sociodemographic
The nurse should seek data about the major cultural and ethnic influences on this client and his health; the effects these beliefs/practices have on his perception of his illness, the health care provider and his prescribed treatment; and any conflicts between his beliefs and the GNP's beliefs regarding health and health care.

Nutritional
The nurse should get data regarding the client's ability to shop for and prepare his own meals; finances available for his nutritional needs; his feelings about eating alone; his smell and taste acuity; foods he typically chooses to eat; his views of eating.

Occupation/meaningful productive activity
The nurse should ask about his employment, employer, job description; reason for working, salary, client's feelings about job, if job requirements are congruent with client's interests, skills and abilities, and fringe benefits. If client is retired ask when this occurred, why, its meaning to him, his feelings about retirement, how he spends his time now (typical day, meaningful activities), what losses occurred with retirement, if these were replaced, if so how and with what, and major changes after retirement.

Past and current medical problems

The nurse should clarify past and current medical problems, their treatment, by whom, results, client's feelings/beliefs about these diagnoses, treatments and care received; effects of current problems on client, and their relationship with his aging changes.

Medications

The nurse should get data about client's beliefs about medicines, usual compliance or non-compliance, self-treatment and use of over-the-counter medications; his ability to take own medications safely and correctly; medications taken in past for extended periods; allergies; total medications client is taking, complexity of drug regime, drug interactions possible, his understanding of why he is on current medications, if medication is in containers he can open, client's ability to read labels, his ability to afford these medications, relationship of his drug therapy to his life style; complete drug history — drugs taken, adverse reactions and compliance; effects of his aging changes on his body's drug utilization.

Health habits

The nurse should assess alcohol intake, amount and length of time; smoking history; preventive health habits — use of dentist and doctor, regular daily exercise, hobbies, interests, recreation, sleep or rest problems.

Environment

The nurse should ask if his environment (home, neighborhood and community) is conducive to his needs and abilities; when and where he feels rushed — with his family, in grocery lines, crossing streets, etc.; length of time lived in his home/neighborhood/community, any changes, feelings about these changes; does his home have indoor plumbing, adequate heat and cooling, hot water, rails on steps, adequate lighting, cooking facilities, grocery and drug store nearby; is neighborhood flat or hilly, near public transportation; is client isolated in home; potential for social and sensory deprivation; condition of sidewalks; curbs a different color than the sidewalk and street; can he hear the phone ring and voices on the phone; can he read prices on commodities in stores; temperature setting of hot water heater; can client smell spoiled food, gas leak or smoke; safety of environment for ambulation, with cane or walker, can he get into community buildings; who cuts his grass/shovels his snow, home in good repair, handrails on tub; emergency numbers near phone, nearest available help in emergency.

Functional ability
Functional assessment of a client should be an analysis of the total data and the relationships between these data. The client's ability to function in all realms — physical, psychological, social and economic — must be evaluated. Can the client handle his activities of daily living (ADL) and demands of daily living (DDL) himself? What is his mobility status? Can he see and hear adequately to do his ADL and DDL? How do his views of aging and illness affect his typical day's activities? How do his mobility, vision, hearing and response time affect his ability to drive his car? How do his pride and autonomy affect his cardiorespiratory status? How do his beliefs about bowel regularity affect his self-care? How do his feelings about himself affect his activities? Will he try new things/make new friends? How does his mental status affect his compliance with medications? Relationships with others? Recognition of internal and external stimuli? Safety in his home? How do his home lighting, bathroom location, vision and nocturia interrelate? How do his beliefs affect his use of internal/external resources?

In functional assessment and problem identification or diagnosis the framework devised by Carnevali & Patrick is applicable. The nurse is concerned with helping the client to achieve and maintain a balance of his activities of daily living (ADL) and demands of daily living (DDL) with his coping resources (CR) and support systems (SS) in ways congruent with his life style. Each of these aspects is influenced by the client's age, health, illnesses, life experiences and life style (Carnevali & Patrick, 1979).

ADL are the behaviors and events usually engaged in by most individuals during a day, e.g. dressing, eating, bathing, walking, shopping, cooking, driving car, etc. DDL are the expectations an individual has of himself or believes others have of him. These expectations help to determine his pace, choices and priorities. For example: I should wash the car today, take my medicines on time, make that dress for my granddaughter, write that article instead of reading that novel, do well in that interview or hurry so I won't be late for that meeting. Coping resources are the internal or personal capabilities that an individual has to draw on in living life, managing problems, coping with stress, etc. These include characteristics such as courage, intelligence, problem-solving ability, self-confidence, endurance, knowledge, creative and adaptive ability, coping strategies, determination, physical strength, and emotional health. Support systems are the individual's external resources which he can utilize to help him in living. These can be personal or material resources such as family, significant friends, health care personnel, own home, neighborhood stores, equipment, money, transportation, social service agencies, etc.

Lifestyle is the person's preferred pattern of living or approach to life — how he usually perceives, thinks, behaves. It is a composite of his unique stable personal characteristics; independent versus dependent; spontaneous/deliberate; of type A/B personality; preferring high/low stress levels, change/stability, structured/unstructured situations, high/low activity level; outgoing/reserved; fast/slow paced; with many acquaintances/few close friends, etc. (Carnevali & Patrick, 1979). This lifestyle is constructed by the self's unique and creative responses to experiences.

This framework is applicable in assessing and planning care with older adult clients; however, certain considerations must be kept in mind. Aging, illness and environmental factors can hamper the older adult's ability to perform his own ADL and DDL. For example, decreasing vision and hearing may make driving hazardous, or failing vision and joint stiffness could prevent sewing or knitting, or living on a hill may prevent an elderly man from mowing his lawn. Attitudes and beliefs about aging and elderly people may alter the older person's demands of daily living, e.g. 'Mother you should rest more', or 'Dad, you shouldn't be up on the roof fixing the gutter at your age', or 'I can't dance anymore now that I'm old', or 'Old people shouldn't live in neighborhoods with kids, they should all go to retirement communities'. Too often biases and ignorance affect reflected appraisals given to older persons, then become internalized by the elder himself and become self-fulfilling prophecies.

Coping resources can increase or decrease with age or illness. Physical strength and endurance may well decrease with normal aging. Most other coping resources are usually enhanced for healthy older adults as a result of their numerous and varied life experiences. Mental status changes and physical or mental illness can hamper most of these coping resources. For many older adults, losses of friends and family through death or moving decrease the number of personal resources in their support system unless meaningful substitutes are found. Also erroneous beliefs of family and friends can prevent personal resources from being supportive to the elder. Sometimes previous material resources can change or diminish, e.g. the drug store three blocks away was convenient until illness decreased the person's ability to walk long distances; a significant drop in income with retirement; buildings which are inaccessible to persons with walkers or wheelchairs;

equipment that breaks down; a bus at the corner with steps too high to climb; social service agencies who can offer help but who antagonise the elderly person by rushing him; and the home loved and owned for years that is now unsafe due to disrepair.

The lifestyle or personality of older adults is even more unique and diverse than in younger years, for it is continually shaped and clarified as one ages and experiences more and diverse life experiences. Understanding the client's lifestyle enables the nurse to better understand how the client perceives his world. Also lifestyle is a pivotal factor affecting an individual's style of aging and life satisfaction.

This framework is most effective when the nurse fits the client's total data into it. Then and only then, can the imbalances (nursing diagnoses) and their causes be clearly defined for the individual client, and appropriate interventions selected with the client and implemented. If the assessment has been done carefully, solutions are usually more readily apparent.

Example client situations
The GNP's role and function in primary care can be seen most effectively in examples of real client situations. These examples also demonstrate the need for GNPs to assess and assist elderly clients in a variety of settings. With each client the emphasis is on effective comprehensive assessment of the individual client and his needs.

Nursing home
Mrs Elder (all names are fictitious) is an 83-year-old widow who was placed in Goodhaven Nursing home after being transferred from three other nursing homes and two hospitals within a two year period. The staff avoided her because they perceived her as 'demanding, confused and unable to be pleased'. As this avoidance continued Mrs Elder became more verbal, crying out frequently, refusing most care, belligerent, tachypnic and tachycardic and very anxious. She ate little, slept poorly, often refused her medications and began accusing staff of abuse. Her family rarely visited, for the distance between their home and the nursing home was too great. After several days spent in observing, listening to and caring for Mrs Elder, the GNP was able to identify five major problems. Mrs Elder had 1) moderate mental status change (delirium) secondary to moderate heart disease, which was thrown out of control by her anxiety and resultant tachycardia; 2) moderately severe anxiety secondary to her new environment, her needs not being met and total loss of her support system; 3) depression secondary to multiple transfers and multiple concurrent losses with

bereavement overload; 4) social and sensory deprivation secondary to her depression and anxiety (with pushing away behavior), her isolation in her room, her decreased vision and hearing and her physical distance from her family; 5) pain and general physical discomfort secondary to her unnecessarily limited mobility and accentuated by her anxiety.

Once the GNP was able to diagnose the priority problems, then interventions were begun to help the staff deal with their feelings about Mrs Elder; learn ways they could effectively help her and thus feel less frustrated with her; stop avoiding her perceive her and her situation realistically; and help her find solutions to her problems. The first step in interventions with the client was gaining Mrs Elder's trust by listening to her, not becoming angry in return, anticipating her basic needs, staying with her for brief and contracted periods, returning on time, bringing her apple sauce (her favorite food) anytime she wanted it, and using touch in ways acceptable to her. Getting the doctor's approval to discontinue her thioridazine hydrochloride, encouraging her family to visit every month, helping her reminisce, getting her out of her room in the wheelchair when she was ready, doing morning care according to her own routine, and showing her she was lovable and acceptable also helped. One aide was caught being physically too rough with three clients, including Mrs Elder, and dismissed. Subsequently Mrs Elder's favorite aide on each shift was assigned to care for her. Within a month after effective care was consistently instituted by the staff, Mrs Elder was behaviorally a different person. She had gained weight, smiled and talked with selected people, did much of her own care and cooperated with the staff. She was no longer tachypnic tachycardic, anxious or 'demanding'. Her mental status improved to normal except for a problem with recent memory, her depression lessened considerably, and her physical discomfort was minimal.

Virgil C. is a 65-year-old ex-accountant with dementia secondary to alcoholic encephalopathy. When he was transferred to our nursing home from another nursing home, he was undernourished, had multiple bruises and was very afraid of people. He was totally unable to perform his own ADL, to recognize his wife or to make his needs known. His usual behavior was to pace the halls constantly, eat anything he could find and avoid everyone.

Key points for the GNP's assessment showed Mr C. to have minimal cognitive ability, and to respond visually to persons who approached him slowly from the front and only to the edge of his personal space. Some of his problems were identified as: 1) realistic severe anxiety and fear secondary to his dementia, transfer to a new location and probable previous physical abuse; 2) severe mental status change secondary to dementia from alcoholic encephalopathy; 3) social and sensory deprivation secondary to his anxiety, and dementia. A team conference was held and care planned. A partial care plan included providing him with his favorite nutritional foods at spaced intervals while he walked up and down (since he was too restless to eat sitting at meal times); working on trust development, with the GNP being the one consistent person to approach him in ways acceptable to him; calling him by name (he nonverbally showed preference for Virgil) each time staff saw him and acknowledging something he was doing or something about him, without violating his personal space; keeping all communication with him at his level, brief, warm and slowly paced; anticipating his basic needs and helping him after telling him what staff member was going to do, e.g. 'Take you to the bathroom', and personalizing his room with his clothing, family pictures and other small personal possessions.

With this approach Virgil made steady progress to his apparent maximal capacity. He still walks most of the day but usually holding hands with some staff member and even venturing outside if the staff member is with him and it is nice weather. He eats walking and at the table. He non-verbally asks for food, to go to the bathroom, and for company on walks. He smiles when his wife visits and at familiar staff members. He also occasionally 'talks' with his wife or staff, though only parts of his conversation are understandable. He has gained weight and no longer shies away from strangers.

Clinic

Mrs Brown is a 63-year-old widow who lived alone in a trailer near her daughter and worked full time as a clerk at a discount store. She had visited the clinic previously for health maintenance appointments and for treatment of a URI and sinusites. One day she called the GNP and asked if she could 'run over during her lunch hour since she felt she had difficulty getting her breath'. She was at the clinic within 15 minutes appearing anxious and slightly dyspnic. The history of her chief complaint was virtually negative. She had begun feeling short of breath two days ago without any associated symptoms. The dyspnea had increased slightly. The physical exam demonstrated only tachycardia, tachypnea and varicose veins. The doctor was consulted and agreed to a chest X-ray and lung scan to rule out pulmonary embolism. The GNP scheduled the tests and called Mrs Brown's daughter, who met her mother at home and continued the observation and reassurance begun by the GNP. Later the GNP met Mrs Brown and her daughter at the hospital. The chest X-ray was normal. The lung scan was positive for a small pulmonary embolism. The doctor was called. He came and met Mrs Brown, admitted her to the hospital and took over her medical care. The GNP saw Mrs Brown every day for continuity of psychosocial care and for health education regarding varicose veins and pulmonary embolism.

Mr Ellis is a 70-year-old Black living with his wife in a small home they own and receiving Social Security and S.S.I. His three children live in different cities and, like him, struggle financially. Mr Ellis was followed at the clinic for moderate hypertension controlled by a low salt diet and medication. On one visit the GNP noticed he seemed preoccupied and his blood pressure was elevated. Upon questioning he admitted he was 'powerful worried because they quit sending him his gold check and he couldn't make it without it'. Because of his financial worries he had economized by not refilling his anti-hypertensive prescription. The GNP gave him some medicine and contracted with him to call the Social Security Administration in town 'since I couldn't get any sense out of them. They don't like to mess with usins'.

The phone call to Social Security produced little clarity about the situation, so later in the week Mr Ellis and the GNP went to the Social Security Administration together. Once there the GNP was able to determine that because of changes in guidelines, he was receiving higher Social Security payments, was no longer eligible for S.S.I., and was ironically then expected to live on less total dollars. The next week on a home visit, Mr and Mrs Ellis and the GNP planned a new budget to fit the reduced income. Mr Ellis was still angry but he felt supported and was again taking his medication. He also promised to come to the clinic before missing any medication again and if he was 'worried'.

Hospital

Mr Crouse, a 69-year-old Black man from a rural area, was transferred to a large medical center by his local M.D. for treatment of breast cancer. When the GNP met him he was lying in bed with the covers up to his nose looking very frightened. Attempts to converse with him proved futile so the GNP gathered data from the staff and by observation. This assessment in part showed that Mr Crouse had been very quiet since admission, had looked at his hospital bed and toilet with wonder and awe, had been 'diagnosed' by the doctors and nurses as being mentally retarded, and had provided the doctors with little personal data. The staff was very angry with Mr Crouse because 'he wouldn't co-operate', and they subsequently talked over and around him. Since Mr Crouse would not talk with any white people or anyone in a white uniform (including the GNP), the GNP got Mrs Parrish, a

Black nursing student in a blue uniform, to agree to be Mr Crouse's nurse. With data gathered by Mrs Parrish and analyzed with the GNP's help, it was determined that Mr Crouse was not mentally retarded. He was in culture shock; very anxious and fearful of the strange doctors, nurses and hospital; severely lacking in support systems due to his distance from home and family, and totally confused and greatly lacking in understanding of his breast cancer and proposed treatment.

The pertinent data and identified problems were shared with the medical and nursing staff, but only one doctor (a junior assistant resident) and one nurse believed this information. Thus, Mr Crouse's care improved only minimally. Mrs Parrish remained his nurse with the GNP as her backup. Mr Crouse did well physically with his surgery, but the attitudes of most of his doctors and nurses severely traumatized him emotionally. Unfortunately for Mr Crouse, the GNP and Mrs Parrish could not change other health care providers' attitudes rapidly enough in order to provide him with quality care. At discharge Mr Crouse stated, 'I'll never see no doctor again'.

Mrs Johnson is a 77-year-old woman with CHF controlled with digoxin, severe arterial insufficiency of her right leg and osteoarthritis. She was admitted to the hospital where after a thorough medical workup a profundaplasty was performed in hope of restoring adequate circulation and saving her right leg. After observation in the hospital for two weeks the decision was made that amputation was the only choice. After her second surgery Mrs Johnson's behavior changed radically. Her memory and judgment were impaired, she was preoccupied and anorexic, she was no longer motivated to help herself and she was very irritable and weak. At this point the GNP became involved in Mrs Johnson's care. Assessment showed strong positive family support, previous personal strength in coping with crisis, no serum $K+$ determination since pre-amputation, a new cardiac arrhythmia, no pre-operative anticipatory help regarding loss of her leg, no recent serum digoxin level and depression secondary to the loss of her leg and her prolonged hospitalization. Subsequent lab studies showed her serum $K+$ to be 2.9 and her digoxin level to be 2.4, so she was hypokalemic and in digoxin toxicity.

In consultation with the doctors she was put on KCL suppliment and her digoxin dose was lowered and monitored. A psychiatric consultant was called in to help her resolve her depression and grief. A staff conference with the doctors and nurses enabled a complete care plan to be devised and carried out by the staff. Her family's support was appreciated and encouraged, and her previous coping strategies were uncovered and supported. Soon her serum $K+$ and digoxin levels were normal, her CHF was again under control and the arrhythmia resolved. Her physical strength, personal motivation and courage returned with help from the psychiatrist and staff. The following month she was discharged to her family with concrete plans to complete her rehabilitation on an out-patient basis.

Public Health Department
 Mrs Robertson was an 87-year-old widow who lived alone in her rural home near her children and their families. She was slowly dying from thalassemia. Her coping resources and family support systems were quite effective and consistent although strained by the slow progressive downhill course of her illness. Her own emotional energies were wearing thin and her children were beginning to bicker over her care. In this situation the GNP had been visiting Mrs Robertson weekly to check on her condition, listen and visit with her, and validate her medication intake.

With recognition of the new stresses, visits were made more frequently and on an 'as needed' basis. The GNP focused on supporting the family and allowing them to ventilate their grief and frustrations, and on being a more frequent and visible part of the support system for Mrs Robertson. This mainly entailed letting her talk about her illness and death with the GNP, thus providing her with this outlet and relieving the family of this emotionally charged burden. Mrs Robertson died quietly and with dignity one day will all her children around her. The family, with the GNP's and each other's support, were able to grieve normally toward resolution and to feel positively about what they had contributed to their mother's life, care and peaceful death.

Independent practice
 Mr and Mrs Coleman called the GNP because of concern about Mr Coleman's mother's new confusion and seemingly less capable condition. They feared she might need nursing home placement. With permission from all three people concerned, the GNP made a home visit to the mother. Assessment of the patient showed delirium probably secondary to malnutrition, early pneumonia and Exlax overuse. Consultation with the family doctor resulted in quick treatment and resolution of her malnutrition, pneumonia and Exlax toxicity. The GNP then focused her efforts on health education for Mrs Coleman, Sr and her son and daughter-in-law regarding aging and preventive health care. Mrs Coleman, Sr now continues to live safely and independently in her own home with understanding and support from her family. All three of them feel free to call the GNP

with any of their health questions with which they are hesitant to 'bother their busy doctor'.

Mr Finch called the GNP because his mother had seemed confused that afternoon. Later in the day he had talked with his sister, who had taken their mother out to lunch two days previously and had also found the mother to be slightly confused. A home visit was made which found Mrs Finch to be dressed in soiled underwear and robe, sitting in a chair and eating ashes from her ashtray. Her conversation was disjointed and irrational. Since the son said she was an insulin dependent diabetic and had other medical problems, the GNP tried to find out what medicines Mrs Finch had taken that day and what she had eaten. Mrs Finch was unable to respond in helpful ways except to take the GNP to a cupboard in the kitchen where 35 to 40 different prescription medications were found. The GNP then did a physical exam, tested Mrs Finch's urine and blood sugar (4+ and negative; high) and called the family doctor who, after hearing all the data, admitted Mrs Finch to the hospital.

Mrs Finch was hospitalized for four weeks and had numerous tests. Her altered mental status slowly returned to normal. The cause of her mental status change was never clearly determined, although the doctors felt it was due to drug interactions and depression leading to decreased control of her diabetes from inadequate nutrition and insulin intake. The GNP took all of Mrs Finch's medicines to the hospital where the doctors there confronted the family doctor (whose name was on all the medicines and who did not remember prescribing them). These medicines were all discontinued except of her insulin and anti-anxiety medicine. The GNP visited Mrs Finch in the hospital, educated the family about aging, diabetes and depression, and later helped Mrs Finch find healthier ways to deal with her loneliness and depression once she was home.

Conclusion

As these client examples demonstrate, the GNP has a viable and very needed role in primary care with older adult clients. The need for the nurse in this role is there, and the demand will increase as more clients and families experience the service which this professional can render, and as GNPs continue to do the needed clinical research and publication on care of older adults with acute and chronic problems.

REFERENCES

American Nurses' Association 1973 Standards for geriatric nursing practice. Kansas City, Missouri

Butler N 1975 Why survive? Being old in America. Harper & Row, New York

Carnevali D L, Patrick M 1979 Nursing management for the elderly. Lippincott, New York

University of North Carolina School of Nursing 1979 Definition of primary care. Chapel Hill, North Carolina

U.S. Department of Health, Education and Welfare 1977 Elderly people: the population 65 years and over. In: Health/United States/1976–1977. Washington, D.C., ch 1, p 3–26

Hospice concepts applied to the aging

DEATH AND DYING EMPHASIS

The Decade for Dealing with Death might well be a title describing the years from 1970 to 1980. Both in North America and Great Britain vast quantities of resource materials appeared focusing on the topics of death and dying. Certainly a popularizer of this universal theme was Dr Elizabeth Kubler-Ross whose small volume, *On Death and Dying*, written in 1969, helped to encourage the flood of related works.

Ten years later Michael A. Simpson (1979) published a critically annotated bibliography and source book of thanatology and terminal care entitled *Dying, Death, and Grief*. His evaluation includes over 750 books, more than 200 films, plus numerous other teaching aids and journals. In the introduction to his book Simpson states: 'Death is a very badly kept secret, such an unmentionable and taboo topic that there are over 750 books now in print asserting that we are ignoring the subject. At no time in history has there been so much attention paid to death as a subject for scholarly and literary study, clinical and research attention, or for cynical commercial exploitation'.

Since the creation of humankind, death has been the inevitable conclusion of physical life. Throughout history different cultures and societies have dealt with it in various ways. Prior to the rise of modern hospitals, persons usually died in the familiar settings of their own homes. With the advance of the 20th century technology, scientific methods have enabled persons to extend their lives. Increasing numbers of people are dying in impersonal settings of sterile institutions, often surrounded by a maze of medical machines.

In the course of this century both birth and death have primarily moved out of the home. As Silverstone & Hyman (1976) noted: 'In this highly efficient and highly sterile atmosphere, strangers may usher in life and usher it out, while those with the deepest personal ties can feel like trespassers'.

Aging and dying

Since the oldest members in our population are, generally speaking, the closest to dying, it is particularly important to give special attention to ways in which the elderly may be assured of an opportunity for a good death. According to Pearson (1979) the first federally sponsored conference in the United States on terminal illness and impending death among the aged was held in 1965.

Early in the 1970s concerned humanitarians in the United States began exploring ways to adapt the British hospice concept in the States. *The Hospice Movement* by Sandol Stoddard (1978) has as its subtitle 'A Better Way of Caring for the Dying'. An even more recent publication, *A Hospice Handbook*, (Hamilton & Reid, 1980) is subtitled 'A New Way to Care for the Dying'. Both works imply that in providing care for terminally ill patients, including the elderly, the hospice approach is superior to other methods of tending the dying.

ATTITUDES TOWARD DEATH

Before discussing the hospice concept in detail and examining its implications for the aging, we will look briefly at attitudes toward terminal illness and death as exhibited by society in general, by medical personnel, and by the aging.

Attitudes of society in general

By now almost all health professionals are acquainted with the stages of death as described by Kubler-Ross (1969). She has helped persons in medical and lay fields to realize that dying persons and their significant others may experience in varying ways feeling of denial and isolation, anger, bargaining, depression, and acceptance. Somewhat in contrast to her listing are seven stages in the grieving process discussed by Kavanaugh (1972). His categories are shock, disorganization, volatile emotions, guilt, loss and loneliness, relief and re-establishment.

However, many patients and families are unwilling to discuss death in any dimension. They treat it as a taboo subject. Two major works lifting up this attitude are Weisman's *On Dying and Denying* (1972) and *The Denial of Death* for which Ernest Becker (1973) won a Pulitzer prize.

Reluctance to accept the reality of death compounds problems for every involved person. Varying levels of awareness exist as patients, health professionals, families and friends face the inevitability of death. If death were not taboo for some people, it could be talked about freely. Direct references might stimulate rather than abort discussion.

Fear of death
Based on review of extensive research, Brink (1979) concludes that persons with strong religious beliefs tend to have somewhat less death anxiety. Those with lower levels of religious activity usually manifest more fear of death. Such fear may be due to other anxieties: the unknown, loneliness, loss of identity, loss of significant others, loss of body, loss of control, regression. Those who have been a failure at living fear death most, whereas those who are having fulfilling life do not show so much fear. In a study of 1269 individuals aged 45 to 74 (Bengston et al, 1979), the middle-aged expressed the greatest fears of death and the elderly the least fear.

Attitudes of health care professionals

Younger and middle-aged persons, the very ones who provide much of the care for the dying elderly, may need to be more conscious of their feelings toward death. Many staff exhibit behavior based on the following attitudes and expectations of their patients (Strauss & Glaser, 1977). 'The patient should maintain relative composure and cheerfulness; he should face death with dignity; he should not cut himself off from the world but continue to be a good family member and be nice to other patients; he should cooperate with staff members who care for him and, if possible, avoid distressing or embarrassing them'.

There is evidence (Mauzey et al, 1977) that death and dying is a topic freely avoided in health histories. Thus, those interviewing patients may be unwilling to discuss that about which the patient has most need to talk.

Ethical decisions also pose problems for care givers. Medical science can prolong death for days, weeks, months, even years. Through the use of surgery, artificial respirators, dialysis equipment and other mechanical devices, life can be sustained almost indefinitely. What are the moral responsibilities, especially as applied to an aging population?

Attitudes of aging toward death

As human beings become septuagenarians, octogenerians and nonagenarians, they often have a changing perception of time. Coupled with the realization that time is becoming more precious, there may also be a sense of emptiness regarding the meaning of time. However, lamenting about the uselessness of the future is not necessarily a death wish.

Losses associated with age

Although aging can be a season for deeply satisfying achievement and fulfillment, accumulated years may bring deteriorations in biopsychosocial functioning. Sensory deprivations are very common; other systems, including the cardiopulmonary, gastrointestinal and nervous, showed marked changes. Loss of status and income resulting in altered self-image may accelerate the process sometimes referred to as social death (Watson & Maxwell, 1977).

Disengagement theory

Gerontologists engage in vigorous debate regarding the inevitability of gradual or rapid withdrawal of an aging person from active life. Some believe that the anticipation of death frees individuals from feeling obligated to participate in the ongoing stream of living, that they willingly disengage. On the other hand, Kastenbaum (1977) reports that many geriatric patients in hospitals or nursing homes invest themselves solidly in a network of interpersonal relations and responsibilities. Such persons may actually intensify their life participation.

Suicide

The extreme example of withdrawal from life is self-inflicted death. The rate of suicide increases sharply with advancing age, especially among men, and unsuccessful attempts are of greater significance in old age than young (Jeffers & Verwoerdt, 1977). Evidence from research studies by Busse and Pfeiffer (1977) indicate that the majority of the older persons committing suicide have been depressed. A smaller fraction is made up of persons who have used alcohol to excess. A still smaller fraction consists of persons with organic brain syndrome. A very small percentage of those committing suicide suffer from an intractable terminal illness.

Other reactions of aging to death

Older persons may respond in many ways to the fact of their impending death. According to Brink (1979), most elders do think about death, but they are not really obsessed with it. Usually it is realistically considered and prepared for. Most of their views on death involve positive recognition that it is frequently an end to suffering.

Staff working with homebound elderly and those confined in nursing homes often observe the incapacitated pleading and praying for death. Still there may be a strong element of fear. In the aged, fear of death correlates positively with living alone and with a low level of education (Brink, 1979).

Fear of prolonged illness. Current studies (Jeffers, 1977) show that death is feared much less than prolonged illness, dependency, or pain. These latter conditions may bring threats of rejection and isolation, as well as the loss of social role, self-determination and individual dignity. Repeatedly the aging express anxiety about becoming a burden to their loved ones. Many may already have lost a spouse through death and have few remaining friends to support them at time of sickness. Kubler-Ross (1974) was asked how to respond to a geriatric patient who said she had lived long enough. Her answer symbolizes the spirit of the hospice concept: 'Yes, you may have lived long enough, but since you are still living, is there anything that we can do to make it more worthwhile so that you can truly live until you die?' Helping people retain a desirable quality in their final days of living is part of the hospice goal.

THE HOSPICE CONCEPT

The term 'hospice' is derived from a medieval word for a place where travelers on a difficult journey could find shelter and care. These shelters were commonly operated by religious orders. The word was again used in the late nineteenth century and into the twentieth to describe very high quality nursing homes in England that specialized in care of the terminally ill and dying.

In the 1960s as Dr Kubler-Ross was breaking the taboo on death and dying in the United States, Dr Cicely Saunders was beginning the modern hospice movement in her pioneering work in England toward better care for the dying. Her work led to the creation of St Christopher's hospice in Sydenham, England, which is viewed as the model hospice by most of the Western world. Present usage of the term 'hospice' implies a medically directed interdisciplinary health care program providing a continuum of home and in-patient service to the terminally ill patient and family which continues into the bereavement period.

The hospice setting

Hospice is a concept, not an institution. It is the characteristic elements that earn a program for the terminally ill the title of 'hospice'.

Hospices may be found in free-standing-institutions such as St Christopher's in England; in special units within a hospital, as the Palliative Care Unit at the Royal Victoria Hospital in Montreal, Canada; in programs that offer only home care, such as Hospice of Marin in California. Hospice may be a team of trained workers serving wherever the terminally ill are located within an entire hospital.

Hospices may offer a combination of the above models and may include day care or night services.

The ideal hospice offers both in-patient care and home care. The aim of hospice is that the concept will permeate all types of health care organizations and institutions and effect a change in the attitude and approach of society to this stage of life.

Round-the-clock care

In the home care setting as well as in the in-patient facility, provision must be made for seven-day-a-week, 24-hour coverage. The anxiety level of both patient and family are greatly reduced by the comforting knowledge that someone is available at time of need.

Medically directed interdisciplinary team

The medical director's role varies. In addition to supervising the medical work of the hospice staff he works as a consultant to the patient's personal physician in areas of symptom control and home care, and in come cases assumes part or all of the medical care of the patient.

The interdisciplinary team includes the patient and significant family members who are encouraged to contribute their concerns and ideas to the plan of care. They also must give it final approval. Other team members include the primary physician, the hospice medical director, nurses, social worker, home health aides, therapists, volunteers and religious leaders. If the hospice works in close conjunction with other community agencies such as district or visiting nurses or cancer society, the job of coordinating and communicating is essential and complex. The team, or as many members of it as feasible, should have periodic case conferences to update each other and to consider the needed changes in the plan of care.

It is the major responsibility of nursing staff to evaluate the patient/family needs and to call upon the various disciplines as needed. Hospice is a holistic approach acknowledging that no one person can meet all the needs of the dying patient and his family. The team works together to extend the family resources to meet these unique needs both efficiently and humanely.

Patient and family: the primary unit of care

The hospice concept considers the patient and family, including any significant relationships, to be the unit of care. The physical problems of the patient may not be the most significant area of need. Of equal importance in facing terminal illness and death will be the emotional, social, economic and spiritual needs of the patient/family.

Symptom control

'I'm sorry, there is nothing more I can do for you' are some of the most devastating words doctors can use. Along with conveying the knowledge of impending death they bring to the patient and family, with no intent by the doctors to do so, the utter feeling of being alone and abandoned, just at the point they need help most.

There remains much that the physician *can* do. Symptom control now becomes the focus of care and requires a holistic approach to the needs of the patient and family by the multidisciplinary team. Dr Walter Modell, Director of Clinical Pharmacology at Cornell University, warned in a lecture as early as 1961 that 'our concentration on diagnosis and cure has resulted in neglect of relieving distress. In treating the terminally ill we must keep in mind that what the symptom causes may be as important as what causes the symptom'.

Pain is a subjective experience that can be measured by no scientific instruments. Pain is also experienced in other realms than the physical and all aspects of pain, to the patient or to his family, affect the quality of life.

Cohen (1979) describes four kinds of pain which make up the 'total pain' that must be faced by the dying and their caretakers. These are social, psychological, spiritual and physical. To achieve 'pain control' the total pain of patient and family must be treated.

Social pain

The discomfort felt by friends and relatives when they come to visit the dying sometimes puts the burden of being the comforter on the patient. At times the patient may be extremely embarrassed about physical deterioration, weight loss, disfigurement by surgery, etc., and the patient may prefer not to see friends or even family members for weeks or months. The patient may feel very isolated and abandoned. There is the acute awareness of losing control: loss of job, independence, ability to be helpful to others. One patient expressed it well by saying, 'I have spent my life being the good Samaritan and find it very difficult to be the helpless, wounded Pharisee'. Then there are the physical losses of vision, hearing, appetite, and mobility. Loss of control of bowel and bladder can be among the hardest to accept, and among the most painful, since one becomes totally dependent in a particularly painful way on another at this time.

Spiritual pain

Spiritual pain is a very individual experience. The patient's own faith and beliefs and how he feels about his own life may play an important part. Some people are in agony until they have been able to go to confession and have last rites; others need to be forgiven by, or grant forgiveness to, someone in their life. Even those who have not been actively religious may wish a religious leader to come to them offering prayers and rituals which may bring great comfort. On the other hand, the patient and family may have great fear that someone will attempt to bring religion to them on the deathbed, and this must be avoided unless it is requested.

There can be great pain if one party feels that the other party is not 'right with God'. On one occasion a hospice received a call asking help to get a whole lifetime in order before the end. The request was for a priest to perform 'one marriage, three baptisms, and last rites'. Occasionally the patient appears ready to die but seems to be waiting until the spiritual problems have been worked out.

Psychological pain

Fear, anxiety, loneliness and anger may well overcome the patient and his family as they face death.

Fear of pain is one of the major causes of psychological stress. Copp (1974) states that the patients often made the statement that 'fear of pain is worse than the actual pain itself'. She also observed what is commonly known to nurses, that fear of pain tends to be much greater than fear of death. It is the process of dying that is feared most. Reassurance that pain and other symptoms will be controlled and demonstration of this promise can alleviate this fear.

Fear of becoming a burden to the family or friends is a great pain. Working with the patient and family to talk this over together and plan realistically often resolves or lessens this fear. Early planning and use of homemaker services, volunteers, or in-patient hospice facilities for occasional respite may prevent exhaustion and illness for the caretaker.

Fear of abandonment by doctors and institutions may distress the patient/family. They may have been sent out of the hospital due to lack of need for skilled nursing or the doctor who feels helpless may have turned over his care to a number of specialists, fragmenting the responsibility and creating a feeling of insecurity. If the family is totally committed to the ongoing responsibility and is able to do so, this assurance must be given to the patient. If, however, the family cannot cope and may already have abandoned the patient, then it is essential that the patient receive assurances that adequate care will be provided to the end.

Loss of control over every aspect of one's life is a great source of pain. Involving the patient in the planning and decision-making allows the patient to maintain some control and a continued feeling of importance.

Financial fears and problems may be a serious concern. The social workers's assistance in working out solutions may be of great help. Mr A. lived 5 weeks beyond his 'death' from a heart attack while his life was sustained with an experimental artificial heart. He taught his wife to operate his business and re-wrote his will three times during this extension of his life. He died very much at peace regarding the future of his young family. The intensive care unit where he was cared for had followed hospice principles in breaking all the rules to allow this to occur, and in this case the time bought with the use of artificial life support machines was appropriate and of great value.

Anger is another psychological pain that needs to be ventilated in nonjudgmental atmosphere. Dealing with any sources of anger that are remediable by clarification of action, and helping the patient/family to sort out which are remediable and which must be accepted can be helpful.

The pain of grief both to patient who will lose his family and to the family who are losing their loved one is great. Grieving should be allowed both in anticipation and following the death. Letting go and having a good cry with an understanding person can be very therapeutic.

Rossman (1977) well states: 'The hospice team must establish a relationship of trust and win the confidence of the family and friends so that they feel free to express their fears, feelings, thoughts and concerns. To accomplish this the team members must be honest, considerate, supportive and dependable'.

Physical pain
The hospice concept stresses that no patient should be forced to wish for death because of pain that is inadequately treated.

Intractable physical pain, often increasing in intensity, sets up a vicious cycle of pain-anxiety-depression which may well be incapacitating to patient and family. Sometimes each of the aspects of the cycle must be treated by various disciplines in order to achieve satisfactory pain control and allow life at the optimum level for patient and family.

Acute versus chronic pain. Nurses and doctors must be aware that the patient with chronic pain often suffers in 'quiet despair' and does not present the same symptoms or complaints as the acutely ill patient.

Assessment of pain: objectives
1. To understand what the patient is experiencing and the effect on the patient/family.
2. To discover any physical phenomena causing, or being caused by,

pain. (It must be kept in mind that the cause of pain may not be the primary untreatable disease process, but may be such things as constipation, fear, musculoskeletal pains, bedsores, blood clots, etc., which may respond to treatment, eliminating or reducing the need for pain medication).

3. To facilitate the creation of an appropriate and effective plan of treatment.

Assessment of pain: method

1. *Listening* to the patient and family and assuming that what they tell you is the truth (remembering that one patient's *perception* of a painful sensation may be very different from the perception of another patient with an equal sensation of pain).

2. *Questioning* the patient using a routine format such as one using the simple mnemonic PQRST:

P Provocative-palliative factors: what provokes and what relieves it?
Q Quality: is it sharp or cutting? burning? deep and aching or throbbing? These are the three standard categories of pain.
R Region: describe where the pain is located anatomically.
S Severity: describe the degree of pain. (Severe pain may be associated with such physical findings as sweating, pallor, increased blood pressure and heart rate).
T Temporal characteristics: describe the duration of the pain.

3. Observe the patient for visible or palpable physical evidence of the source of pain. An abscess, an inflamed joint, etc., may be the cause.

4. Document and evaluate the information gathered and formulate a plan of action.

Method of achieving pain control (Mount, 1976)

1. Determine the cause of pain.

Prevent the pain before it occurs. In chronic pain it is necessary to individualize the medication and dose for each patient and then to give the medication on an around-the-clock basis, not waiting for the pain to re-appear.

3. Erase the memory of pain through the achievement of total pain control and an attitude of sincere concern and confidence. (Reduction of anxiety and fear may allow the reduction of the medication dose).

4. Use medications in such a way as to achieve pain control while keeping the patient alert and minimally sedated. Use the right dose of the right medication for the patient. In general a drug should be chosen that has a minimum effective time span of four hours. Those skilled in palliative pain control use a stepladder of three groups of

drugs: aspirin or aspirin-like drugs, codeine or its synthetic counterparts, and morphine or its equivalents.

When increased doses of drugs of one level no longer work, a change is made to another level of drug, never laterally within the same group. The strong narcotics of choice are morphine, methadone, and dilaudid. Diamorphine continues to be a drug of choice in some of the English hospices, though its popularity seems to be fading.

Brompton's mixture, or a variation of this liquid medication, continues to be widely used. A variation of the Brompton formula which is a simple solution of morphine in water is gaining in popularity. This eliminates the expensive cocaine which has been shown not to increase pain relief and may cause side-effects, and also eliminates the alcohol which may burn throats and add to sedative effect. Oral morphine solution can be made in an increasingly potent solution which prevents the difficulty of administering ever increasing amounts of solution, if pain increases, to an increasingly debilitated patient. Other medications in liquid form may be added to the mixture so the patient requires only one dose.

5. Ease of administration of drugs is a key factor in freeing the patient from paraphernalia allowing him to remain in his own environment as long as possible. Oral route is preferred.

The role of volunteers

Almost no other area of health care has welcomed the volunteer so warmly or involved the volunteer so extensively in every aspect of the work as has the hospice movement. There is no job in hospice that cannot be performed by a willing volunteer. Receptionist, bookkeeper, nurse, social worker, medical director; any of these and other jobs can be filled by unsalaried people, depending on skills, education and time commitment at hospice.

It is imperative that volunteers be very carefully screened and selected. Then begins a thorough training program of basic hospice concepts. This training should include exploring personal feelings about illness and death, communication skills, various aspects of death and dying such as physical and spiritual problems and needs, the hospice movement, and special skills related to specific assignments.

The hospice volunteer is a key factor in the success of the hospice movement, not only helping provide top quality care at minimum cost but enabling hospice to go far beyond the technical and professional 'tasks' needed by the patient and family, to become the 'loving, supportive presence' that typifies the hospice concept.

Those volunteers who become members of the patient/family care team will have varying roles, but often they become surrogate family members. One of the highest compliments paid a hospice volunteer was from a man who said, 'I want to be with my wife when she dies, but if it is the hospice volunteer who is with her it will be all right because I have come to realize that our volunteer is an extension of me'.

Psycho-emotional support for the volunteer who inevitably participates to a degree in the suffering and bereavement is essential. This is often done in peer groups, at social events, and in one to one sessions with staff working on the case.

Bereavement support

To stop care at the time of death is to leave the survivor alone to face the pain of grieving, loneliness, depression, and even despair. Hospice offers support to survivors in facing bereavement and re-establishment in a variety of ways. The peer support of other survivors is important. Many times these people have become acquainted and have informally begun to meet and support each other during the terminal phase of their loved ones life. Or they may meet at a social gathering sponsored by the hospice or at a more serious group session where they are invited to come to share with each other their struggles, feelings and problems.

Group or individual therapy sessions, one-to-one support from staff and volunteers who have worked on the case or from a special bereavement team, and help from social workers in working out the many problems of finance and living adjustments are all elements of the bereavement program of hospice. If necessary, the survivor may be carried in a formal relationship to the hospice as long as a year following the death.

Since the hospice movement is still comparatively young, it is difficult to assess the full impact and the lasting benefits of bereavement support. However, evidence is mounting to show the value of letting survivors know they have not been forgotten. No doubt such support contributes significantly to improved mental and physical health of those who kept vigil with the dying.

Cost containment

Hospice care in the home setting is considerably more cost-effective than hospital care. When in-patient hospice care is compared to hospital or nursing home cost it is harder to compare and the literature does not contain a definitive cost comparison study. Certain costs are obviously reduced. This saving may be offset by the need for increased nursing staff.

However, let us not measure the effectiveness of hospice work in terms of money saved but in terms of quality care for patient and family at a time when physical, social, psychological and spiritual needs are at maximum.

Research and education

During the past several generations the psychology that ill people belong in hospitals and that only doctors and nurses have the skills to care for the sick and dying has been created. Now, with the high cost of hospitalization and hospital bed shortages, we are sending gravely ill people home when further curative treatments will be of no avail and they no longer need 'skilled nursing care'.

We have a society both educationally and psychologically unequipped to cope with this home care. It is therefore imperative that the hospice movement begin serious research into the needs of the dying patient and the family and better methods of responding to those needs. Controlled studies of approaches to symptom control and palliative care must also be done.

Since no one will escape the impact of death, education based on sound research findings is needed at every level, from the medical community to the general public, to create awareness of the needs and to give professionals as well as non-professionals better skills to cope with death and all of its ramifications.

IMPLICATIONS OF HOSPICE FOR THE AGING

Although the hospice concepts described above are applicable to any age, they have special meaning for those who have lived seventy, eighty, or more years. Leaders in psychology and medicine (Busse & Pfeifer, 1977) state that the developmental task in late years should focus on integrity. Failure to achieve an integrated being can lead to despair. Hospice seeks to help patients and families integrate the remaining days of life and thus enhance the quality of living.

Butler (1979) notes that there has been little comment in the hospice literature about the very special problems of the elderly. However, it is possible to discuss implications of hospice care as it affects the aging person's quality of life in the following areas: physical, psychosocial, financial and spiritual.

Implications for physical wellbeing

Control of pain and other physical symptoms requires special attention to pharmacology related to the elderly. Since drugs are metabolized differently in older people than they are in younger people, it is important to be aware of the varying metabolic dimensions including absorption, distribution, destruction, excretion, kinetics of drug binding, and alterations in biological ryhthms (Busse & Pfeiffer, 1977).

Patients in advanced years may become more easily disoriented. Hence, it is very important to avoid heavy sedation which could further contribute to confusion. Fear of pain can produce intensified problems. The aim is that the patient should be alert and that he should be independent (Saunders, 1969). Physical as well as emotional independence have great meaning for the aging who are experiencing increased losses, so every precaution should be taken to assure their maintaining self-worth.

Although, as cited earlier, the aging have a higher rate of suicide than other segments of the population, it is revealing to read (Dienstfrey & Lederer, 1979) that suicide is extremely rare among the hospice elderly whether as inpatients or at home. This could suggest that elderly hospice patients may have less fear of pain and are perhaps being kept more comfortable than aging persons not receiving hospice care.

Implications for psycho-social wellbeing

As important as phsycial care for hospice patients is the emotional care. Aging persons participating in a hospice program are aware that they are dying. The very awareness removes much of the secrecy and sometimes deceit which too often surround the patient/family unit. Dr Robert Butler, Director of the National Institute on Aging, writes, 'Every person has the right to know when he is dying. It gives him some control over his own life, if not his death. He can make arrangements for any bequests and order his relationships with friends and loved ones as well as prepare himself psychologically and spiritually' (1975).

In addition to having an awareness of impending death, aging hospice patients also benefit from the knowledge that they will not be deserted nor left alone at time of death. As aging may bring an increase of chronic diseases, such conditions, including loss of hearing and vision, tend to isolate individuals and contribute to feelings of loneliness. Through sensitively trained hospice staff and volunteers, the patient and family know that a loving presence will help sustain them through long hours preceding death.

Sharing in decision making is more likely to be evident in hospice than in non-hospice settings. Pearson (1969) points out that when implicit judgment of social death accompanies institutionalization, we are likely to see that families and acquaintences make a variety of decisions that hopefully would have involved the opinions and desires of the elder. In non-hospice settings the patient is too seldom consulted, even if it involves concerns such as pets.

According to Kubler-Ross (1974) older people generally know when their time of death is close and they are usually right. Their very death awareness makes them prime prospects for hospice treatment which will offer natural opportunities for conversations about thoughts and feelings regarding the unfamiliar experience of death. If, instead, there is a 'wall of silence' as described by Silverstone (1976), that silence can deprive the patient and those who care for him or her of the comfort and support at the time when it is most needed. Hospice goals include removing such artificial walls and barriers.

Implications for financial wellbeing
Older citizens are often living on fixed incomes with primary financial support coming from pensions and social security payments. When retirement years mean the end of employment and regular paychecks, new financial burdens may develop. In the United States maintaining severely impaired persons for an extended time under hospital care poses serious financial problems to patient and family. In other countries where socialized medicine exists, there are still additional expenses accompanying prolonged illness. It is expected that the fledging hospice movement will flourish in the years ahead, not only for humanitatian reasons, but because of the comparative costs: inpatient facilities are about 27 per cent less expensive that acute-care hospitals, while hospice-supervised home care is the least expensive of all (Dienstfrey & Lederer, 1979).

Implications for spiritual wellbeing
Many older persons find great comfort and strength in religious beliefs which, in some cases, have nourished them throughout their lives. In writing about the role of religion, hospice pioneer Lamerton (1973) states that all religions demand that those ministering to the dying shall preserve as peaceful an atmosphere as possible for the patient. All major religions agree that after death the body must be treated with respect and gentleness. Such attitudes and environment typify hospice care. The same author also observes that people who had not given a thought to religion and those with a very strong religion died more peacefully than those with a lukewarm faith whose ill-considered assumptions collapsed under stress. Medical personnel are well advised to be conscious of the religious faith component within the dying person and his family.

Although hospice organizations may or may not be sponsored by agencies with religious affiliations, there is much evidence that many persons helping to develop such care do so through religious motivations. Both the Seattle Hospice and Hospice of Marin County in California received strong impetus from church-sponsored courses on death and dying. In the first United States hospice located in New Haven, Connecticut, one of the founders was Ed Dobihal, a United Methodist minister. He writes, 'Being spiritual in the hospice context is offering love, kindness, mercy and understanding'. (Abbott, 1978). Such qualities which add meaning to life at any age can certainly bring increased solace and comfort to the dying elderly.

Rights of the dying

Various advocacy movements have created documents identified as a Bill of Rights. Moreover, American Hospital Association as well as the American Association of Homes for the Aging each has lists of rights belonging to patients or residents. While an Associate Professor of Nursing at Wayne State University, Amelia Barbus conducted a workshop on 'The Terminally Ill Patient and the Helping Person'. From that event emerged a Bill of Rights for the Dying embodying many principles important for elderly hospice patients. Included in the sixteen items are rights pertaining to maintaining a sense of hopefulness, having questions answered honestly, retaining individuality and not being judged for decisions which may be contrary to beliefs of others.

Life review

A right which carries therapeutic value is that which is often called life review. Those providing care for the dying should encourage this review of personal history which may assist patients and families in accepting impending death. Such a review, useful for all older persons, involves reflecting on past experiences and working through unresolved conflicts (Butler, 1979).

Varied settings for hospice

In private homes

Of persons in the United States aged 65 or over, about 50 per cent are living in their own domicile. Of that number, some five per cent may be considered homebound or bedbound (Brickner, 1978). In several of her books, Kubler-Ross (1969, 1974) extols the value of arranging for dying persons to remain at home. This, also, is one of the major goals of hospice. Of the 59 operating hospices surveyed by the General Accounting Office of the United States (*Hospice Care*, 1979), 68 per cent reported that they were providing home health care. Next to bereavement, this was the service offered most frequently.

Aging patient at home. Consequences of this for elderly persons are illustrated in the case of Mr A. At age 79, he and his 77-year-old wife had moved two years previously to a mobile home park in Florida. They enjoyed the mild climate, met a few friends in the park, and lived a simple, contented life with two cats. Mrs A. developed cancer of the liver which quickly metastasized to her lungs. Both husband and wife, married for 59 years, dreaded thoughts of her dying in a strange hospital. When physicians determined there was no cure to be expected, they referred the couple to the local hospice. During the final 14 weeks of Mrs A.'s life, the hospice staff and volunteers supported husband and wife, enabling them to remain in their mobile home with cherished pets. Mr and Mrs A. often expressed deep appreciation to the hospice for being able to experience death as naturally as possible.

Following Mrs A.'s death, Mr A. looked to the hospice friends as his surrogate family. They provided bereavement counseling and medical referrals regarding his increasing problems with arthritis and congestive heart failure.

In nursing home
Only 5 per cent of persons over age 65 reside in nursing homes. The public often sees such institutions as 'warehouses for death' (Kuhn, 1977). Many nursing home patients, if adequate community resources were available, could no doubt be sustained in their own homes. However, some long-term care facilities are experimenting in ways to provide hospice-type care for the dying. Georgetown University Hospital in Washington, D.C. for 30 years had home care provided for cancer patients. It has now linked with The Washington Home, a long-term care establishment, to provide a six-bed unit where hospice services are available (Osterweis & Champagne, 1979).

In Phoenix, Arizona, staff at the Beautitudes Campus of Care, a residential facility with a continuum of care for the aging, are experimenting in giving hospice care not just in the skilled care section but especially in the intermediate section which is less institutionalized. Nursing and social service personnel there report that such individualized attention has been particularly satisfying as it involved surviving spouses living in apartments on the campus.

In free-standing hospice
The British model which Americans study so carefully often features a separate institution such as St Christopher's at Sydenham, England. Actually, this is a hybrid of institution and home for a large, multigenerational 'family'. A separate wing contains 16 one-room

apartments for well and self-sufficient aged men and women. The hospice also has a day-care center for pre-school children of mothers working at St Christopher's. Often old persons who are terminally ill respond very positively to the presence of children (Heifitz, 1975).

Hillhaven Hospice in Tucson, Arizona, represents the first freestanding facility of its type in the United States. It is housed in a complex shared with a skilled nursing facility and a residential facility. It is physically and functionally separate except for its corporate affiliation and a contractual agreement with the nursing home for dietary, laundry, and housekeeping services (Osterweis & Champagne, 1979).

At Hillhaven Hospice grandchildren and other young relatives are a common sight. Children from local schools visit at holidays and other special times. Infants have been passed from parents' arms to nurses and from nurses to patients, with every patient holding the child. Holding life in its young form means a great deal to dying patients (McIntier, 1979). Older persons, yearning to contribute to younger generations, may find this particularly meaningful.

In hospital settings

Most hospice patients prefer to die at home, but according to Kubler-Ross (1974) a few prefer to die in hospitals. Mothers or grandmothers who do not want to expose children to the final crisis, or people who have been very lonely and have had poor family relationships sometimes prefer to die in an institution.

An outstanding example of a hospital-based hospice is found in the Royal Victoria Hospital Palliative Care Service in Montreal, Quebec, Canada. The stated purpose of this unit is 'to further define the needs of terminally ill patients, and to initiate ways of meeting these needs more appropriately within a general hospital setting' (Palliative Care Service, 1977). The well-documented report from this major teaching hospital acknowledges that 'when movements are restricted and strength fails, total care may mean a good back rub and a nurse's hand to hold'. One of the 16 conclusions of the extensive document states that 'it is possible for a Palliative Care Service to provide a positive atmosphere of welcome and confidence rather than a negative one of a home for the dying'.

As older men and women seek hospice support during terminal illness, they look for it in any one of its varied forms. Each community must determine what style of hospice care is most appropriate for meeting its needs. Flexibility is a basic guideline for hospice developments. Cautions against commercialization and establishment of a hospice industry should be heeded. Senior citizens have been exploited in many fields, so professional care givers must assure that the aged will not be exploited at the time of their death.

IMPLICATIONS FOR SURVIVORS OF AGED PATIENTS

Spouses of the deceased elderly are usually quite old themselves. The surviving widow or widower may already be disabled by chronic conditions which become more prevalent with aging. Long hours of caring for the dying at home or even keeping vigil at the bedside in a more institutionalized setting may tax the remaining strength of the widowed person.

However, realizing that the husband and wife had no doubt agreed to participate in the hospice program, the survivor may find support in knowing that the one who died was never abandoned. An eighty-eight-year-old widower stated, 'I suffered right along with my wife, but I thank God we could be together until the very end'.

Adult children with aging parents are often very busy persons with many business, professional and social involvements. In addition to caring for a dying mother or father, they may be supporting children in higher education or giving other types of attention to their offspring. In this era of high mobility, families are often quite separated geographically. Knowing that hospice staff and volunteers are giving personalized attention to a dying parent can be a comfort to fully scheduled adult children.

Grandchildren and greatgrandchildren often have their first experience with death at the time a grandparent dies. If this elder relative has been receiving compassionate hospice care, the child's attitudes towards death may be affected in a manner which will have a positive influence for the rest of that young person's life.

Hospice volunteers must also be given special attention as a category of surviving friends. In many cases, particularly where the aged patient has no spouse nor any family in the vicinity, the volunteer becomes one of the most significant care givers during the terminal illness. Although the death of one who has lived long years may be easier to accept than death of a younger person, the loss felt by volunteer can still be acute. Questions may haunt volunteers who wonder if they made correct decisions, provided adequate support or gave sufficient comfort. These are important reasons for enabling hospice volunteers to gather periodically for peer support.

Conclusion

Only a small number of the elderly will at present benefit directly from hospice provisions. Moreover, as Simpson (1979) noted: 'Some hospices or clinics using that title provide extremely bad terminal care; some hospitals and some family doctors and general practitioners provide excellent terminal care. The modern movement back to better care for the dying is only partially related to hospices and still involves a number of people not working in a hospice'.

It is to be hoped that the hospice will permeate care in all types of institutions and will benefit the dying, be they old or young. Every vocation upholding this approach — including medicine, therapy, counseling — can find satisfaction in knowing that it has contributed to bringing comfort and meaning at time of death. Then each can affirm the Latin phrase identified with 'Make Today Count', 'a national organization for terminally ill, 'dum vivimus vivamus — while we live, let us live'.

REFERENCES

Abbott J 1978 New way to help the dying. A D 7: 7, 19–23
Bengston V L, Cuellar J B, Ragan P K 1979 Stratum contrasts and similarities in attitudes toward death. In: Hendricks J, Hendricks C D (eds) Dimensions in aging. Winthrop, Cambridge, Massachusetts
Benoliel J, Crowley D 1977 The patient in pain: new concepts. Nursing Digest 5 (2): 41–48
Brickner P W 1978 Home health care for the aged. Appleton-Century-Croft, New York
Brink T L 1979 Geriatric psychotherapy. Human Sciences Press, New York
Butler R N 1975 Why survive? being old in America. Harper & Row, New York
Butler R N 1979 The need for quality hospice care. Death Education 3 (3): 215–225
Cohen K P 1979 Hospice: prescription for terminal care. Aspen Systems Corporation, Germantown, Maryland
Copp L 1974 The spectrum of suffering. American Journal of Nursing 74 (3): 491–495
Cox M S 1979 The Connecticut Hospice Inc. volunteer report. Hospice Institute, New Haven
Craven J 1975 Hospice care for dying patients. American Journal of Nursing 75 (10): 1816–1822
Dienstfrey H, Lederer J 1979 What do you want to be when you grow old? Bantam Books, New York
Dunn M K 1979 The making of the staff team for working with the dying. Speech at University of Michigan, Institute of Gerontology. Issues in hospice care for the elderly: a forum
Garvin R M, Burger R E 1968 Where they go to die. Delacorte Press, New York
Gosnell D 1977 Know your community resources. How available are health care services to the elderly. Journal of Gerontological Nursing III (3): 65–66
Grollman E A 1974 Concerning death — a practical guide for the living. Beacon Press, Boston
Homilton M, Reid H F 1980 A hospice handbook: a new way to care for the dying. Eerdman Publishing, Grand Rapids
Harper B C 1977 Death: the coping mechanisms of the health professional. Southeastern University Press, Greenville
Heifetz M D 1975 The right to die. Putnam, New York

Hendricks J, Hendricks C D 1979 Dimensions of aging: readings. Winthrop Publishers, Cambridge, Massachusetts
Hessel D 1977 Maggie Kuhn on aging. Westminster Press, Philadelphia
Hospice Care — a growing concept in the US 1979. General Accounting Office, Washington, DC
Jeffers F C, Verwoerdt A 1977 How the old face death. In: Busse E W, Pfeiffer E (eds) Behavior and adaptation in late life, 2nd edn. Little Brown, Boston, ch 9, p 142-157
Johnson M 1976 Pain: assessment. Nursing 76 (9): 48-50
Kassakian M G, Bailey L R, Rinker M, Stewart C A, Yates J W 1979 The cost and quality of dying. A comparison of home and hospital. Nurse Practitioner 4 (1): 18-23
Kastenbaum R 1977 The foreshortened life perspective. In: Wilcox S A, Sutton M (eds) Understanding death and dying. Alfred Publishing, Port Washington, New York, p 137-147
Kavanaugh R E 1972 Facing death. Penguin, New York
Klutch M 1978 Hospices for terminally ill patients: the California experience. Western Journal of Medicine 129 (No. 7): 82-84
Kubler-Ross E 1969 On death and dying, Macmillan, New York
Kubler-Ross E 1974 Questions and answers on death and dying. Collier, New York
Lack S A, Buckingham R W 1978 First American hospice: three years of home care. Department of Public Information, Hospice, Inc. New Haven, Connecticut
Lamerton R 1973 Care of the dying. Priority Press, London
Mannes M 1974 Last rights. Morrow, New York
Mazey M, Rauchhorst L, Stokes S A 1977 The health history of the aged persons. Journal of Gerontological Nursing III (3): 47-51
McInteir Sr T M 1979 Hillhaven hospice: a free standing family centered program. Hospital Progress 67: 68-72
Mount B M 1976 The problem of caring for the dying in a general hospital: the palliative care unit as a possible solution. Canadian Medical Association Journal 115: 119-121
Mount B M 1976 Use of Brompton mixture in treating the chronic pain of malignant disease. Canadian Medical Association Journal 115: 122-124
Osterweis M, Champagne D S 1979 The US hospice movement: issues in development. American Journal of Public Health 69 (5): 492-496
Palliative care service 1977. Royal Victoria Hospital, McGill University, Montreal
Parsons J 1977 Needs of the cancer patient. Nursing Digest 5: 2, entire volume
Pearson L 1969 Death and dying: current issues in the treatment of the dying person. The Press of Case Western Reserve University, Cleveland and London
Plant J 1977 Finding a home for hospice care in the United States. Journal of the American Hospital Association 51 (7): 53-62
Safford F 1977 Introducing a hospice program to a long term care facility. Paper Presented to Western Gerontological Society, San Francisco
Saunders C 1965 The last stages of life. American Journal of Nursing 65 (3): 70-75
Saunders C 1976 Control of pain in terminal cancer. Nursing Times 72 (28): 1133-1135
Saunders C 1978 Hospice care. American Journal of Medicine 65: 726-728
Schoenberg B, Carr A C, Peretz D, Kirtchner A 1970 Loss and grief: psychological management in medical practice. Columbia University Press, New York
Shephard D 1977 Principles and practice of palliative care. Canadian Medical Association Journal 116: 522-526
Silverstone B, Hyman H K 1976 You and your aging parent: the modern family's guide to emotional, physical and financial problems. Pantheon Books, New York
Simpson M A 1979 Dying, death and grief: a critically annotated bibliography and source book of thanatology and terminal care. Plenum Press, New York
Stoddard A 1978 The hospice movement: a better way of caring for the dying. Stein & Day, New York

Strauss A L, Glaser B A 1977 Awareness of dying: In: Wilcox S A, Sutton M (eds) Understanding death and dying. Alfred Publishing, Port Washington, New York, p 124-136

Watson W H, Maxwell R J 1977 Human aging and dying: a study in sociocultural gerontology. St. Martin's Press, New York

Weisman A D 1972 On dying and denying: a psychiatric study of terminality. Behavioral Publications, New York

Families living and coping with the cognitive impaired

Purpose

This research proposed (1) to explore the factors influencing a family to continue living with and caring for an old person with irreversible senile brain disease; (2) to describe their problems in daily living; and (3) to describe the strategies these families devised for handling the problems. In this presentation I will focus upon the factors influencing a family to continue the care of the senile brain diseased person in the home, versus those leading a family to consider institutionalization.

Study sample

The study sample consisted of 30 white families living in one household in San Francisco, half of them Jewish. The age and sex distribution of these families in caregiving relationships is similar to that reported in the literature.[1] It is the middle-aged and old woman who carry the burden of care for her ailing spouse or parent. Nevertheless, it is noteworthy that in this study 27 per cent of the caregivers were men who assumed the full responsibility for the care of their often very impaired spouse or parent. Table 8.1 shows the age and sex distribution of the study population. Two-thirds of the caregivers were spouses and one-third were children caring for a parent. While the study population fell into all SES categories, all families had at least a minimal income covering the cost of food, housing, and medical expenses which seems necessary for families to attempt to care for a severely impaired person in the home.

All impaired subjects had the diagnosis of senile brain disease in their medical record. The distribution on the Short Portable Mental Status Questionnaire (SPMSQ) are shown on Table 8.2. Nearly half of the impaired sample had trouble getting to the bathroom on time, 40 per cent needed 24-hour nursing care and supervision, 37 per cent tended to wander or had got lost, and 27 per cent had sensory aphasia or were completely unable to communicate verbally.

Table 8.1 Sex and age of impaired persons and their caregivers (N = 60)

	Sex				Range	Age Mean	Mode
	M		F				
	N	%	N	%			
Impaired persons	18	60	12	40	59–92	80	87
Caregivers	8	27	22	73	45–88	69	66

Table 8.2 Distribution of impaired persons' cognitive functioning on short portable mental status questionnaire (SPMSQ) (N = 30)

	N	%
Mild cognitive impairment (3–4 errors)	7	23
Moderate cognitive impairment (5–7 errors)	4	13
Severe cognitive impairment (8–10 errors)	19	64
	30	100

Study instruments

The study instruments consisted of the OARS Multi-dimensional Functional Assessment Questionnaire[2], in-depth focused interviews, and participant observation. The impaired persons' and their main caregiving family members' physical health, mental health, social resources, economic resources, and performance levels for activities of daily living were assessed by the OARS and the problems these families were facing in the presence of senile brain disease were explored in the interviews. I gathered the data in the families' homes in two to five sessions with the main caregiver and one or two sessions with the impaired person within a two-week period.

Findings

The findings show that a wide array of problems resulting from the disease itself, the caregiving situation, and the wider social context confront these families.

In this study the crucial variable determining a family's ability to continue caring for a senile brain diseased person in the home was mutuality which emerged as the major parameter in qualitative data analysis. Mutuality was defined as the caregiver's ability to find gratification in the relationship with the impaired person and meaning from the caregiving situation. Another important component to mutuality was the caregiver's ability to perceive the impaired person as reciprocating within the relationship by virtue of his/her existence.

The study population fell into four distinct groups according to this parameter regardless of the actual severity of the disease or any of the sociodemographic variables:

Group 1 — high mutuality from within the caregiver: impaired person relationship ('internally reinforced mutuality')
Group 2 — high mutuality due to circumstances ('externally reinforced mutuality')
Group 3 — low mutuality
Group 4 — no mutuality 'survived'

These groups constitute four major management-relationship patterns, as they emerged from the interview data, characterizing these families' lives.

All names used in the following case-studies are fictitious.

Group 1 — High Mutuality 'Internally Reinforced'

In this group (N = 7), all impaired members had moderate to severe cognitive impairment and three impaired persons had severe physical problems as well. Despite their severe impairment, these impaired persons had all retained an important function in the lives of their caregivers. All of these caregivers considered the imagined loss of the impaired person as a major loss in their own lives. Although managing, everyday life was fraught with severe problems due to the impaired person's impairment, these caregivers considered themselves to be managing well under the circumstances.

Eighty-seven-year-old Mrs. Gold, aphasic, incontinent, with severe cognitive impairment, was sitting in a wheelchair while her 57-year-old son was caressing her. He was a self-employed accountant, responsible for his mother's care for the last four years. He had hired nurses for the time he was at work:

> 'Only the nurses' salaries are over £20 000 a year and I take care of mother at night. For me this is the only thing to do and while I give a lot, she gives a lot in return. I really want to spend time with her, so I decided to give up some clients. It is a calculated gamble, because I am not sure I will earn enough to cover our expenses. On the other hand, I might wake up one day with the money and my mother will be gone. So what good will the money do me? Yes, I often think about losing her and this is why it is good now. I am lucky that I can take care of her. I take one day at a time. It is a good day if she moves her hand and feels well. Like today — she had a good bowel movement; it is a good day. If I would wait for the big things to happen, like her lifting her arm, or leading a real conversation, there would be no good days. It is down to the real basic things if you are happy or not.'

Group 2 — High Mutuality 'Externally Reinforced'

In this group (N = 6), the presence of the impaired person is essential to the caregiver's style of life. As a family unit they are able to do together what neither of them could do on his or her own. In these families there was little difference in the overall mental, physical, or socioeconomic competence levels of the impaired person and the caregiver, which ranged from mild to severe impairment.

Mrs Franklin was 66 years old and lived with her 87-year-old mother, who was at times confused and 'crazy'. Both women had handicapping physical problems and both lived on minimal income. While the daughter gave her mother practical help with shopping, getting dressed, etc., the mother provided the apartment, which the daughter would be unable to afford. Neither have close relatives or friends; they are each other's closest human support:

> 'As long as my mother is not violent — and this is now taken care of by the medicine — we manage a good life together. I will take care of her as long as she lives.'

Group 3 — Low Mutuality

In this group (N = 8), all caregivers considered the cognitive impairment, whatever its actual severity, an immense problem in their ability to relate emotionally to the impaired person. These families were so overwhelmed by the impact of the disease upon everyday life that the value they attached to the impaired person's continued presence was in jeopardy.

Mr Green was 78, but looked at least ten years younger. He had a pleasant smile and a vacant expression and his answers were limited to: 'I don't know'. His wife:

> 'Three times he was missing; he just walked out of the house, once for 72 hours. His memory cells are absolutely smashed. He doesn't remember if he eats or where he lives. I cannot go away with him because every minute I have to watch him. Let's say if he has to go to the men's room. I have to stand at the door and wait; he might walk off in the opposite direction and get lost. He can still play chess; he is an intelligent man and sometimes he plays bridge not badly. He had terrific knowledge, but he never shared it with anyone. He is very selfish. Nothing bothers him. This is not very commendable, but it is true. We have been married for 35 years and it is hard to imagine living without someone that you have shared life with for so long. But he is not quite a comfort to me. Gradually his sickness and the way his family treats me healed the shock or the unbelievable loss his death would have been, should it happened earlier. I have so many problems and worries, so much unhappiness from this situation that I am not sure how I would feel now. There is only the fear of being all alone in the world. I am alone now, but somehow it is a habit to take care of someone, to share with someone. He can't answer me and I can't come to him with my problems, but somehow you are not alone. And, he is not a help, but he is there.'

Group 4 — No mutuality 'Survived'

In this group (N = 9), the impaired persons range from mildly to totally impaired with the one common factor that none of these impaired family members seem to play any 'positive' role in their caregivers' lives. All of these caregivers would be relieved to know that their impaired member is well taken care of in an institution; some would be relieved by the impaired person's death.

Seventy-three-year-old Mrs Moraga had been caring for her severely impaired 87-year-old husband for the last three and a half years:

> 'You see, all the doors have three locks; he wants to go out and he wets the bed every night. I have to change the bed at least two to three times a night, but the worst is that he screams — he talks of other times, he pushes me away. When I give him supper he says 'I never get anything to eat' and he eats a tremendous amount of food. No, he definitely does not appreciate me; he doesn't even know. This has been going now for nearly four years. He sits, stares, and then screams that he is scared. I tell him I protect him and then he asks if I am sure to protect him. He calms down for a minute and then he forgets again. No, medications don't help. The only thing that does help is to take him for a drive in the car, but at night it is too dangerous. Whenever our daughter comes — they always loved each other so much — he says 'I don't have a daughter; get out of my house!' It is not a life. Yes, it would be easier if he would die; I am honest about it. I am quite active and I cannot do anything I would like to do.'

Knowledge of the factors which influence a family to continue home care for a senile brain-diseased person or to consider institutionalization, is of major importance for the planning of services. In this study population none of the social, demographic, or health (impairment) characteristics of either the impaired person himself or of his/her caregiver made a statistically significant difference in the above considerations. On the other hand, mutuality, a family's management ability (their capacity to find help), morale and tension (the number of highly valued unmet needs) the disease and caregiving situation cause influence the decision to institutionalize an impaired family member. The higher the mutuality, the more unlikely was the caregiver to (even) consider institutionalization as a possible alternative to home care. This applies also to high management ability and to high morale. Severe tension (regardless of the level of mental or

Table 8.3 Caregiver's attitude toward institutionalization according to caregiver and impaired member morale and tension and caregiver mutuality and management ability

	Caregiver's Attitude toward institutionalization	
	Pearson R	Significance
Caregiver mutuality	0.90	0.000
Caregiver management ability	0.56	0.001
Caregiver morale	0.42	0.032
Impaired person morale	0.61	0.000
Caregiver tension	0.71	0.000
Impaired persons tension	0.59	0.001

physical impairment) correlated with a caregiver's likelihood to consider institutional care.

Implications
I had chosen to organize the implications of these findings for health services in an equation describing the interrelationships of the crucial variables along with the role that can be played by nursing intervention in maximizing a family's capacity to care for a severely disabled old person:

$$\text{Capacity to care for a senile brain diseased person in the home} = \frac{\text{Management ability} + \text{mutuality}}{\text{tension}} \cdot \text{Nursing intervention}$$

Whenever the numerator of management ability and mutuality do not outweigh the denominator tension, families reach a precarious balance, which is likely to develop into crisis or a state of feeling overwhelmed. Appropriate intervention will be geared either toward meeting some of these families' unmet needs and thereby reducing the tension, and/or toward increasing these families' management abilities. After these interventions, it might in certain cases even be possible for families to regain mutuality, destroyed by the overwhelming burden of the caregiving situation. Nursing intervention might enable the caregiver to redefine his reality and perceive mutuality and meaning once tension is reduced and management strategies improved.

The major areas of tension for these families amenable to intervention were: the supportive family member's health problems related to the caregiving situation, being 'tied down', and the caregiver's lack of free time and feelings of resentment, helplessness, hopelessness, and guilt. Health visiting services for preventive, maintenance, and curative home care for both the cognitively impaired person and his/her caregiver would answer a large need. Special attention should be paid to such stress-related diseases as high blood pressure, tension headaches, obesity, and cardiovasulcar problems.

For temporarily relieving caregivers, a wide array of services are needed: (1) a free or low-cost 'granny-sitter' service; (2) low-cost comprehensive day care services ready to accommodate individuals who are both mentally and physically impaired; (3) respite services enabling the caregiver to take a 'vacation'.

Whenever the above alternatives and a wide array of other possible interventions are not effective or desired by the caregiver to reduce the family's tension, these families deserve the prerogative of choice with appropriate, financially accessible institutions providing good nursing care. No one should be made to feel guilty for their 'failure' to keep a person with senile brain disease at home.

This study also suggested the need for research in four major areas: (1) methological research to establish the armamentaria necessary to measure family impact; (2) added knowledge on the development of family coping over time in relation to the length of the caregiving situation, the kind of impairment, and the point on the individual and family life cycle; (3) evaluative program research in regard to services for families living with senile brain disease; and (4) cross cultural research on families in caregiving situations.

NOTES

[1] Isaacs B, Livingstone M, Neville I 1972 Survival of the unfittest. Routledge & Kegan Paul, London

Robinson B, Thurner M Parental care-taking: A family-cycle transition. Paper presented at the 29th Annual Scientific Meeting of the Gerontological Society, New York, October 13-17, 1976

Treas J 1977 Family support systems for the aged: Some social and demographic considerations. Gerontologist 17 (6): 486-491

[2] Pfeiffer E 1975 Multidimensional functional assessment: the OARS methodology. Center for the Study of Aging and Human Development, Durham, N.C.

REFERENCES

Anonymous Death of a mind. The Lancet, 1950, Saturday, May 27th, 6613

Berezin M A 1970 Partial grief in family members and others who care for the elderly patient. Journal of Geriatric Psychiatry 4: 53-64

Bartol M A 1979 Nonverbal communication in patients with Alzheimer's Disease. Journal of Gerontological Nursing 5: 21-31

Botwinick J 1977 Intellectual abilities. In: Birren J E, Schaie K W (eds) Handbook of the psychology of aging. Van Nostrand Reinhold, New York, p. 580-605

Burnside I M 1970 Clocks and calendars. American Journal of Nursing 70: 117-119

Burnside I M 1973 Touching is talking. American Journal of Nursing 73: 2060-2063

Burnside I M 1976 Group therapy with regressed aged people. In: Burnside I M (ed) Nursing and the aged. McGraw-Hill, New York

Burnside I M 1979 Alzheimer's disease: an overview. Journal of Gerontological Nursing 5: 14-20

Cath S H 1972 The institutionalization of a parent — a nadir of life. Journal of Geriatric Psychiatry 5: 25-46

Corsellis J A N 1977 Observations on the neuropathology of dementia. Age and Ageing 6: Supplement 20-29

Eisdorfer C, Stotsky B A 1977 Intervention, treatment, and rehabilitation of psychiatric disorders. In: Birren J E, Schaie K W (eds) Handbook of the psychology of aging. Van Nostrand Reinhold, New York, p. 251-275

Eisdorfer C, Wilkie F 1977 Stress, disease, ageing and behavior. In: Birren J E, Schaie K W (eds) Handbook of the psychology of ageing. Van Nostrand Reinhold, New York, p. 251-275

Ernst P, Beran B, Safford F, Kleinhauz M 1978 Isolation and the symptoms of chronic brain syndrome. The Gerontologist 18: 468-474

Gruenberg E M, Hagnell O, Ojesjo L, Mittelman M 1976 The rising prevalence of chronic brain syndrome in the elderly. Paper presented at the Society, Stress and Disease Aging and Old Age Symposium, Stockholm

Gunner-Svensson F, Jensen K 1976 Frequency of mental disorders in old age. Examples of comparability of epidemiological investigations in relation to utility in planning. Acta Psychiatrica Scandinavia 53: 283-297

Hirschfeld M 1976 The cognitively impaired older adult. American Journal of Nursing 76: 1981-1984

Hirschfeld M 1978 Families living with senile brain disease. Doctoral dissertation, University of California, University Microfilms No. 295 400, San Francisco

Isaacs B 1971 Geriatric patients: Do their families care? British Medical Journal 4: 282-286

Isaacs B 1979 The evaluation of drugs in Alzheimer's disease. Age and Ageing 8: 1-7

Isaacs B, Livingstone M, Neville I 1972 Survival of the unfittest. Routledge & Kegan Paul, London

Jury M, Jury D 1976 Gramp. Grossman, Viking Press, New York

Kane R L, Kane R A 1976 Long-term care in six countries: Implications for the United States. Fogarty International Center Proceedings No. 33. DHEW Publication No. (NIH) 76-1207, Washington D.C.

Kendall M J 1979 Will drugs help patients with Alzheimer's disease? Age and Ageing 8: 86-91

Kinsbourne M 1977 Cognitive decline with advancing age: An interpretation. In: Smith W L, Kinsbourne M (eds) Aging and dementia. Spectrum, New York, p. 217-235

Kleban M H, Lawton M P, Brody E M, Moss M 1976 Behavioral observations of mentally impaired aged: those who decline and those who do not. Journal of Gerontology 31: 333-339

Kraus A S, Spasoff R A, Beattie E J, Holden D E W, Lawson J S, Rodenburg M, Woodcock G M 1976 Elderly applicants to long-term care institutions. II. The application process; placement and care needs. Journal of the American Geriatrics Society 24: 165-172

Labouvie Vief G 1976 Toward optimizing cognitive competence in later life. Educational Gerontology 1: 75-92

Lawton M P, Nahemow L 1973 Ecology and the ageing process. In: Eisdorder C, Lawton M P (eds) The psychology of adult development and ageing. American Psychological Association, 619-674, Washington, D.C.

Libow L S 1977 Senile dementia and pseudosenility: clinical diagnosis. In: Eisdorfer C, Friedel R O (eds), Cognitive and emotional disturbance in the elderly. Clinical Issues, Year Book Medical Publishers, Chicago

Liston E H 1979 The clinical phenomenology of presenile dementia. A critical review of the literature. Journal of Nervous and Mental Disease 167: 329-336

Pfeiffer E A 1977 Psychopathology and social pathology. In: Birren J E, Schaie K W (eds) Handbook of the psychology of ageing. Van Nostrand Reinhold, New York, p. 650-671

Phillips M 1979 Theoretical aspects of psychometric testing in the elderly. Age and Ageing 8: 294-298

Plath D W 1973 Japanese psychology through Japanse literature. Cares of career and careers of caretaking. Journal of Nervous and Mental Disease 157: 346-357

Powell C 1977 The use and abuse of drugs in brain failure. Age and Ageing 6: Supplement, 83–90

Rabbitt P 1977 Changes in problem solving ability in old age. In: Birren J E, Schaie K W (eds) Handbook of psychology of ageing. Van Nortrand Reinhold, New York, p. 606–625

Roslaniec A, Fitzpatrick J J 1979 Changes in mental status in older adults with four days of hospitalization. Research in Nursing and Health: 177–187

Sainsbury P, Grad de Alacron J 1970 The effects of community care on the family. Journal of Geriatric Psychiatry 4: 23–41

Sanford, J R A 1975 Tolerance of debility in elderly dependents by supporters at home: Its significance for hospital practice. British Medical Journal 3: 471–473

Savitsky E, Sharkey H 1972 Study of family interaction in the aged. Journal of Geriatrics Psychiatry 5: 3–19

Schaie J P, Schaie K W 1977 Psychological evaluation of the cognitively impaired elderly. In: Eisdorfer C, Friedel R O (eds) Cognitive and emotional disturbance in the elderly. Clinical issues. Year Book Medical Publishers, Chicago

Shanas E 1973 Family-kin networks and aging in cross-cultural perspective Journal of Marriage and the Family 35: 505–511

Shaw J 1979 A literature review of treatment options for mentally disabled old people. Journal of Gerontological Nursing 5: 36–42

Sheldon J H 1948 The social medicine of old age. Report of an Inquiry in Wolverhampton. Oxford University Press, London

Smith C M, Swash M 1979 Possible biochemical basis of memory disorder in Alzheimer's disease. Age and Ageing 8: 289–293

Soyer D 1972 Helping the family to live with itself. Journal of Geriatric Psychiatry 5: 52–65

Spark G M, Brody E M 1970 The aged are family members. Family Process 9: 195–210

Stipe J, White D, Van Arsdale E 1979 Huntington's disease. American Journal of Nursing 79: 1428–1433

Sussman M B 1976 The family life of old people. In: Binstock R H, Shanas E (eds) Handbook of aging and the social sciences. Van Nostrand Reinhold, New York, p. 218–243

Taulbee L R 1976 Reality orientation and the aged. In: Burnside I M (ed) Nursing and the aged. McGraw-Hill, New York, p. 245–254

Treas J 1977 Family support systems for the aged: Some social and demographic considerations. The Gerontologist 17: 486–491

Wang H S 1977 Dementia of old age. In: Smith W L, Kinsbourne M (eds) Ageing and dementia. Spectrum, New York, p. 1–24

Wells C E 1979 Pseudodementia. American Journal of Psychiatry 136: 895–900

Wershow H J 1977 Reality orientation for gerontologists: some thoughts about senility. The Gerontologist 17: 297–302

9

Sally J. Redfern

Evaluating care of the elderly: a British perspective

Britain, like other Western nations, is an ageing society with increasing numbers of very old people who require a disproportionate amount of care from the national health and social services. These services are becoming increasingly inadequate in the current inflationary climate, and how they can best meet the rising demands made upon them is largely unknown. It is particularly during times of severe economic stringency that we need to know to what extent the care given to our old people is effective. How can care be evaluated, and what kind of evaluative research has been carried out in Britain?

These are some of the questions which prompted this chapter. In the first section I have looked at the nature of evaluation and have drawn on the writing of Doris Bloch (1980) as well as British writers in an attempt to clarify some issues. Karen Luker's evaluation continuum (1980, 1981) has provided a suitable framework which distinguishes the completely subjective evaluation undertaken when delivering care to a patient from the more objective evaluation research with its problems of criteria formulation, measurement, control and generalization.

Following this is a description of the demographic trends of the elderly in Britain and a brief overview of their residential needs and provision. Even though most old people live happily at home either alone or with relatives, increasing numbers of women, especially, without spouse or children become too frail to cope any longer and require some kind of permanent care.

Finally, I have selected some examples of British research related to the elderly which refers to care given or to care received. In recommending the most appropriate research strategy for evaluating complex issues like health care, I have argued that this inevitably depends on the nature of the research problem. It is feasible to select quasi-experimental research designs when fairly specific items of care are to be evaluated, but with complex, comprehensive care evaluation, a more subjective and realistic approach such as 'illuminative evaluation' is more appropriate.

What is evaluation?

In the U.K. we have been much slower to see the need for evaluating nursing care in a systematic way than appears to be the case in the U.S.A. McFarlane (1970) searched the literature for research relating to quality of nursing care and could find no British studies which attempted to establish criteria of quality. All the studies she found were American or Canadian in origin. Since then, however, the amount of interest given by researchers to this area is increasing.

As Bloch (1980) observes, ambiguities surround the meaning of evaluation, evaluation research, and assessment of nursing care. Woody (1980) regards evaluation research as an 'oxymoron — a figure of speech which combines contradictory words, such as 'sweet sorrow' — because evaluation and research are two nearly opposite processes ... evaluation is an overview of nursing care; research is a biopsy of nursing care. They are different.' Bloch (1980), on the other hand, sees 'evaluation' and 'evaluation research' as lying at opposite poles of a continuum. At the one end is evaluation, which can be equated with assessment of the quality of nursing care. This is done as part of everyday delivery of care and it is not normally concerned with scientific rigour, measurement tools, sampling methods, reliability and validity etc. At the other end of the continuum is evaluation research which imposes a systematic rigorous scientific research study rather than involving the assessment of day-to-day care. Bloch sees a continuum which specifies varying degrees of rigour rather than a dichotomy which indicate presence or absence of rigour. She proposes a 'marriage' between evaluation and evaluation research so that the 'offspring' produced are quality assessments which inspire confidence. All evaluation requires some component of subjective judgment, but the closer the evaluation is to the rigorous end of the continuum, the more valid Bloch sees that judgment as being, and the greater the confidence which can be put into decisions based on such judgments.

The nursing process, which is receiving an increasing amount of British attention (e.g. Kratz, 1979; Hunt & Marks-Maran, 1980; McGilloway, 1980), is an appropriate means of linking evaluation with evaluation research. In the context of the care of the elderly, Luker (1980, 1981) made this link in the study of the effect of focused health visitor intervention on elderly women living alone at home. Both evaluation and the nursing process begin with a recognition of values, and Luker views the components of the nursing process (problem identification, goal setting, care planning, implementation and evaluation) as very similar to those of the process of evaluation. She regards evaluation as a circular continuum which incorporates the nursing process and evaluation research (Fig 9.1).

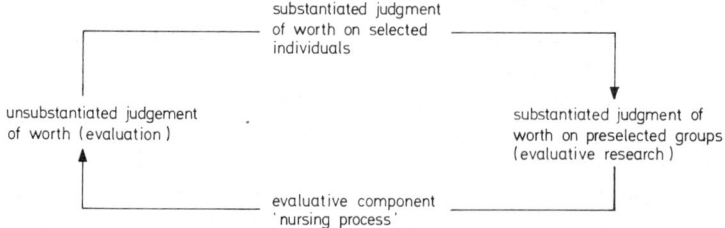

Fig. 9.1 The evaluation continuum (Luker, 1980) (reproduced by permission of the author)

Luker (1980) refers to Donabedian's (1969) three approaches to evaluation of nursing care. In 'structure evaluation', it is assumed that if environmental features (like equipment, staffing levels, management styles, nurse characteristics) have reached acceptable standards, then the care given will be good and the recipients of the care will benefit. The second approach, 'process evaluation', examines the nurse's decision-making and what she does in delivering care. Nursing audits (e.g. Wiseman, 1976a & b, 1977a & b) are means of appraising nurse performance, and the assumption is that if the care given reaches a certain standard then the recipient will benefit. 'Outcome evaluation' assesses the effects of nursing care upon the recipient, with the emphasis on the recipient rather than the nurse. Bloch (1975) suggests a fourth approach, 'process-outcome evaluation', in which the outcome is related to the process which brought it about. As she points out, it is relatively sterile to concentrate on outcome evaluation alone without seeking to establish what led to the favourable or unfavourable outcome. For 'only an evaluation that encompasses both process and outcome has the potential for great impact on the quality of care' (Bloch, 1975, p. 258).

The problem of identification and measurement of appropriate criteria of care is one of the main constraints to evaluating quality of care. The Study of Nursing Care project set up by the Royal College of Nursing and the Department of Health and Social Security (McFarlane, 1970; Inman, 1975) was no attempt to develop methods of measuring quality of care. Twelve small scale studies were completed by inexperienced nurse researchers, which became some of the first pieces of research into nursing practice in Britain. These studies focused on a variety of different aspects of patient care (e.g. bowel function in hospital patients, patient anxiety on admission to hospital, the 'unpopular' patient, teaching and practice of surgical dressings), but nearly all were descriptive studies and could not achieve the ambitious aim of the project. In the final monograph of the project, Inman (1975) developed a proposal for extending the study which aimed to develop comprehensive measures of ward care. Inman argued, like Bloch (1975), how necessary it is to combine aspects of process evaluation (such as ward organisation and planning skills) in any study which attempts to measure the effects of nursing care on the welfare of patients in hospital wards.

Inman proposed that direct observation and a patient satisfaction questionnaire should be used to examine aspects of care which related to four main categories: nursing activities which related to patients' well-being, nursing activities which demonstrated technical skill, activities which related to the general management of the ward, and the effects of these activities on patient welfare. Inman did not believe that the problems of measuring quality of care could be solved by examining only specific areas of nursing care. Both specific and global studies are required if the effect of a total system of nursing care on patient welfare is to be assessed. Unfortunately, the Study of Nursing Care project came to an end before Inman could complete the follow-up research.

Taking a wider perspective than quality of care given to patients, a number of authors have tried to tackle the criterion problem with reference to the quality of life of old people (Peace, Hall & Hamblin, 1979). Government statistical reports concentrate on objective indicators like income, expenditure, taxation, production of goods and services etc., which tell us very little about the quality of peoples' lives, their needs, attitudes, expectations, hopes, fears etc. This lack of appropriate criteria to assess social needs and policy requirements has led to the development of 'social indicators', which refer to things like housing, education, health and health care, leisure and crime, that is, aspects which are said to indicate the nation's quality of life. However, these indicators remain objective and cannot describe a person's experience which must be fundamental to describing his quality of life. Peace et al (1979) refer to an American study which shows that objective social indicators like these are not reliable criteria of quality of life. This study showed that although the economic and social indicators of living standards rose rapidly between 1957 and 1972, the proportion of the population describing themselves as 'very happy' fell steadily, and this was particularly so amongst the most affluent.

What is needed in addition to objective social indicators are measures of individual wellbeing and satisfaction which take into account a person's personality, aspirations, expectations and values. Work along these lines has been started in Britain (see Peace et al's review, 1979) in that attempts have been made to develop 'subjective social indicators'. The aim is to correlate them with objective social indicators to see if the subjective indicators emerge as reliable and valid indices of social change. Results from these studies suggest that subjective satisfaction ratings are sufficiently sensitive to objective conditions and provide useful indices of satisfaction or distress which results from certain living conditions, lack of facilities and so on. Peace et al (1979) concluded that the measurement of the quality of old people's lives in residential homes using both objective and subjective social indicators provides potentially valuable information for policy makers. Who better to advise on their quality of life than the old people themselves?

Returning to the evaluation-evaluation research continuum, how far are strictly controlled laboratory experiments feasible and appropriate in natural settings with all their variation in social conditions? Is it possible to evaluate care by controlling the setting sufficiently in order to assess the effect of some defined intervention upon the welfare of the patient or client? In drug trials, the randomised controlled experiment is appropriate and feasible because it fulfils the requirements of the classic experimental design:

1. The primary objective of the intervention can be unequivocally specified

2. It tests the effectiveness and/or efficiency of a given product or process in achieving the goal compared with alternative interventions or with no intervention

3. It has precise, foreseeable, and measurable control over the nature and quality of the input

4. Influences extraneous to the measured input, the controlled intervention process, and the measured output can be excluded by research design

5. The criterion of success is uncontroversial and can be measured on a single dimension (Illsley, 1980, p. 113).

Such an approach is usually not possible in social settings with human subjects because of ethical constraints, lack of measurable criteria and equality of intervention, subject and researcher bias, unforeseen and uncontrollable consequences or events, and so on. Furthermore, it is important to recognise the multidimensional nature of the care recipients receive and to take account of the multiple interaction between people and events rather than the events alone. The researcher is often concerned with evaluating a natural intervention in a social setting and, as Illsley (1980) notes, the researcher tries to tailor his approach to the natural setting rather than controlling and, therefore, changing the situation to fit his rigorous experimental design. But in doing so he will be less successful in determining goals, controlling input and measuring or evaluating output.

There are examples where quasi-experimental research designs have been used successfully to evaluate the effect of specific items of care on patient welfare, such as the growing literature on the effect of structured information on patient anxiety, pain and stress after surgery (Hayward, 1975; Boore, 1978) and during barium X-rays (Wilson-Barnett, 1978). Also with the elderly, the effects of focused health visitor (Luker 1980, 1981) and social worker (Goldberg et al, 1972) intervention have been assessed with experimental approaches. In all these examples the effect of an intervention has been evaluated, one which was imposed on the experimental group of patients or clients and comparisons made with a control group of individuals who received 'usual' care. When evaluation of a more comprehensive service is required or a service which has occurred naturally rather than imposed by the researcher, then a less formal methodology is necessary which allows uninterrupted continuation of the service, is flexible enough to include changes in service over time, and which caters for the inevitable multiplicity of outcomes.

An example of an appropriate and less formal methodology is what sociologists call 'illuminative evaluation' which takes into account the complex contingencies surrounding events as well as the events themselves. This research approach involves documenting the experiences of the patient or client and the service providers, advisers and helpers so that an account is compiled of the effects of the service on the patient/client. The researcher would have a list of research questions and topics he/she would want to discuss but he/she would use informal, unstructured interviews and observation to collect the information. This strategy has the advantage that it records what happens as and when it happens and very little structure is imposed on the subjects of the research; but it is expensive in terms of time and cost because the interviewer must be a trained professional social scientist who can interpret an unstructured situation. He/she cannot hire survey interviewers to collect the data. Other disadvantages of the case-study approach are that replication is impossible and analysis of the mass of information collected is open to criticism of subjective bias and selective reporting. Such bias can be tempered to some extent by using 'triangulation' where different methods and sources of information are used to provide different types of data relating to the same problem. Such an approach to evaluation research is expensive in terms of time, manpower and funding because it requires a team of researchers working together on a long-term basis. Longitudinal research is necessary if we are to find answers to the social problems of our time, but the organisations which typically fund sociological and nursing research in Britain are not sympathetic to research proposals which require a large financial outlay and which may not provide the answers that policy makers want.

Demographic trends

Improvements in standards of living, in hygiene and in health care during the twentieth century have resulted in a rapid increase in the numbers of elderly people in Western industrial societies (Hughes & Wilkin, 1980). In 1976 14 per cent of the population of England and Wales were aged 65 years and over which amounted to some seven million people. The increase of people in this age group was estimated to be 20 per cent between 1966 and 1976, and it is expected that by 1986 the rise in the proportion of people over 75 years will be 24 per cent. This trend for the very old is expected to be particularly dramatic. In 1976, one in 104 of the population of England and Wales was aged 85 and over. By 2001 this is put at 1 in 65 (Department of Health and Social Security, 1978). This change towards an ageing population is to a large extent the result of an increased life expectancy at birth. Life expectancy for men rose from 49 years in 1911 to 70 years in 1978, and for women, from 52 to 76 years (DHSS, 1978). Most of the elderly in Britain, particularly the very old (over 75 years), are women, a large proportion of whom are widows or single and who live alone.

Over the next 20 years little change in the total number of people over 65 years is forecast, but the number of the over 75-year-olds will continue to increase for a decade or so and is expected to level off towards the end of the century (Hughes & Wilkin, 1980). As Hughes & Wilkin observe, the implications of these trends have serious consequences: a heavier demand on families, especially children who are themselves past retirement age, and greater pressure on health and welfare services and for hospital and residential care for old people whose families cannot provide constant support and supervision. The growth in numbers of the very old has not been accompanied by a corresponding increase in such provision, and the proportion of people in the 45 to 60 year age group, that is, those who do most of the caring, is decreasing.

The pressure to provide additional effective health services for the elderly is as much a problem in the U.S.A. as in the U.K. In both countries many old people retire to warmer, coastal areas, like Florida in the U.S.A. and the south coast in the U.K., away from the colder, industrial, urban areas. In the coastal towns of the U.K. the elderly comprise more than 30 per cent of the population compared with less than 10 per cent in the expanding suburban, semi-rural areas and the new towns built in the 1950s and 1960s (Jeffrys, 1978). The implications for resource allocation and provision in these areas is serious and expanding with the current cutbacks in health and social service provision and the pressure on health authorities to produce economies of scale by moving health care provision from many small, accessible community hospitals to fewer large, centralized district general hospitals.

Residential needs and provision for old people

Many old people in Britain live in what is, oddly, known a 'the community', that is in houses, bungalows, flats, rooms etc. which are owner-occupied or rented. Residential homes run by state or private authorities are also regarded as part of 'the community', but hospitals, some of which are 'home' for many people, are seen to be outside the community. It seems that 'the community' starts at the hospital gates.

Living at home

The ability of old people to support themselves independently in their own homes depends very much on the kind of home and the facilities available and the support they receive from families, friends and the health and social services. Over one-quarter of pensioner households lack a fixed bath, hot water supply or inside W.C. (DHSS, 1978). There is no doubt that improving the standard of accommodation of many old people would enable them to maintain their independence for some time. No longer being able to cope with the necessary requirements for daily living in housing which is inconvenient, insanitary, badly lit and badly heated often results in relatives of old people looking for residential or hospital accommodation, a solution which neither the old person nor her family may want. The problem could be eased considerably by providing more sheltered housing in the form of bungalows or flats grouped together under the watchful eye of a warden. Local authorities and housing associations are encouraged to provide more accommodation of this type but in 1976 it was estimated that only about two or three per cent of the elderly population in the U.K. were living in sheltered housing (Jeffrys, 1978).

A profound change which has occurred in Britain over the last 20 years has been the increase of people living alone. In 1951 the proportion of one-person households was 11 per cent of all households, and this increased to over 20 per cent in 1975 (Abrams, 1978). Contrary to popular belief, it is the elderly rather than young people who are responsible for the increase: in 1975, 74 per cent of the one-person households were occupied by a man or a woman aged 60 or more. In 1977, Abrams (1978) carried out a survey of elderly people living in selected areas of England: a middle-class south coast town, an outer London borough, an inner city area which received much slum clearance but little subsequent rebuilding, and a medium-sized, prosperous Midland town. Abrams found that nearly half the sample (47 per cent) of over 75-year-olds lived alone and the proportion was higher (52 per cent) in the south coast town and the slum-cleared inner city. Most (85 per cent) of these very old people living alone were women, and 98 per cent were widowed or had never married.

Residential homes

It is not surprising that it is these very old, single or widowed women who form the majority of people living in residential homes in the U.K. Approximately 46 000 old people live in voluntary or privately run homes and about 105 000 live in local authority homes, 80 per cent of whom are over 75 and nearly 35 per cent over 85 (DHSS, 1978). A recent review of research relating to care of the elderly in residential homes in the U.K. confirms these trends (Hughes & Wilkin, 1980). The evidence from Hughes & Wilkin's review does suggest that with increasing numbers of very old people living in residential homes, and given the established relationship between age and infirmity, the number of residents who are dependent, incontinent and severely confused is increasing. The aim of residential homes for the elderly is to provide a homely atmosphere for old people who do not require specialist medical and nursing care to live out their lives in comfort, security and company. It has become clear that this aim is not now being achieved because these frail old people require nursing care, care which the homes are providing (Wilkin & Jolley, 1978), and the kind of life they lead may not be what the residents want.

Although it is considered possible to place old people in appropriate accommodation according to their physical and mental functioning, a proportion is always misplaced, be it in hospital, residential home or in private dwellings (Dodd, Clarke & Palmer, 1980). This may be largely because an initial placement has become inappropriate as a change in condition has not resulted in removal to accommodation thought to be more suitable. Keeping old people in familiar surroundings may be the wisest decision, particularly if that is their choice. Of much more concern are those living in long stay geriatric wards who have slipped through the rehabilitation net, yet are capable of regaining the independence required to cope in residential care or sheltered housing. The evidence does suggest that of those misplaced in residential homes, a larger proportion (up to 54 per cent) could have returned to private accommodation in the community than should have been in hospital (up to 17 per cent: Hughes & Wilkin, 1980). It seems that one of the main reasons that return to living alone in the community is so uncommon is that so few old people receive domiciliary services such as meals on wheels, home help, community nursing, laundry services and chiropody. Hughes & Wilkin (1980) reported that less than 20 per cent of the old people newly admitted to residential homes received such services.

Hospitals

Advancing age results in increasing frailty and infirmity and so it comes as no surprise that more than half the hospital beds are occupied by old people and a third by those over 75. This is the case even though only 2.5 per cent of old people are in hospital at any one time (DHSS, 1978). The rapid increase in Britain in the number of geriatricians and departments of geriatric medicine reflects present policy that old people are happiest at home and to this end an energetic approach to treatment and rehabilitation is proposed. Many of these acute geriatric units are located in hospitals which contain other acute medical specialties, which means that a full range of diagnostic and therapeutic facilities and specialist advice is available as much for old people as for anyone else.

The patient who does not respond quickly enough to this energetic approach is considered unsuitable for rehabilitation and is moved to the longstay ward for 'continuing care'. Although rehabilitation and eventual discharge from hospital is the explicit aim for many patients in longstay wards, in practice this is not achieved. These wards are normally sited in old and unsuitable hospital buildings which contain only geriatric beds; sufficient numbers of nursing staff of the right calibre are hard to find; there is a general atmosphere that this is the 'end of the road' and the feeling of having been left behind, leaves the morale and energy of staff and patients at low ebb.

The evidence about the various kinds of accommodation typically occupied by old people suggests therefore, that the large majority is coping contentedly at home either independently or with the help of friends and relatives. Contrary to what is often assumed, there is no widespread evidence that families of old people are failing to accept their responsibilities towards their aged kinfolk (Jeffrys, 1978). The family provides the bulk of care. It is those old folk who have no family or friends nearby and who have become too frail to cope at home who need the support of the health and social services. Some can continue at home with support, others require residential care, and a minority requires permanent hospital care. The concern over the growing proportion of old people in residential homes and in hospital wards, who require nursing care but not active therapeutic intervention and so are misplaced in their present accommodation, has led to the suggestion that nursing home provision within the National Health Service is the answer (DHSS, 1978; Harrisson & Ayton, 1979). The need for and feasibility of developing nursing homes for the elderly is the subject of a research study recently commissioned by the DHSS (Wade, 1980).

These old people in longstay wards are perhaps the most neglected of those in institutional care today. The geriatrician finds them an embarrassment because, as well as blocking his acute geriatric beds, they do not respond to his medical model of diagnosis, treatment, cure and discharge and no-one else is prepared or able to take over his responsibility for them. He moves them to the longstay ward and typically finds time to make infrequent visits, visits which function more to show the nurses working in the longstay wards that he cares about them, than to be therapeutic to the patient. If the nurse in charge of the longstay ward were in a position to take over responsibility for the patient's care from the geriatrician, then improvements could occur. However, she typically has not been prepared for such a role. Her training has been oriented to the disease-centred medical model; she has been encouraged by her training and by doctors to be the submissive handmaiden to medical authority, with the result that she has not the understanding nor the capacity to organise the patient's care in a way which caters for their physical, psychological and social needs on an individual and continuous basis. Wherever these old people are placed, whether it is in National Health Service nursing homes or in longstay geriatric wards, their quality of life will not improve until nurses are given appropriate and adequate training to meet the needs of this vulnerable group, and until the nurses are able to take responsibility for such a group and the accountability that goes with it. This requires a major change in attitude both for the doctors to release that responsibility and for the nurses to take it.

Some recent evaluation research
In essence, structure evaluation emphasises characteristics of the environment which facilitate care, and process evaluation refers to what the nurse or other care provider does during the delivery of care. The assumption is that if the care provided is of 'high' quality then the recipient of the care will benefit. Thus, research concerned with the process of care focusses primarily upon the behaviour of the nurse in the course of caring for the patient. Process approaches to measuring quality of care have received more attention than outcome or process-outcome approaches both in the U.S.A. and in the U.K. (Miller, 1978; Ventura, 1980), although there is much more research into the

evaluation of nursing care from any perspective in the U.S.A. Miller (1978) documented 19 pieces of American research published after 1965 of which nine were concerned with process evaluation, four with outcome evaluation, and six with both process and outcome. In contrast, she described only four British studies, Adams & McIllwraith's (1963) study of staffing levels of geriatric wards, the Blackpool Audit (Wiseman 1976a, 1976b, 1977a, 1977b) which is concerned with structure and process evaluation, the Rhys Hearn Workload Package (e.g. Rhys Hearn 1979a, 1979b; Rhys Hearn & Howard 1980) which calculates staffing levels based on individual patient needs, and the Aberdeen Formula (e.g. Mackley, Heslop & McAllister, 1979a, 1979b) which purports to define acceptable standards of nursing care and the nursing staff requirements to meet those standards.

Workload and patient — dependency
Although the quantity of research carried out in Britain is much less than that in the U.S.A., the literature on patient-nurse dependency, staffing levels and deployment of nurses is relatively large (see reviews by Barr, Moores, and Rhys Hearn, 1973; Wilson-Barnett, 1979). This kind of research typically regards nursing as a series of activities which can be defined, observed and counted, the nature and duration of which can be calculated according to the patient's dependency level. With such information, the claim is that the staffing levels required to deliver care to groups of patients with different dependency needs can be calculated. This kind of approach assumes that the nursing care a patient requires is observable, finite and measurable, and that there is an optimum length of time to perform certain activities according to different dependency categories.

The work by Rhys Hearn and her colleagues (Rhys Hearn, 1979a, 1979b; Rhys Hearn & Potts, 1978; Rhys Hearn & Howard 1980) is a long-term study designed to develop a tool suitable for determining workload and staffing requirements based on individual needs. The aim is to produce a 'package' for nurse managers to use to determine the number and grade of nursing staff required to deliver care to patients at a specified standard. The first package is being developed in geriatric wards, chosen because these wards are often considered to suffer from continuous shortages of staff. The trials have shown that ward staffing levels fell short of that required to deliver care which the nurses themselves had specified as 'ideal'. However, when staffing was increased to do this 'ideal' level, the care given still did not match the care prescribed yet the nurses thought they were giving 'ideal' care. Rhys Hearn concludes that until an agreed policy on standards of care has been developed based on research into the outcomes of care, work into staffing levels will not progress sufficiently to determine the most rational deployment of scarce resources.

Most of the research published on patient-nurse dependency and staffing requirements has been confined to the physical needs of patients in general or geriatric wards. Savage, Widdowson & Wright (1979) however, examined the care of the elderly in a psychiatric hospital which formed part of a longitudinal study (The Hospital Innovation Project at Fulbourn Hospital) in which the staff caring for the patients were encouraged to recommend and implement changes designed to improve care. The initial study which looked at workload of staff showed that most (nearly half) of the nurses' time was spent on physical nursing activities like dressing, feeding, toiletting and only one-fifth of the total nursing time was directed towards the patients' psychosocial needs (talking with patients, group discussions, etc). Furthermore, when more staff were on duty, the extra time available was spent in physical care activities rather than in talking to patients, which is very similar to the picture which emerges from studies in general hospitals. Savage et al found that it was the patients who were moderately dependent on staff for their physical and psychosocial needs but could do some things for themselves and could make themselves understood but with difficulty, who received the least amount of attention from the staff. Those who were totally independent as well as the heavily dependent received more attention. The findings which emerged from this initial study in the Hospital Innovation Project led to the implementation and evaluation of changes in patient care. For example, the strict routine of the physical care activities (getting patients up and putting them to bed, washing, dressing, feeding etc.) were changed to incorporate more flexibility and autonomy for both patients and staff. The result has been that patients do more for themselves and others, staff spend more time in discussions with patients and morale is higher.

This describes only one example of the longitudinal action research study at Fulbourn Hospital (Towell & Harries, 1979). The Hospital Innovation Project showed how changes initiated by nurses, managers, doctors, social workers, etc. within the psychogeriatric service led to improvements in care which were tried, tested and maintained. Although maintaining such improvements depends largely on the commitment and motivation of individuals, innovations are more likely to become normal practice if developed from within the organisation than imposed from outside.

The kind of work and the problems faced by nurses working in geriatric wards have been examined by Wells (1980) and Baker (1978), and a depressing picture emerges. Wells found that although nurses in geriatric wards had positive attitudes towards working with old people, these attitudes were expressed in terms of patronage, and martyrdom as well as for altruistic reasons and wanting to be needed. She concluded that the nurses worked extremely hard and were well-meaning but about the wrong things, and they were convinced that the solution to all their problems, particularly to criticisms about poor standards of care, was to have more staff. Wells maintained, however, that it was the system of delivery of care rather than the shortfall of nurses which was the main problem.

> Clearly, nurses on geriatric wards are not to blame for their lack of knowledge and skill. These nurses are a product of a training system that taught them a series of tasks and neglected to provide adequate information about care of the elderly. The central problem in geriatric nursing is the central problem in all of nursing: nurses do not know why they do what they do (p. 129).

The emphasis on ritualistic routines has prevented nurses from learning how to give individualized care to their patients based on individual problems, and how to evaluate the effects of their nursing activites. Wells lay the blame squarely in nursing education's court. Without being taught to provide nursing care from an individualized, problem-solving approach, few nurses responsible for the delivery of care will be in a position to stimulate change and improve the quality of that care.

Baker (1978) used participant observation in longstay geriatric wards in order to describe what nurses did and how they perceived their jobs and their patients. The typical style of nursing was 'routine geriatric' which supports much of Wells' (1980) findings. Baker widened the focus of attention to include not only the problems occurring at the point of delivery of nursing care but also the problems which are inevitable for a low status branch of medicine. Geriatric medicine, together with other low status sections of care like mental handicap, psychogeriatric and community care, which also cater for large and increasing numbers of old people, has been starved of resources. The outcome is that professional standards are at risk, high calibre doctors, nurses and other professionals find the specialty unattractive, and the nursing and medical hierarchy implicitly endorse the 'routine geriatric' style as a means of maintaining some kind of control over standards of care. Baker recommends that longstay geriatric patients should be removed from the medical model of the geriatric department to units managed by nurses. National Health Service nursing homes have been suggested and the D.H.S.S. is planning some feasibility studies (Dopson, 1980), but until nurses receive the kind of training that Wells (1980) proposes, which would enable them to take responsibility and accountability for these longstay patients, it is likely that such nurse managed units will become off-shoots of existing hospital geriatric departments and extensions of the geriatrician's empire.

Activities of daily living

A considerable amount of research has been published on methods of assessing patients' functional disability after catastrophes such as a stroke and during the recovery and rehabilitation period. Most of the methods developed have been attempts to measure to what extent a person can perform activities of daily living (ADLs) which are regarded as essential to life, and so are confined to mobility self-care and domestic activities (transferring from bed to chair, walking, dressing, washing, toiletting, feeding, preparing food etc.) The aim typically is to produce an overall score of disability based on ADLs from checklists, profiles, or summed scores. These are used by people involved in rehabilitation, such as occupational therapists, who tend to develop their own checklists and scoring systems without paying too much attention to the reliability and validity of the measures. This problem is recognised and some work has been done to evaluate ADL measures in terms of their reliability and validity, such as the Northwick Park ADL Index (Benjamin, 1976).

A major limitation of ADL indices is that they are usually confined to assessing a person's physical functioning in hospital. They cannot assess, with confidence, a patient's ability to function independently at home or in residential care unless the assessment is made within the context of the patient's future living environment. This essential relationship between outcome (patient's functional capacity) and structure (home environment) is one of the objectives of a research study into the effectiveness of a Stroke Rehabilitation Unit at the Royal Victoria Hospital in Edinburgh (Smith, Garraway, Akhtar & Andrews 1977; Walton, Hockey & Garraway, 1978). The aims of the study are to assess the levels of independence achieved by elderly patients after suffering a stroke, and to establish their degree of dependence in relation to their home circumstances so that their needs and their capacity to cope at home can be determined. The patient is assessed the week before being discharged from hospital in a unit which is designed structurally to simulate room layout, equipment and facilities at home. Comparison is being made between patients assessed in the Stroke Unit and others receiving conventional care in medical units in Edinburgh hospitals in order to compare the effectiveness of different methods of organising stroke rehabilitation. As well as the structural simulation of the home environment, the Stroke Unit provides specific, integrated treatment designed to meet an individual patient's requirements according to his disability, and is directed toward retraining in activities of daily living.

A recent pilot study assessed the feasibility of an augmented home care scheme for elderly patients who had acute or subacute illnesses but who normally would have been admitted to hospital (Currie, Burley, Doull, Ravetz, Smith & Williamson, 1980). An ADL scale was developed specifically for the study because no appropriate scale was available. The preliminary findings suggested that rapid mobilization of medical, nursing and domestic help in the patient's home prevented admission to hospital and provided appropriate and adequate care to the patient at home. Patient satisfaction was reported to be high, although how this was measured was not specified. The authors were aware that more research which made comparisons with a control group cared for in hospital was needed before any conclusions could be drawn. It would be important too to estimate the true costs in terms of providing food, warmth, shelter at home and the possible loss of earnings by a relative who cares for the sick person, as well as the direct costs of taking services to the patient's home. Providing care at home is not necessarily cheaper than providing care in hospital (Opit, 1977).

Quality of life and consumer satisfaction
There now exists a considerable literature on the quality of life of old people in residential care (Peace et al, 1979; Hughes & Wilkin, 1980; Ward, 1980). As Hughes & Wilkin (1980) make clear, the measurement of quality of life and life satisfaction of old people living in institutions must take into account theories of ageing and of organizations, the difficulty of identifying sensitive and valid criteria of quality of life, the characteristics of the individual and the environment which affect quality of life and the difficulty of finding life satisfaction scales suitable for use with the elderly.

Concern about the quality of life of old people in residential homes has arisen for two main reasons. One is that researchers and the public generally believe that the physical, mental and social changes which alter and limit a person's activities as a result of ageing must constitute a decline in that person's quality of life. The other reason is the belief that a reduced quality of life resulting from the aging process is made even worse by the effects of institutionalization imposed on the old person by the residential home (Hughes & Wilkin, 1980). Any attempt to identify what constitutes a 'good' quality of life must consider both the effect of institutional living on quality of life and quality of care, and current theories of what constitutes 'normal' or 'successful' ageing (e.g. disengagement, activity and exchange theories). For example, how much physical, mental and social change or deterioration must occur before quality of life decreases? Do the elderly have different expectations of what constitutes quality of life or do the expectations they had when younger remain?

The characteristics of the individual which have been regarded as important to quality of life are:

a. Mortality and morbidity — these objective indices are often thought to be higher after relocation of old people in residential homes. As indices of quality of life, however, they are extremely dubious because the assumption is that to be dead is to be worse off than to be alive, and *continuing* to live is an index of *quality* of life

b. Functional dependence — the assumption is that there is a negative relationship between dependence and quality of life

c. Psychological dependence — such as loss of autonomy, decision-making, internal control and self-esteem

d. Life satisfaction and morale — the assumption is of a direct relationship with quality of life (Hughes & Wilkin, 1980)

The characteristics of the environment thought to affect quality of life are:

a. The physical environment — the belief is that it affects the social behaviour and functional dependence of the elderly

b. The social environment — the assumption is that residential homes should provide 'normal' patterns of life for the elderly by imposing organised activities to overcome the apparent lack of stimulation observed. The traditional picture of large lounges containing apathetic old people seated around the perimeter remains true, but imposed organised activities may increase the negative effect of institutional living. Individual activities with one or two close friends are probably preferable.

c. The care providers — these people are accorded low status, labour turnover is high and only 12 per cent have any kind of qualification. Those with qualifications are nearly all nurses, and so the style of care provided parallels that given by nurses in geriatric hospitals and does not tend to promote a homely atmosphere. 'Staff appear to view the residents as objects to be serviced.' (Hughes & Wilkin, 1980, p. 57).

The life satisfaction measures which have been developed are reviewed by Hughes & Wilkin (1980), and Ward (1980). Three scales appear to have been used with elderly samples. The Life Satisfaction Index developed by Neugarten et al was developed with wealthy, middle-class Americans but has been used widely with non-institutionalized elderly. The evidence tends to suggest that higher levels of activity and social interaction correlate with life satisfaction which apparently supports the activity theory of ageing. The Philadelphia Geriatric Center Morale Scale was developed specifically for American old people in institutions, and consists of three factors: agitation, attitude to own ageing and dissatisfaction with loneliness. Bradburn's Affect Balance Scale is the third scale described by Hughes & Wilkin, and it regards life satisfaction as having a positive and a negative dimension. Happiness occurs when the individual is in 'positive balance', that is, the positive items outweigh the negative items. This scale has been validated but its use with the elderly has been limited. Peace et al (1979) used it with elderly people in residential homes and found it extremely difficult to administer because the old people did not understand many of the questions. Hughes & Wilkin (1980) concluded that there are considerable problems in using life satisfaction scales with the elderly. They are difficult to administer and old people often do not convey their true feelings because they fear the consequences of being critical. Thus validity of the scales is dubious. The terminology used by researchers is often unclear, with terms like life satisfaction, morale, happiness and psychological wellbeing being used interchangeably. The reliability of the scales is not well-established, particularly for the institutional elderly and most of the scales take a global view of life and do not refer to the specific environment.

A considerable amount of research has been published on the effects of the physical environment on old people's behaviour in residential homes (see Hughes & Wilkin's review, 1980). The evidence suggests that grouping old people in small numbers does increase social interaction but territorial behaviour is common which means that 'low status residents' (the confused and those displaying anti-social behaviour) are found more often in the 'worse' seats and are often isolated by the more lucid residents. The 'more successful' homes are homely without repetitive units, long corridors, and confusing colours. Self-contained flats with supportive rather than caring staff are preferred by staff because residents are said to be more mobile, mentally alert, continent, active and eager to engage in social interaction than those in residential homes. A scheme which encouraged group living within homes found that the prevalence of confusion and incontinence decreased, fewer sleeping pills were consumed, functional dependence decreased and activity increased. The evidence does suggest that there is a trend in residential homes against the 'warehousing' model which encourages apathy and dependence (Miller & Gwynne, 1972).

With respect to social activities, there is little evidence that the initial increase in activities (such as tending an indoor garden) is maintained once the initiators have left, and it is probably the enthusiasm of the initiators which stimulated the old people's interest rather than the activity itself. Encouraging old people to continue an existing interest and facilitating continuing friendships with individuals inside and outside the home will probably be more effective in terms of their satisfaction with life than imposing an unfamiliar group activity on them. Peace et al (1979) warn that the current generation of old people have low expectations and will accept any residential care that is not 'the workhouse'. They do not expect the luxury of autonomy and choice. There is the danger that residents and planners and policy makers will regard poor provision as acceptable, whereas future generations brought up with the Welfare State may have different expectations. Peace et al maintain that policy makers should consult consumers for an indication of the quality of life as distinct from the quality of care. In their study in which they assessed the residents' quality of life in various old people's homes, no one home stood out as universally liked. Although the residents reporting the highest satisfaction with their lives lived in small homes which were high in resident autonomy, the picture was more complex than this. The personality of the residents varied to such an extent that it was impossible to say that certain types of individuals were suited to certain types of home.

Turning now to hospital care, Miller (1978) evaluated the care given to patients with dementia in psychogeriatric wards. She described the care the patients received in terms of the checklist of care recommended by the Report of the Working Party on Improving Geriatric Care in Hospital (British Geriatrics Society and Royal College of Nursing, 1975) and evaluated the care received according to the extent to which the patients were 'disengaged'. Miller found that each patient spent, on average, 41 per cent of their time 'engaged', that is, in contact with people and/or manipulating moveable objects. The remaining 59 per cent of the time was spent 'disengaged'. The emphasis of care in most of the wards was on routine, physical care where patients were 'batch processed'. The patients had very little independence or autonomy and the nurses always attributed their difficulties to staff shortages. The primary task of staff in these wards appeared to be long term and terminal care but longstay patients and deaths were regarded as failures and patient discharges as successes. Miller recommended that individual care based on patient rather than task allocation, with more activities designed to increase the incidence of 'engaged' behaviour, would improve the patients' quality of life.

Miller's patients were not, generally, in a position to tell her about their quality of life and what could be improved. It is generally acknowledged that patients do not complain, and say they are very happy with their care. A survey of the opinions of old people in geriatric hospitals (Raphael & Mandeville, 1979) showed that it was possible for patients to admit to dissatisfaction in their care by asking them to specify what could be improved. These patients specified such things as lack of privacy for toilet activities, noise, excessively heavy meals, lack of social activities, and insufficient information from doctors and attention to minor disabilities. The patients had great admiration for the nurses but considered them too short-staffed to provide all the care required. Like Miller (1978), Wells (1980) and Baker (1978), Raphael & Mandeville pointed to the need for individualized care.

Conclusions
In my choice of research studies evaluating care of the elderly, I have selected examples from workload/dependency, activities of daily living and quality of life/consumer satisfaction research in order to illustrate the range of approaches taken in this kind of research.

What should we recommend as the most appropriate research strategies for evaluating complex social issues such as health care? Inevitably it depends on the nature of the research problem but the ideal would be to strike a compromise between the objectivity and generalizability that the controlled experiment provides and the subjectivity essential to realistic evaluation of complex health care issues. Complete control of relevant variables is impossible in a natural setting (except for randomized controlled drug trials), but a quasi-experimental design where it may not be possible to control all extraneous variables, is feasible and appropriate when relatively specific items of care are to be evaluated (such as the effect of information giving, continence training programmes and lotions for cleaning wounds).

This kind of approach has been taken in evaluating the care of the elderly (Goldberg et al, 1972; Luker 1980, 1981). Goldberg et al carried out the first relatively controlled field experiment in Britain which attempted to assess the effectiveness of social work with elderly people. The old people were assigned randomly to either the experimental group which received care from trained and experienced social workers, or to the control group which were cared for by local authority welfare workers who were experienced but had trained 'on the job' and had no special social work training. The findings showed that significantly more elderly people in the experimental group had regular contact with the social workers; the social workers identified more problems in their clients, worked more selectively according to clients' needs, made greater use of individual and family casework techniques, encouraged more outings and visits, and worked more closely with medical and voluntary agencies. The results could not confirm, however, that the improvements in the experimental group were the result of social work training. It is more likely that the lighter caseloads given to the experimental social workers, their personality, motivation and commitment to the study, and their knowledge that their work was being scrutinized accounted for the differences found between the groups. Although this study showed that the old people in the experimental group had fewer social needs after the social work intervention, and that the decrease in the number of needs was greater than for the controls, the findings say little about the difference in *quality* of care received with reference to those needs that remained. For example, there was a significant improvement in life satisfaction over time in both the experimental and the control group, but the difference between the groups was not significant.

Luker (1980, 1981) conducted a similar kind of controlled experimental study in which she evaluated the effect of focused health visiting given to elderly women living alone at home. She found that the number of health problems which improved was greater for the old people who received the focused health visiting compared with the control group. Luker could not, however, be conclusive about the nature of care required to improve the client's health status and quality of life.

Although these two experimental studies attempted to evaluate a fairly comprehensive type of care, the need for definition, measurement and control inherent in such research designs necessarily determine the kind of results which emerge. Inevitably, the research setting becomes artificial over time because, as Luker found, new problems in the client's health status and changes which occurred to existing problems could not be included in the evaluation after the study started (although they could, of course, be treated).

When the aim is to evaluate complete and comprehensive systems of care such as the effects of different institutional styles of care on the quality of life of old people, than an experimental design is too simplistic and controlled, and a more subjective and realistic approach such as illuminative evaluation is appropriate. This kind of approach is the one described by Helen Evers in Chapter 3 of this volume. She described the different patient careers and staff goals which emerged during her study of old people in longstay geriatric wards, and she was able to identify the main differences which distinguished the 'personalised' from the 'minimal warehousing' wards.

In the context of Luker's (1980) evaluation continuum (Figure 9.1), the kind of evaluation research used to provide 'substantiated judgements of worth on pre-selected groups' will vary in scientific rigour depending upon the nature of the problem. Otherwise the continuum can remain as it stands. The evaluative component of the nursing process, in which care given is evaluated with reference to the goals specified to meet the patient's/client's nursing problems, leads to the identification of an 'unsubstantiated judgement' that such care is effective. This belief can be tried out with selected individuals and if supported, it becomes a 'substantiated judgement of worth' which can then be put to the more stringent test inherent in evaluation research.

REFERENCES

Abrams M 1978 Beyond three-score and ten: a first report on a survey of the elderly. Age Concern Publications, Mitcham, Surrey

Adams G F, McIlwraith P L 1963 Geriatric nursing: a study of the work of geriatric ward staff. Nuffield Provincial Hospitals Trust, Oxford University Press

Baker D E 1978 Attitudes of nurses to the care of the elderly. Unpublished PhD Thesis, University of Manchester

Barr A, Moores B, Rhys Hearn C 1973 A review of the various methods of measuring the dependency of patients on nursing staff. International Journal of Nursing Studies 10 (3): 195-208

Benjamin J 1976 The Northwick Park ADL Index. Occupational Therapy December: 303-306

Bloch D 1975 Evaluation of nursing care in terms of process and outcome: issues in research and quality assurance. Nursing Research 24 (4): 256-263

Bloch D 1980 Interrelated issues in evaluation and evaluation research: a researcher's perspective. Nursing Research 29 (2): 69-73

Boore J R P 1978 Prescription for recovery: the effect of pre-operative preparation of surgical patients on post-operative stress, recovery and infection. Royal College of Nursing Research Series, Royal College of Nursing, London

British Geriatrics Society and Royal College of Nursing 1975 Improving geriatric care in hospital. Royal College of Nursing, London

Carver V, Liddiard P (eds) 1978 An ageing population: a reader and source book. Hodder & Stoughton with Open University Press, Sevenoaks, Kent

Currie C T, Burley L E, Doull C, Ravetz C, Smith R C, Williamson J 1980 A scheme of augmented home care for acutely and sub-acutely ill elderly patients: report on pilot study. Age and Ageing 9: 173-180

Department of Health and Social Security 1978 A happier old age: a discussion document on elderly people in our society. HMSO, London

Dodd K, Clarke M, Palmer R L 1980 Misplacement of the elderly in hospitals and residential homes: a survey and follow-up Health Trends 12: 74-76

Dopson L 1980 A step closer to home. Nursing Times, 76: 2125, 2134

Goldberg E M, Mortimer A, Williams B T 1972 Helping the aged: a field experiment in social work. Allen & Unwin, London

Harrisson S, Ayton M 1980 The dependence of elderly people in residential homes. Nursing Times 76 (24): 105-112 Occasional Paper

Hayward J C 1975 Information — a prescription against pain. Study of Nursing Care Series 2 Number 5, Royal College of Nursing, London

Hughes B, Wilkin D 1980 Residential care of the elderly: a review of the literature. Unpublished Research Report Number 2, Departments of Psychiatry and Community Medicine, University of Manchester

Hunt J M, Marks-Maran D J 1980 Nursing Care plans: the nursing process at work. HM + M Publisher, Aylesbury, Buckinghamshire

Illsley R 1980 Professional or public health sociology in health and medicine. The Rock Carling fellowship, Nuffield Provincial Hospitals Trust, London

Inman U 1975 Towards a theory of nursing care: an account of the RCN/DHSS Research Project 'The Study of Nursing Care'. Concluding monograph, Royal College of Nursing, London

Jeffrys M 1978 The elderly in society. In: Brocklehurst J C (ed) Textbook of geriatric medicine and gerontology. 2nd edn. Churchill Livingstone, Edinburgh, ch 22, p. 763–782

Kratz C R (ed) 1979 The nursing process. Ballière Tindall, London

Luker K A 1980 Health visiting and the elderly: an experimental study to evaluate the effects of focussed health visitor intervention on elderly women living at home. Unpublished PhD Thesis, University of Manchester

Luker K A 1981 An overview of evaluation research in nursing. Journal of Advanced Nursing (March) (to be published)

Mackley B, Heslop T, McAllister D 1979 The Aberdeen formula: evaluation on the larger scale (1) Nursing Times 75 (7): 29–32 Occasional Papers

Mackley B, Heslop T, McAllister D 1979 The Aberdeen formula: evaluation on the larger scale (2) Nursing Times 75 (8): 33–36 Occasional Papers

McFarlane J K 1970 The proper study of the nurse: an account of the first two years of a research project The Study of Nursing Care. Series 1. Introduction. Royal College of Nursing, London

McGilloway F A 1980 The nursing process: a problem-solving approach to patient care. International Journal of Nursing Studies 17: 79, 90

Miller A E 1978 Evaluation of the care provided for patients with dementia in six hospital wards. Unpublished MSc Thesis, University of Manchester

Miller E J, Gwynne G V 1972 A life apart: a pilot study of residential institutions for the physically handicapped and the young sick. Tavistock, London

Opit L J 1977 Domiciliary care for the elderly sick — economy or neglect? British Medical Journal 1: 30–33

Peace S M, Hall J F, Hamblin G R 1979 The quality of life of the elderly in residential care. Unpublished Report, Research Report Number 1, Polytechnic of North London Survey Research Unit

Raphael W, Mandeville J 1979 Old people in hospital: a survey of opinions of patients, visitors and staff. King Edward's Hospital Fund, London

Rhys Hearn C 1979a Staffing geriatric wards: trials of a 'package' — 1. Nursing Times 75 (11): 45–48 Occasional Paper

Rhys Hearn C 1979b Staffing geriatric wards: trials of a 'package' — 2. Nursing Times 75 (12): 52 Occasional Paper

Rhys Hearn C, Howard J 1980 The relationship of nursing needs, resources and standards in geriatric wards. In: Department of Health and Social Security, Management services and the nurse. Unpublished Report, Department of Health and Social Security, London

Rhys Hearn C, Potts D 1978 The effect of patients' individual characteristics upon activity times for items of nursing care. International Journal of Nursing Studies 14: 23–30

Savage B, Widdowson T, Wright T 1979 Improving the care of the elderly. In: Towell D, Harries C (eds) Innovation in patient care: an action research study of change in a psychiatric hospital. Croom Helm, London

Smith M E, Garraway W, Akhtar A J, Andrews C J A 1977 Measuring the outcome of stroke rehabilitation. British Journal of Occupational Therapy 40 (3): 51–53

Towell D, Harries C (eds) 1979 Innovation in patient care: an action research study of change in a psychiatric hospital. Croom Helm, London

Ventura M R 1980 Correlation between the Quality Patient Care Scale and the Phaneuf Audit. International Journal of Nursing Studies 17: 155–162

Wade B 1980 Study of different care provision for the elderly: some of the problems involved in survey assessment of self-care ability. Paper presented at a symposium on Improving the Care of the Elderly, University of Exeter

Walton M, Hockey L, Garraway W 1978 How dependent are stroke patients? Nursing Mirror 147 (14): 56–58

Ward P 1980 Quality of life in residential care: a review of measures of quality of life and quality of environment in residential institutions for elderly people. Unpublished report, Personal Social Services Council, London

Wells T J 1980 Problems in geriatric nursing care: a study of nurses' problems in care of old people in hospitals. Churchill Livingstone, Edinburgh

Wilkin D, Jolley D J 1978 Mental and physical impairment in the elderly in hospital and residential care 1. Nursing Times 74 (29): 117–120 Occasional Papers

Wilson-Barnett J 1978 Patients emotional responses to barium Xrays. Journal of Advanced Nursing 3 (1): 37–46

Wilson-Barnett J 1979 A review of patient-nurse dependency studies. Unpublished report. Department of Health and Social Security, London

Wiseman J 1976a A nursing audit of basic care, in nursing ABC — 1. Nursing Times December 2: 169–172 Occasional Papers

Wiseman J 1976b A nursing audit of basic care, or nursing ABC — 2. Nursing Times December 9: 173–176 Occasional Papers

Wiseman J 1977a A nursing audit of basic care — 1: further developments and a critical evaluation. Nursing Times 73 (43) 137–140 Occasional Papers

Wiseman J 1977b A nursing audit of basic care — 2: further development and a critical evaluation. Nursing Times 73 (44): 141–144 Occasional Papers

Woody M F 1980 An evaluation perspective. Nursing Research 29 (2): 74–77

The protection of aged human subjects in the clinical research setting

The protection of human subjects involved in clinical research, for so long unattended responsibility in social, scientific, and health care communities, has been addressed seriously in the past decade. Organizations, societies, academies, and health science organizations, including professional nursing in various countries, have issued guidelines which help individuals monitor the rights of patients in research studies and clinical trials in health care facilities. Evidence of a working knowledge of the Declaration of Helsinki, the Nuremberg Code, and documents which have evolved from them is apparent in the deliberations of committees reviewing proposals to evaluate the risks and benefits of human subject research. Guidelines change because decisions concerning risks and benefits are becoming more difficult. As society and technology are becoming more complex, so too are the issues arising from them. Wrestling with these issues is espected and required, not only by official protectors of human rights assigned to monitoring roles of responsibility, but also by those who attempt to maintain the therapeutic aspect of the patient care environment and those who interact in it. When the patient and potential research subject are elderly and vulnerable, cognizance of what is at stake becomes part of the nurse's professional role. Advocating or obstructing intrusive research measures and practices can be therapeutic or non-therapeutic. Today dozens of associated factors must be taken into consideration.

Some years ago Campbell, Sechrest, Schwarts, and Webb stated that more than an ethical code is needed. They believed that what is required is 'a specification of the multiple interests potentially threatened by social science research: the privacy of the individual, his freedom from manipulation, the protection of the aura of trust on which the society depends, and by no means least important, the good reputation of social science'.

Those participating in research in the clinical setting believe that the application of this statement to the health professions is apparent.

Confronting the risks

And what of the scientific and technical community? Lowrance (1976) urges us to take upon ourselves matters of conscience. Some principal kinds of risks which ought to be taken upon the conscience of the technical community are, in his opinion:

1. Technically complex risks whose intricacies are comprehensible only to highly trained people
2. Risks that can be significantly reduced by applying new technology or by improving the application of existing technology
3. Risks constituting public problems whose technical components need to be distinguished explicitly from their social and political components so that responsibilities are assigned properly
4. Risks whose possible consequences appear too grave or irreversible, so that prudence dictates the urging of extreme caution, even before the risks are precisely known
5. Technological intrusions on personal freedom made in the pursuit of safety.

In this chapter I will be considering the last point. But at the same time I would urge the professional community to become involved in health care of clients and to develop a heightened sensitivity to the ethics, politics, and perhaps the psychology of research.

The patient's right to research

The term 'protection' of human rights or protection of human subjects can conjure up a literal picture in which the nursing staff bars access to a patient's door from the increasing numbers of researchers asking entry. That very similar scenes do occur cannot be denied, especially in large medical complexes and teaching institutions where the commitment is to care, education and research. It is all too easy to couple the terms 'intrusion' and 'research', which has the unfortunate effect of poisoning people's attitudes toward research and the research process. That process should neither be viewed with suspicion nor should it be enshrined. The purposes of research and the values held by those who promote it, pay for it, and do it are and should be constantly open to scrutiny.

The staff nurse at the bedside of the elderly is learning to question the intrusions into the patient care setting made in the name of research which will lead to improved patient care. Even more subtle than the nurse's questions about the patient's right to be spared from research, are the questions about the right of the elderly to be included in research. The elderly as well as those who care for them are profoundly affected by both alternatives. The dangers of intrusion, on the one hand, are associated with dangers of manipulation. The dangers of non-intrusion, on the other hand, are associated with dangers of dehumanization or neglect by a routinized, institutionalized, unquestioning staff. Both points of view are over-stated as two extremes for purposes of discussion. What are the other points on the continuum between these two extremes? What patient and staff rights are involved?

The patient's right to know

Informed consent, vastly different from mere compliance or consent, is an integral part of nursing research. The elderly have the right to know the purpose of the research proposed; the credentials of those involved; the methods which will be employed to protect their identity, their bodies, their peace of mind; and what demands will be made on them if they elect to participate in the research. What may seem straightforward is not always so, as Kelly & McCelland (1970) point out in their work regarding consent forms and disclosures to aged clients. There is a struggle between related issues as protection is sought for the subject, the staff, the researcher, the public, and the integrity of the research itself.

Informed consent is only protective insofar as the subject understands what is involved. And understanding is dependent on effective communications: verbal, non-verbal, and written. The focus, then, is upon those who inform and those who are informed and the effectiveness of communication skills. It should be noted that the elderly subject may present special problems for the researchers, some of which are highlighted in the next section.

Questions to be answered regarding informed consent procedures with aged patients or clients

Can he read the informed consent?
Many of the elderly cannot do so because of lack of education or because they do not speak the prevailing language fluently.

Can he see to read the informed consent?
Many of the elderly cannot find, do not wear, and deny having spectacles. Holding the instructions in his hand, he may not be able to see to read them and may not confess the problem or ask for help.

Can he hear the instructions and terms of the informed consent?
Covering up hearing deficits is a precise art for some older persons. They smile, agree, nod appropriately, and fill the silences with

Fig. 10.1 Informed consent for participation of human subjects in a research project

Date..............................

Name of Participant: ....

    Project Title: ....

Principal   ....
    Investigators:
    ....

I voluntarily agree to participate in this nursing study which I understand is to determine how I react to shift work and to non-shift work. The benefits to be derived from this research will be that new information will be obtained about the body's reaction to changes as it relates to the way different people organize time. I understand that I can terminate my participation at any point.

The investigation has been explained to me by..............................
..........................She/He has answered all of my questions. I hereby authorize him/her and/or such assistants or agents as may be selected by the investigators to measure certain aspects of my person. I understand that I will be asked to:

1. Undergo physical examination.
2. Complete written questionnaires.
3. Do performance tasks and tests.
4. Submit temperature data and urine specimen.

The methods by which the data will be collected will be by:

1. Observation: Mechanical and direct
2. Interview
3. Questionnaires
4. Records and Reports
5. Specimen of urine.

My participation is subject to the following conditions:

1. That adequate safeguards be provided to maintain the privacy and confidentiality of my records.
2. That my name and family's name not be used to identify said material, but code numbers be used.
3. That my individual scores on tests not be reported; that data be reported as aggregate or group scores.
4. That said material be used only for purposes of nursing study and research.

....
Participant's Signature

Witness to Participant's Signature: ....

This form is an example of an informed consent form and is used with permission of Dr Gereldene Felton in conjunction with her research study 'Body Rhythm Effects on Rotating Work Shifts'. Journal of Advanced Nursing 1975 (March-April 16–19).

appropriate responses. But they do not understand their rights as a research subject because they are not, in fact, hearing them.

Can he understand the instructions given by the informant?
Jargon, technical terms, and scientific concepts which subjects cannot comprehend have no place in consent documents. The onus is on the researcher to be clear and to provide reasonable assurance that the subjects understands, through careful choice of words and definitions of terms.

Can he ask questions?
Aphasia, communication blocks, and cognitive impairment may erode mental alertness of the patient's ability to communicate. The loss of previously effective communication tools frustrates and depresses him. An unhurried atmosphere where questions are welcomed is essential. Patients often require composure time.

Can the informant answer his questions appropriately?
Informers may be forced to communicate through writing or a third person, an intermediary who brings the consent form to the potential subject. What understandings and authority does the interpreter of the form have? What effect does he have on the subject and those involved in research or in patient care?

The patient's right to 'no!'
Basic to the protection of human dignity in research is the need to make clear to the subject that participation is a matter of free choice, that it is not required by the institution or care-givers, and that no alteration in his treatment, length of stay, quality of care, or personal feelings toward him as a result of his decision will occur.

The aging client must understand that he or she is free to: (a) decline at the onset; (b) reconsider an initially positive decision and withdraw as a subject during the stay; or (c) ask that the data represented his contribution to the study to be destroyed or go unused after the fact. These options and the methods by which they are implemented should be part of the informed consent process.

It is not always easy to disguise disappointment if a client or patient chooses not to participate. But this can be a subtle form of coercion and must be avoided as must other methods of eliciting data in devious ways which result from the researcher's or interviewer's style. Edward Shils (1959) was adamant about this over two decades ago, noting that even the less intrusive measures must be sharply limited by ethical considerations. He criticised methods of interviewing in which there

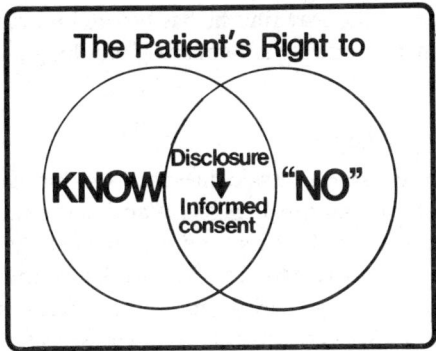

Fig. 10.2 Informed consent

is, on the part of the interviewer, 'the simulation of warmth to insure rapport' or 'giving the appearance of agreement to answers on controversial questions to encourage the expression of unpopular attitudes'. These opinions, which at one time were thought to be too extreme, are now being reappraised as our awareness of ethical and political considerations become more sensitive. Another problem arises with regard to disclosure of the design of the research project. In some cases disclosure would put into jeopardy the credibility of the entire project. In more recent and perhaps more litigious years, subjects have demanded to know if they are in the treatment or control group of an experimental design. Upon disclosure, if it was forthcoming, the subject has demanded that he or she be placed in the groups of his or her choosing — the control group if the treatment were thought to involve risk, the experimental group if the treatment were perceived therapeutic, albeit unproven. Unwillingness to comply with such requests has meant a threatened lawsuit on the part of the subject toward the researcher. The issue is a real one but is no longer of significance if the study has already been scuttled due to irreparable damage to the 'double-blind' design.

As is the case whenever ethical problems over-ride legal ones, there is a need to negotiate conflicting values. Both the researcher and the would-be subject have compelling arguments. As the pendulum begins to swing back toward placing more value on the integrity of the research we sense that the 1980s are likely to bring legal, ethical, political and professional issues to the forefront. We anticipate a reconsideration of the rights of the researcher and those of the human subject, as well as a review of the associated economics of research. The aging patient may find himself in a bewildering world of power politics from which he cannot extricate himself. As he tries to view the counter-arguments, he may find he has before him more than a two-pronged argument. 'And what happens if anything goes wrong?', he asks.

Other aspects at 'risk'
Informed consent, as we have said, means disclosure of risks so that the subject can make an informed choice. Warning the subject of the risk implies that knowledge of the risk and the implications resulting from it are known by the researcher. But we know that as medicine, technology, genetic engineering and other fields move forward, associated questions — not answers — emerge. As far as possible we must confront the risk and must help the patient to, if not an answer, an awareness of the considerations. How good are we at assessing risk? Data about risk is conflicting — experts communicate opinion, conjecture, speculation, changing views. Risk motivates not only institutional and public policy but 'research on research', that is, related research to assess risk of the original research.

In assessing risk to the subject, we should remind ourselves of four lines of investigation promoted by Lowrance. He states that measurements are made in order to:

1. Define the conditions of exposure
2. Identify the adverse effects
3. Relate exposure with effect
4. Estimate overall risk.

Although he is addressing science and the determination of safety, it would seem his lines of investigation may also apply to this problem of the assessment of risks in research.

We must recognize also that there are times when unforeseen, surprising, fluke events make us ask 'what went wrong?' The human being whom we sought to cure, heal or help is further damaged by the research process which was to give him hope. What is to be done about it?

Assessing blame
In Great Britain the Royal College of Physicians of London held a conference in 1980 (May 8) 'Liability — When Things Go Wrong — Who Is Responsible? Who Makes Amends?' Concurrently through 1970 and 1980 a Ciba Foundation Study Group under the Chairmanship of Dr David Evered put together a formidable panel* of

*Members: T. Binns, L. H. Blumgart, A. Diamond, C. T. Dollery, R. H. T. Edwards, R. Huws Jones, D. R. Laurence, J. K. Lloyd, R. Porter, Sir Charles Wilson, D. C. Evered

experts to discuss issues and write a paper which was entitled 'Medical Research: Civil Liability and Compensation for Personal Injury'. This group concluded:

> ...that the present system based upon negligence and supplemented by exgratia payments from research funding bodies is unsatisfactory. The Group does, however, consider that whatever system of compensation is adopted, it should be open to participants in research to seek redress through the courts on the basis of negligence if it is suspected that this has occured. ... The Group has concluded that a no-fault scheme would provide the most satisfactory means for compensating participants for injuries received as a consequence of medical research.

It went on to recommend the establishment of a centrally operated Fund to provide compensation on this basis. They agree that this does not diminish the rights of the participant to bring an action in the event of negligence on the part of the investigator or an action under the law relating to product liability against the manufacturers of defective equipment or drugs. This statement would appear to be an important beginning on which related considerations by other groups can be built.

The nurse as research informant

As mentioned, earlier, informed consent requires an informant and the investigator as an informant is clearly the most straightforward mode of communication with the elderly about the specifications and implications of the research proposed. Serious problems arise when the clinical researcher-physician, nurse, social worker, dentist, pharmacologist, sociologist, psychologist, etc. sends someone else to be the informant. Equally researchers informing subjects may bring with them bias and delay. Untrained informants may bring wrong information or they may lack the ability to make responses. They too may bring bias and delay to the project. When the informant is not a researcher, not a trained interviewer by the primary investigator, but rather a professional nurse, it is yet another matter. Regardless of her willingness, some role conflict may ensue.

Smith & Davis (1980) describe the environmental context in which ethical problems are exacerbated. The ingredients include an institutional environment, role conflict and lack of power — all of which work in the situation discussed above of the nurse as an informant.

They discuss in a recent article situations in which:

1. Nurses, as employees, work under policies established by others
2. Nurses experience conflict between meeting a patient's needs and following institutional procedures

3. Nurses have responsibility but not accountability and authority
4. Nurses generally have either limited or no input into decisions that they are responsible for implementing.

When a nurse is 'told' to get the informed consent signed by a patient for inclusion in a research project, she may sometimes be being exploited. In those cases where she has no role in the research team, and no information or understanding, she may be forced into questionable and unethical behaviour. The nurse relinquishes a therapeutic role, an advocacy role to the aged patient, and through her established patient-nurse relationship address the subject as informant. She knows no more of the research protocol than what she reads on the form. She knows little of the credentials or trustability of the researcher. She is unsure of the purpose of the research or how the results will be used. This activity takes her reluctantly away from other duties. Though improperly informed herself she 'informs' the human subject.

If the research proves to be relevant, adding to the growing body of clinical knowledge about the subject, meeting high research standards, and is eventually published in a respected research professional health journal, even this activity can be interpreted in the nurse's mind as a defendable extension of her role. If, however, the researcher is proved to be questionable in credentials, experience, technique, intention or ability; if the design proves faulty past the point of acceptability by the professional community; if the treatment in any way brings risk to the elderly patient in her charge, it will cast a cloud over all whom the experience has touched. The nurse may gradually feel that she has been inadvertently involved in manipulation of her patient. The nurse and the elderly patient were vulnerable. The nurse and her patient are victims.

Meeting research and ethical standards

Bailey asks: 'If we have a scientific interest in demonstrating the way harmful effect on people is caused, but an ethical interest in avoiding such harm, how can we solve the dilemma by serving both goals and demonstrating harmful effects without harming people?' Fortunately he suggests a number of approaches but reminds us that they all have both advantages and disadvantages.

The approaches include consideration of the use of these methods:

1. Animal studies (We must of course remember the need for protection of animal subjects as well as human.)
2. Computer simulation approaches

3. Finding a condition in which the negative effects already exist so that the researcher is not responsible for producing them

4. Application of only a very low level of the cause, or for only a short period of time, so that the effects, though negative are very mild

5. Informing respondants (Human subjects) of the possible negative effects and securing their permission through an informed consent procedure

6. Rationalization of the part of the researcher that the study is in some way justified (i.e. because it is a lesser evil than the harm the investigator is attempting to cure)

7. Use of samples rather than complete populations so that fewer subjects are harmed

8. Maintenance of privacy through publication of aggregate data only.

Nursing practice in research settings

Moving past the consideration of informed consent problems, those associated with research design and sampling, and the intrusive and unobtrusive approaches to researching clinical problems, the nurse faces other subtle ethical issues in those cases where care of the aging coexists with research. The following list is a brief noting of such issues as examples which the reader may be able to use to bring to mind others in their settings.

Issue A. Transplant and limited access to experimental techniques or technology: Who chooses, who decides, who tells the nurse to tell the elderly patient he will not be afforded the innovation? How do aged clients fare when they are chosen — or when they are excluded as recipients?

Issue B. Medication for the older client: Who orders, who administers the medication which is research or experimental in nature? After informed consent is agreed to, who answers the questions asked by the elderly patient as he observes changes after the treatment drug is administered?

Issue C. When the elderly client in the research study fails and/or dies: Who answers the nurse's questions and deals with her worry and guilt? Who counsels the staff to enable them to counsel the family?

Issue D. The therapy, whether proven or experimental, may hurt. How much pain is justified in the name of therapy? How much pain in the name of research? When should the nurse refuse to continue to inflict pain? Where is the thin line between treatment and torture?

Issue E. According to agreed upon research protocol, when is it justified to withhold an explanation or modify the truth? When does reassurance or comforting mislead, avoid, deny, or sidestep the facts?

What is cover-up and what constitutes a conspiracy of silence between staff?

Issue F. Patient advocacy/patient neglect: What happens when no one advocates for the patient who cannot speak for himself? What happens when various health team members are at odds in the name of patient advocacy?

Issue G. Life sustaining practices: Who decides the quality of life? The quality of death? What about robbing the patient of his opportunity to stay conscious, use his own inner resources, and even to experience death? Who decides one's right to suffer and/or to die?

Issue H. Let the record show: Errors of unethical commission or omission on the charts of the elderly patients are whose responsibility?

No one individual or group can decide but multidisciplinary groups can discuss ethical issues surrounding patient care in research settings. Davis & Aroskar (1978) suggest that 'nurses should, at least, be able to articulate and develop positions on these dilemmas that confront them as individuals and professionals. Ethical rounds for nurses, death and dying courses in basic nursing education, and continuing education efforts in the area of health care ethics provide forums for doing this within the nursing community and with other health disciplines'.

Summary

Research settings involving aging patients and their professional nurse caregivers reflect value systems of both individuals and society. When there is open communication, respect for the dignity of the individual, an articulation of shared value systems, even the most complex of research and ethical issues is not too large to address. Similarly, no query, speculation, or worry about human rights is too insignificant to share. Protection of human subjects means avoiding manipulative practices affecting elderly patients, professional staff, and family. Both health care and the community at large benefit.

REFERENCES

Bailey K D 1978 Methods of social research. Free Press, New York, p 382–383
Ciba Foundation 1980 Medical Research: Civil liability and compensation for personal injury. Portland Place, London
Davis A J, Aroskar M A 1978 Ethical dilemmas and nursing practice. Appleton-Century-Crofts, New York, p 131
Kelly K, McCelelland E 1970 Signed consent: protection or constraint? Nursing Outlook 27: 40–42
Lowrance W W 1976 Of acceptable risk. William Kaufmann, New York, p 18, 120
Reich W T 1978 Ethical issues related to research involving elderly subjects. Gerontologist 18: 326–337

Shils E A 1959 Social inquiry and the autonomy of the individual. In: Lerner D (ed) The human meaning of the social sciences. Meridan Co, p 114–157

Smith S J, Davis A J 1980 Ethical dilemmas: Conflicts among rights, duties, obligations. American Journal of Nursing 80: 1463–1466

PART TWO

Bibliographies

General sources of reference

With the advent of computerized library retrieval services, bibliographical review on a large scale or complex cross references are now realistically available to the writer-researcher. National services such as the National Library of Medicine (8600 Rockville Pike, Bethesda, Maryland 20014) publish not only their retrieval services but printed bibliographies on a wide variety of subjects previously retrieved. Similarly large agencies caring for the ill and aged own country- and system-wide retrieval computers (i.e. Central Office Library, Veterans Administration, Department of Medicine and Surgery, 810 Vermont NW, Washington, DC 20429). Retrieval across all systems is possible by the Smithsonion Institution (Washington, DC) retrieval which monitors in-process research. Listed here are some of the published bibliographies which particularly concern issues related to the aging population and those who care for them.

Analysis and Selection of Training Resources in Aging. Duke University Center for the Study of Aging and Human Development 1977-1978
Bibliography of articles, reports, data and congressional hearings researched during study: final report for study of health manpower needs for services to older Americans. CSF Ltd., Rockville, Maryland 1978 1 Apr
Catalog of publications: Health Resources Administration Washington, DC — US DHEW 1978
Current literature on aging (Quarterly subject guide to selected publications in the field of aging and related areas). The National Council on Aging, Inc. 1828 L. Street, NW-Washington, DC 20036
Delgado M, Finley G E The Spanish-speaking elderly: a bibliography. The Gerontologist 1978 Aug; 18 (4): 387-394
Depression, grief and suicide in the aged: bibliography US-DHEW, National Institute of Mental Health 1976 Sept
Directory: project summaries and addresses — fiscal year 1974 — model projects on aging program: older Americans act, title III, Section 308. US-DHEW, Office of Research, Demonstrations, and Manpower Resources Agency on Aging 1975
Directory: State agencies on aging and regional offices. US-DHEW. Agency on Aging 1978 Aug
Feinglos S Searching the literature of aging: Gerontology reference sources. Duke University Medical Center Library 1978
Medical-oriented references on thanatology and gerontology published by ARNO Press. New York: New York Times Co

National Clearinghouse on Aging Thesaurus 2nd edition. US-DHEW, Agency on Aging 1977 Jul

National Directory of Medicare Home Health Agencies. US-DHEW 1976 Dec

National Council on Aging Publications List 1977 Fall/Winter. Washington, DC 1977 Sept

Nurse Planning Information Series. Washington DC: HEW-Division of Nursing; Bureau of Health Manpower, Health Resources Administration; Hyattsville, Maryland 20782:

> Nurse practitioners and the expanded role of the nurse 1978; 5 a bibliography. DHEW publication no. (HRA) 78-20
>
> Nurse staffing requirements and related topics: a selected bibliography. DHEW publication no. (HRA) 79-39; 1979
>
> Home health care programs: a selected bibliography. DHEW publication no. (HRS) 79-60; 1979
>
> Community health nursing models: a selected bibliography. DHEW publication no. (HRA) 79-61; 1979
>
> Quality assurance in nursing: a selected bibliography DHEW publication no. (HRA) 80-30; 1980
>
> Continuing education in nursing: a selected bibliography. DHEW Publication no. (HRH) 80-31; 1980
>
> Computer technology in nursing: a comprehensive bibliography. DHEW publication no. (HRA) 80-65; 1980

Poteet G W Death and dying: a bibliography (1950-1974). Troy, N.Y.: Whitston, 1976. 192

Planning for retirement: a bibliography of retirement planning literature. Washington, DC: NRTA-AARP, 1978

Shock N W Current publications in gerontology and geriatrics. Journal of Gerontology 1978 Nov; 33 (6): 895-950

Supplemental review of literature and bibliography: final report for study of health manpower needs for services to older Americans. Rockville, MD: CSF Ltd. 1978 1 Apr

Tichy M K Health Care Teams: an annotated bibliography. NY Praeger Publishers. 1974

Specialised bibliographies

AGING AND CHANGE

Learning what aging is, being sensitive to the experience of growing old, and having an interest in aging as part of the life experience are gradually assuming their proper place in the professional literature. Classical literature as well as many modern writers still provide the insight often missing in health care literature. Best sources are the reports written by the people who are themselves experiencing aging, and research through primary sources is beginning to become evident.

By far the most encouraging type of literature is that which sees aging more positively, stressing the life-cycle review. All these sources provide evidence from some aged persons of what can be, but often is not, the 'golden age'. Unfortunately there is a dearth of publications in this area which could provide continuity and an important legacy to others doing research.

Benjamin H Biologic versus chronologic age. Journal of Gerontology 1947; 2: 2-7
Chronbach L J, Furby L How shall we measure 'change' or should we? Psychological Bulletin 1970; 74: 68-80
Clark J W Aging dimension: a factorial analysis of individual differences with age of psychological and physiological measurement. Journal of Gerontology 1960; 15: 183-187
Garland M H A symposium on care of the elderly. The challenge of geriatric medicine. Nursing Mirror 1977, 3 Nov; 145 (18): 15-6
Gubrum J F Time roles and self in old age. Human Sciences Press, NY: 1976: 363
Maas H S, Kuypers J A From thirty to seventy: a forty-year longitudinal study of adult life styles and personality. San Francisco, California. Jossey-Bass 1974: 240
Marris P Conservatism, innovation and old age. International Journal of Aging and Human Development 1978-79; 9 (2): 127-35
Mindel C H, Vaughan C E A multidimensional approach to religiosity and disengagement. Journal of Gerontology 1978 Jan: 33 (1): 103-8
Neugarten B L Time, age and the life cycle. American Journal of Psychiatry 1979 Jul; 136 (7): 887-94
Lieberman M A Social and Psychological determinants of adaptation. International Journal of Aging and Human Development 1978-79; 9 (2): 115-126
Lowenthal M F, Thurnher M, Chiriboga D Four stages of life. San Francisco, California, Jossey-Bass 1976: 292
Strumpf N Aging — a progressive phenomenon. Journal of Gerontology Nursing 1978 Mar-Apr: 4 (2): 17-21

To understand the aging process: The Baltimore longitudinal study of the National Institute on Aging, Washington, DC. Department of Health Education and Welfare. National Institute on Aging 1978

Weiner M B The life review process. Caring for the elderly. Journal of Nursing Care 1979 Jun; 12 (6): 34

Weiner M B Caring for the elderly. The concept of 'Being Old' — part I. Journal of Nursing Care 1978 Dec; 11 (1): 9

DEATH AND DYING

Writers in trends in health care did not find it necessary to raise the awareness of the elderly about the fact and phenomenon of death — death is an integral concept of human life-span development. This was not the case, however, with medical and nursing caregivers or those who deliver health services in and out of institutions. The group denial of death and the taboo associated with it made early research about attitudes, practices, and needed reform in care of the dying difficult for those who addressed themselves to research, reform, and education. In the past five years, however, death and dying have been the subjects of a wave of publications in all health professional fields. Books of bibliographical listings are now available. Listed here is a selection of these bibliographical entries. Observation, research, and evaluation will attempt to determine if 'the discovery of death' by health professionals has better catered for the needs of the aging.

Ayd F J Treatment for the terminally ill incompetent: who decides — courts or physicians? Medical-Moral Newsletter 1978 Apr; 15 (4): 13–6

Black P M Focusing on some of the ethical problems associated with death and dying. Geriatrics 1976 Jan; 31 (1): 138–41

Callahan D On defining a 'natural death'. Hastings Center Report 1977 Jun; 7 (3): 32–7

Church of England On dying well: an anglican contribution to the debate on euthanasia. London: Church Information Office, 1975

Garfield C A, ed Psychosocial care of the dying patient. New York: McGraw-Hill, 1978. 430 P

Gonda T A Coping with dying and death. Geriatrics 1977 Sep; 32 (9): 71–3

Gow C J, Williams I Nurses' attitudes toward death and dying. Social Science and Medicine 1978 Feb; 11 (3): 191–8

Hopkins C The right to die with dignity. In: Caughill R E, ed. The dying patient: a supportive approach. Boston: Little, Brown, 1976. p 73–94

Killian B A Attitudes to death and bereavement among the elderly. World of Irish Nursing 1978 May; 7 (5): 2–3

Kolbe R Inside the English hospice. Hospitals 51: 13

Kraus A S, et al Potential interest of the elderly in active euthanasia. Canadian Family Physician 1977 Mar; 23: 123+

Lemasters G The effects of bereavement on the elderly and the nursing implications. Journal of Gerontological Nursing 1978 Nov-Dec; 4 (6): 21–5

Masterman J How the right to die could improve the quality of life. Times (London) 1976 20 Oct: 10

Pattison E M, ed The experience of dying. Englewood Cliffs, N.J.: Prentice-Hall, 1977. 335 P
Plant J Finding a home for hospice care in the USA. Hospitals 51: 13
Raible J A The right to refuse treatment and natural death legislation. Medicolegal News 1977 Falls; 5 (4): 6–8+
Reid J, Yunupingu L, Yunupingu D Caring for the aged and dying in an Australian aboriginal community. Australas Nurses Journal 1978 Aug; 7 (12): 22–6
Raymond E A A plea to let the old die peaceably. New York Times 1977 25 Sep; sect. 4: 15
Rizzolo P J, et al The living will. Journal of Family Practice 1978 Apr; 6 (4): 881–5
Saclier A L Good death: responsible choice in a changing society. Australian and New Zealand Journal of Psychiatry 1976 Mar; 10 (1): 3–6
Simms L M Dignified death: a right not a privilege. Journal of Gerontologic Nursing 1975 Nov-Dec; 1 (5): 21–5
Tayback M Death with dignity. Journal of Gerontologic Nursing 1975 Jul-Aug; 1 (3): 42–4
Watson W H, Maxwell R J Human aging and dying: a study for socio-cultural gerontology. New York: St. Martin's Press, 1977
Winner A Death and dying. Journal of the Royal College of Physicians 1970 Jul; 4 (4)

DRUGS

There is a real need for more published literature on drugs designed for the elderly and their special needs. Articles are available on drug abuse, problems of administration to impaired individuals, problems associated with drug education of the elderly, the need for pharmacy services in the client's home or extended care facilities. Less available are research findings reporting the effect of pharmacological treatments on the aging process. In this respect publications from the Research Resources Information Center (1776 East Jefferson Street Rockville, Maryland 20852) or articles appearing in the Research Resources Reporter are particularly helpful.

Bachinsky M Geriatric medications: how psychotrophic drugs can go astray. Nursing 1978 Feb; 41 (2): 50–5
Butler R N Pharmacological interventions of the aging process. Advanced Experimental Medical Biology 1978; 97: 231–41
Cooper J W, Bagwell C G Contributions of the consultant pharmacist to rational drug use in the long-term care facility. American Geriatrics Society Newsletter 1978 Sept; XXVI (9): 404–408
Glenn W L, et al Pharmacy services in a federal extended care facility as provided by a pharmacy student. American Geriatrics Society 1978 Jul; XXVI (7): 331–335
Miller R L, Algee J Noncompliance and drug toxicity in black, poor, and aged patients. Journal of the National Medical Association 1978 Oct; 70 (10): 733–6
Tower O B, Brands A Psychotropic drugs: approaches to psychopharmacologic drug use. National Institute of Mental Health (5600 Fisher's Lane, Rockville, MD 20857) 1979. Department of Health Education and Welfare-PHS Alcohol, Drug Abuse, and Mental Health Administration. Department of Health Education and Welfare Publication (ADM) 79–758

ECONOMICS AND LAW AFFECTING THE AGING

The finances and economics of aging and the aged are inextricibly involved with the presence of a national health scheme, federal, regional, and local laws which are governmentally regulated and enforced. No bibliographical listing will have wide applicability as state, national and international borders are crossed. Nevertheless, the bibliographic citations below serve as a reminder of bibliographic sources which may yield helpful publications on specific issues. Congressional Records, Proceedings of parliaments and legislative bodies cite primary sources for laws providing special advantages for the aging and elderly.

Other sources are found in publications on health planning and health policy.

Bricker B A quick guide to helping the elderly understand health insurance. Medical Economics 1979 23 Jul; 56 (15): 161–5

Butler R N The economics of aging: we are asking the wrong questions. National Journal (Washington) 1978 4 Nov; 10 (44): 1792–7

Callahan J J, Diamond L D, Giele J Z, Morris R Responsibility of families for their severly disabled elderly. Health Care Financing Review 1980 Winter: 29–48

Chatfield W F Economic and sociological factors influencing life satisfaction of the aged. Journal of Gerontology 1977 Sept; 32 (5): 593–9

Elderly exploited in selling of Medigap coverage. Aging 1979 May-Jun; (295–296): 2–5

Federal Responsibility to the Elderly (Executive programs and legislative jurisdiction). U.S. House 1975 Dec Washington, DC US Government Printing Office 1976

Herman T When Medicare stops: here are guidelines for buying supplementary health insurance. Wall Street Journal (Midwest Ed) 1979 18 Jun; 59 (171): 40

Herzog B R Aging and income: programs and prospectus for the elderly. NY: Human Sciences Press 1978

Hess A E A ten year prospectives on medicare. Public Health Reports 1976 Jul-Aug; 91 (4): 229–302

History of the Provision of Old-Age, Survivors, Disability, and Health Insurance. 1935–1975. Washington, DC — DHEW-Social Security Administration, Office of the Actuary 1976 Sept

Hudson R B State Politics, federalism, public policies for older Americans. Brandeis University: Florence Heller Graduate School for Advanced Study in Social Welfare 1973

Inglehart J K The cost of keeping the elderly well. National Journal (Washington) 1978 28 Oct; 10 (43): 1728–31

Improving legal representation for older Americans hearing: US Senate Special Committee on Aging. 1976 Sept 28, Washington DC Government Printing Office 1977

Lenders can no longer use age alone as the reason for denying credit Geriatrics 1976 Sept; 31 (91): 14–6

Older Americans Act: House Passage. Congressional Quarterly 1978 27 May; 1336–1337

Politics of Aging Society 1978 Jul-Aug; 15 (5: 22–75 (whole issue))

Strickland L, Thomas M P The law and the elderly in North Carolina. University of North Carolina at Chapel Hill, Institute of Government. 1978

EDUCATION FOR GERONTOLOGICAL AND GERIATRIC NURSING

The opportunity to teach nurses and other health professionals to deal with the problems of aging and the aged is once again being incorporated into the professional nursing curricula both at the graduate and the undergraduate levels. Informal investigation as well as more formal research is attempting to discover how attitudes of young practitioners to older clients, patients, and community members affect career selection and satisfaction.

Gerontology and geriatric nursing is attempting to establish itself as a creditable and accreditable discipline. The expanded scope of nursing practice has placed nurses with physical assessment skills in undeserved areas in both community and clinical settings. Specific curricula prepare nurses for primary care work. Often holding graduate degrees they work with multidisciplinary teams. Interdisciplinary educational practices place together learners who will deliver services to the elderly later on. They include members of such professions as nursing, medicine, social work, pharmacology, dentistry, nutrition, and the clergy.

American Nursing Association. ANA resolutions related to gerontological nursing. American Nurse 1978 Apr; 10 (4): 8. Journal of Gerontologic Nursing 1978 Nov-Dec: 43

Anderson S F How geriatric medicine is being taught at the University of Glasgow. Geriatrics 1976 Aug: 102-112

Bahr R T Gerontological nursing: a sequence in the Master of Nursing program, University of Kansas College of Health Sciences, School of Nursing. Kansas Nurse 1978 Aug; 53 (7): 4

Bahr R T, Gress L D Nursing care of the aging in comtemporary society: a course evaluation. Journal of Gerontologic Nursing 1978 Jul-Aug; 4 (4): 16-7

Bahr S R T Editorial. Journal of Gerontologic Nursing 1980 Mar; 6 (3): 116

Baldwin E Senior center experience of a student nurse. Journal of Gerontologic Nursing 1979 Mar-Apr; 5 (2): 22-4

Barrier M C, Guy A (Geriatric education). Soins 1979 5-20 Jul; 24 (13-14): 95-103

Beattie W M Gerontology Curricula: multidisciplinary frameworks, interdisciplinary structures and disciplinary depth. The Gerontologist 1974 Dec: 545-549

Brock A: Madison A The challenge in gerontologic nursing. Nursing Forum 1977; 16 (1): 96-105

Brower H T A study of the content needs in graduate gerontological nursing curriculum. Journal of Gerontologic Nursing 1979 Sept-Oct; 5 (5): 21-28

Cape R D T Geriatric medicine: a plea for specialization. Geriatrics 1980 April: 126-132

Cassell E J On educational changes for the field of aging. The Gerontologist 1972 Autumn; 1: 316-318

Chamberland G, Rawls B, Powell C, Roberts M J Improving students' attitudes toward aging. Journal of Gerontologic Nursing 1978 Jan-Feb; 4 (1): 44-5

Etten M J Gerontological nursing education at the associate degree and diploma levels. Journal of Gerontologic Nursing 1979 Jul-Aug; 5 (4): 32-9

Everson S J, Mealey A R Baccalaureate nursing students as leaders in geriatric groups. Journal of Nursing Education 1978 Jun-Sept; 17 (7) L17-26

Freeman J Gerontology's educational profile. Geriatrics 1976 Oct: 115–116

Gerdes J W Geriatric nurse practitioners: key in improving quality care Oregon 1978 Dec; 43 (5): 8–9

Gerdes J W In anticipation of the geriatric nurse practitioner. Nurse Practitioner 1978 Nov-Dec; 3 (6): 14, 39

Goldman R Geriatrics as a speciality-problems and prospects. The Gerontologist 1974 Dec: 468–472

Henderson M, Penta M Q An educational model for geriatric nurse practitioner curricula. Journal of Gerontologic Nursing 1978 Nov-Dec; 4 (6): 53–6

Hogstel M O Nurses' attitudes toward care of elderly hospital patients: can inservice education bring about positive change? Journal of Nursing Administration 1979 Jun; 9 (6): 26

Hudis A An introductory course in gerontology. The Gerontologist 1979 Aug: 545–549

Jacobson R L Gerontology said to lack identity as an academic discipline. The Chronical of Higher Education 1980 Mar 17

Libow L S The issues in geriatric medical education and postgraduate training: old problems in a new field. Geriatrics 1977 Feb: 99–102

Marten M L A university program to improve nursing care to the aged. Journal of Continuing Education of Nursing 1978 Jan-Feb; 9 (1): 7–10

Mutzebaugh C A, Mueller A L Nursing homes for student learning. Nurse Educator 1978 Jan-Feb; 3 (1): 14–6

Nichols E Preparation of leaders in gerontological nursing: the program at University of California at San Francisco. Journal of Gerontologic Nursing 1979 Sept-Oct; 5 (5): 21–28

Redford K M Non-clinical projects for the trainee nurses. Nursing Times 1978, 21 Sept; 74 (38): 1564–5

Roa D B The team approach to integrated care of the elderly. Geriatrics 1977 Feb: 88–96

Roberts M J, Powell C The rape of geriatrics by fundamentals nursing instructors. Journal of Gerontologic Nursing 1978 Sept-Oct; 4 (5): 4–6

Scott M L To learn to work with the elderly. American Journal of Nursing 1973 Apr: 662–664

Seltzer M Education in gerontology: an evolutionary analogy. The Gerontologist 1974 Aug: 316–318

Steffl B M Nursing education in gerontology in the United States. Arizona Nursing 1978 Nov-Dec; 31 (5): 4–6

Stilwell E M More on the nurse training act of 1978. Journal of Gerontologic Nursing 1979 May-Jun; 5 (3): 11

Stone V The Nurse and the aged. RN 1976 Feb: 21–26

Tuck B R The geriatric nurse, pioneer of a new speciality. Registered Nurse 1972 Aug: 35–38

Winitana M M A staff development programme for hospital aids at Riverton (Southland). New Zealand Nursing Journal 1978 Sept; 71 (9): 18–20

Wise H, Beckheard R, Rubin I, et al Making Health Teams Work. Cambridge, Massachusetts: Ballinger Publishing Company 1974

EPIDEMIOLOGY OF AGING

In the Second Conference on the Epidemiology of Aging, R. N. Butler of the National Institute on Aging noted that the legislative language of the Research on Aging Act of 1974, in the U.S.A., under which the institute was created, mandated a broad approach which includes biomedical, social, and behavioral research in which epidemiologic investigations have a role. There are seven other institutes on aging established in the industrialized nations of Japan, Rumania, Czechoslovakia, the Soviet Union, Israel, France, and Holland. Sweden is in the process of considering the establishment of such an institute. Members of the Institute consider aging through the following organizing concepts: Definition of Aging, Biomedical Correlates of Aging, Social, Psychological, and Functional Correlates of Aging, and Demographic Trends and Health Care Complications. These considerations are published in the National Institutes of Health Publication No. 80-969-July, 1980, *Epidemiology of Aging:* U.S. Government Printing Office, Washington, D.C. 20402. Other related bibliography are listed below.

Abrahams J P, Hoyer W J, Elias M F, Bradigan B Gerontological research in psychology published in the Journal of Gerontology 1963-1964: Perspectives and progress. Journal of Gerontology 1975 (30): 668-673

Atchley R C The Sociology of Retirement. New York 1976 Halsted Press

Bourestom N, Tars S Alterations in life patterns following nursing home relocation. Gerontologist 1974 (14): 506-510

Bourgeois-Pichat J Future outlook for mortality decline in the world. Presented at the meeting of the United Nations, Ad Hoc Group of Experts on Demographic Projections New York 1977 Nov

Branch L G Understanding the health and social service needs of people over age 65. Report to the Administration on Aging. Washington, D.C. Administration on Aging 1977

Bynder H, New P K Time for a change: From micro to macro-sociological concepts in disability research. Journal of Health and Social Behavior 1976 (17): 45-52

Everitt A V The nature and measurement of aging. Hypothalamus, Pituitary and Aging. Springfield, Charles C. Thomas 1976 5-42

Furukawa T, Inoue M; Kajiya F, Inada H, Takasugi S, Fukui S, Takeda H, Abe H Assessment of biological age by multiple regression analysis. Journal of Gerontology 1975 (30): 422-434

Glueck C J, Fallat R W, Spadafora M, Gartside P Longevity syndromes. Circulation 1975 (52): 272

Gruenberg E M, Hagnell O The rising prevalence of chronic brain syndrom in the elderly. Society, Stress and Disease, Aging and Old Age London, Oxford University Press

Harris L The Myth and Reality of Aging in America Washington, D.C., National Council on the Aging, 1976

Havighurst R J, Sacher G A Prospects of lengthening life and vigor. Proceedings of the University of Chicago Conference on Social Policy, Social Ethics, and the Aging Society. Washington, D.C., National Science Foundation, 1977

Heikkinen E, Kiiskinen A, Kayhty B, Rimpela M, Vuori I Assessment of biological age: Methodological study of two Finnish populations. Gerontology 1974 (20): 33-43

Hollingsworth J W, Hashizuma A, Jablon S Correlations between tests of aging in Hiroshima subjects: an attempt to define 'physiologic age.' Yale Journal of Biological Medicine 1965 (38): 11-36

Inkeles B, Innes J B, Kunta M M, Kadish A S, Weksler M E Immunological studies of aging. III. Cytokinetic basis for the impaired response of lymphocytes from aged humans to plant lectins. Journal of Experimental Medicine 1977 (145): 1176

Jackson G, Pierscianowski T A, Mahan W, Condon J R Hypertension in the elderly. Lancet 1976 (2): 1317

Jalavisto E, Makkonen T On the assessment of biological age. I. A factor analysis of Physiological measurements in old and young women. Annals of Academic Science, Finland (Med) 1963 100: 1-34

Kasl S V The effects of the residential environment on health and behavior: review. The Effect of the Man-Made Environment on Health and Behavior. DHEW Pub. No. (CDC) 77-8318, Washington, D.C., U.S. Government Printing Office 1976 65-127

Klawans H, Tufo H Neurological examination in an elderly population. Disorders of the Nervous System 1971 (32): 274-279

Kovar M G Health and health care of the elderly. Public Health Report 1977 (92): 9-19

Kuller L H Epidemiology of cardiovascular diseases: Current perspectives. American Journal of Epidemiology 1976 (104): 425-456

Lawton M P The dimension of morale, research planning and action for the elderly. The Power of Social Science. New York 1972 Behavioral Publications Incorporation

Lawton M P, Nahemow L Ecology and the aging process. The Psychology of Adult Development and Aging. Washington, D.C., American Psychological Association 1973 619-674

Makinodan T, Yunis E Immunology and Aging. 1977 Plen Publishing Corporation

Markus E, Blekner M, Bloom M, Downs T The impact of relocation on mortality rates of institutionalized aged persons. Journal of Gerontology 1971 (26): 537-541

Martin J, Doran A Evidence concerning the relationship between health and retirement. Sociology Review 1966 (14): 329-343

McMahon C A, Ford T R Surviving the first five years of retirement. Journal of Gerontology 1955 (10): 212-215

Murnaghan J E Long-term Care Data. Medical Care 14: 1976 (Supplement)

Nam C B, Ockay K A Factors contributing to the mortality crossover pattern: Effects of developmental level, overall mortality level, and causes of death. Paper submitted to the XVIII General Conference of the International Union for the Scientific Study of Population, Mexico City 1977; 8-13 Aug

Nuttall R L How many functional ages are there? In Publication No. 6, Normative Aging Study. Boston, Veterans Administration Outpatient Clinic 1973 12-22

Obrist W D Cerebral physiology of the aged: Influence of circulatory disorders. Aging and the Brain. New York, Plenum 1972 117-133

Palmore E Health practices and illness among the aged. Gerontologist 1970 (10): 313-316

Palmore E, Stone V Predictors of longevity: A followup of the aged in Chapel Hill. Gerontologist 1973 (13): 88-90

Planek T W The aging drive in today's traffic: A critical review. Aging and Highway Safety: The Elderly in a Mobile Society. North Carolina Symposium on Highway Safety 7, Chapel Hill, University of North Carolina Highway Safety Research Center 1972 3-38

Rosow I, Breslau N A Guttman Scale for the aged. Journal of Gerontology 1966 (21): 556-559

Sacher G A Life table modification and life prolongation. Handbook of the Biology of Aging. New York, Van Nostrand Reinhold 1977 582-638

Sauer H I Geographic variation in mortality and morbidity. Mortality and Morbidity in the United states. Cambridge Harvard University Press 1974 105-129

Siegel J S Demographic aspects of aging and the older population in the United States. U.S. Bureau of the Census. Current Population Reports, Special Studies, Series P-23, No. 59, Washington, D.C., 1976 U.S. Government Printing Office

U.S. Bureau of the Census. Projections of the population of the United States: 1977 to 2050. Current Population Reports, Series P-25, No. 704, Washington, D.C. 177 U.S. Government Printing Office

U.S. Bureau of the Census. Social and economic characteristics of the older population, 1974. Current Population Reports, Series P-23, No. 57, Washington, D.C. 1975 U.S. Government Printing Office

Waldron I Why do women live longer than men? Part I. Journal of Human Stress 1976 2 (1): 2-13. Social Science Medicine 1976 (10): 349-362

Waldron I, Johnston S Why do women live longer than men? Part II. Journal of Human Stress 1976 2 (2): 19-29

Walford R L, Smith G S, Meredity P J, Cheney K E the immunogentics of aging. Genetics of Aging. New York 1978 Plenum Publishing Corporation

ETHICAL ISSUES

The preoccupation with ethical issues has been stimulated by biotechnology as well as research. Ethics, at one time more alive outside hospital walls than in, has become of major concern to nurses, doctors, donors, families, consumers, and members of the health team. Discussion groups, monitoring groups, compliance procedures, informed consent documents — all have ethical issues as their basic consideration. Moreover, nurses have the opportunity to take courses in the ethics of health practice and to select ethics as courses of study and themes of theses and dissertations. University schools of nursing interact with centers for ethical studies. Nurses have been selected for fellowships in ethics and have become ethicists. Books on ethics in nursing, previously unwritten by nurses, have come to our attention these past five years, as have increasing numbers of scholarly articles discussing ethical issues in health. Ethical issues specifically related to the aging and care of the elderly are fewer in number but are increasingly coming to our attention. A selection of these is given below.

Bodmer W F Social concern and biological advances. Journal of the Royal Society of Arts 1977 Mar; 125 (5248): 180-194

Culliton B J The Haemmerli affair: is passive euthanasia murder? Science 1975 Dec; 190 (4221): 1271-1275, 26

Darnborough J, et al Does the end result justify the expense? Journal of Medical Ethics 1975 Dec; 1 (4): 187-192

Davis A J, Aroskar M A Ethical Issues and Nursing Practice. NY: Appleton-Century-Crofts 1978

The Ethical Challenge: Four Biomedical Case Studies. Parts I and II. Science and Mankind 1975 White Plains, NY

Harris S L, et al Behavior modifaction therapy with elderly demented patients: implementation and ethical considerations. Journal of Chronic Diseases 1977 Mar; 30 (3): 129-134

Jonsen A R Principles for an ethics of health services. In: Neugarten, Bernice L; Havighurst R J, eds. Social Policy, Social Ethics, and the Aging Society. Washington US Government Printing Office 1976; p 97-104

Kanoti G A Needed: a geriatric ethic. Hospital Progress 1977 Sept; 58 (9): 104+

Lasch C Aging in a culture without a future. Hastings Center Report 1977 Aug; 7 (4): 42–44

Linklater J Hemlock on the NHS. Spectator 1974 Nov; 233 (7638): 627

MacDonald M L The ethics of using behavior modification with the institutionalized aging: a practical analysis. Journal of Long-Term Care Administration 1976 Spring; 4 (2): 42–46

Mannes M Last Rights. New York: Morrow 1974

The Mount Sinai Hospital and Medical Center Symposia on Medicine and Halacha (Jewish Law). Chicago: Mount Sinai Hospital Center 1976 72p

Ramsey P The strange case of Joseph Saikewicz. In: his Ethics at the Edges of Life: Medical and Legal Intersections. New Haven: Yale University Press 1978 p 300–317

Rexed B, Juda D Planning for scarcity in Sweden: an interview with Bror Rexed. Hastings Center Report 1977 Jun; 7 (3): 5–7

Simmons R G, Klein S D, Simmons R L Transplantation and changing norms: cultural lag and ethical ambiguities. In: their Gift of Life: The Social and Psychological Impact of Organ Transplantation. New York: John Wiley 1977 p 9–44

Triche, C W, Triche D S The Euthanasia Controversy 1812–1974: A Bibliography with Select Annotations. Troy, NY: Whitson 1975

Yondorf B The declining and wretched. Public Policy 1975 Fall; 23 (4): 465–482

Voluntary Euthanasia Society of Victoria. Legislation for Voluntary Euthanasia: A Submission to the Royal Commission on Human Relationships. Unpublished document 1975 22p Available from the Voluntary Euthanasia Society of Victoria, P.O. Box 71, Mooroolbark 3138, Victoria, Australia

Van den Berg J H Medical Power and Medical Ethics. New York: W. W. Norton 1978 91p

ETHNICITY

Perhaps the most salient factor of ethnicity in regard to aging is the stabilizing influence to be gained from the continuity of the close-knit ethnic community and culture. For the nurse professional, ethnicity has a significant impact on the relationship between the caregiver and the care-receiver.

American Indian Population 55 years of age and older. Washington, DC — Dept HEW. Statistical Reports on Older Americans 1977 Mar.

Barta J The aged refugee immigrants. Australas Nurses Journal 1978 Dec; 8 (4): 28

Eribes R A, Bradley-Rawls M The under utilization of nursing home facilities by Mexican-American elderly in the southwest. The Gerontologist 1978 Aug; 18 (4): 363–371

Jackson J S, Bacon J D, Peterson J Life satisfaction among black urban elderly. International Journal of Aging of Human Development 1977–1978; 8 (2): 169–79

Kartmann L L Jewish ethnicity and its relevance for gerontological practice. Journal Gerontologic Nursing 1978 Jan-Feb; 4 (1) 34–9

Nahemow N The honorable elders: a cross cultural analysis of aging in Japan. Social Science in Medicine 1977 Feb; 11 (3): 221–222 Book review.

Ross H Comparative study of the development of black elderly and white european elderly neighborhood families: low-cost consumer-based service models. Gerontological Society Conference, Dallas 1978

Spector R E Cultural diversity in health and illness. NY: Appleton-Century-Crofts 1979

HEALTH PLANNING AND POLICY

Both international and national policies influence to some extent the health policies which extend care and services to the aged. With or without written policy, the use of resources indicates the values and priorities attached to the elderly population of a given country. In Great Britain for example, as in other countries with established national health plans or schemes, priorities established by the Department of Health and Social Security are reflected in DHSS publications, as well as in goals at the national, regional, and community level. Nursing service objectives reflect these priorities.

In the USA, in 1979, the Surgeon General's Report on Health Promotion and Disease Prevention was entitled HEALTHY PEOPLE. (U.S. Government Printing Office, Washington, D.C. 20402: Stock No. 017-001-00316-2.) A goal set for 1990 was to achieve the following:

> To improve the health and quality of life for older adults and, by 1990, to reduce the average annual number of days of restricted activity due to acute and chronic conditions by 20 per cent, to fewer than 30 days per year for people aged 65 and older.

Subgoals included:

(1) Increasing the number of older adults who can function independently, and

(2) Reducing premature death from influenza and pneumonia.

It is incumbent on professional nurses to determine the ways in which they can contribute to the achievement of this goal through nursing education, nursing services, or nursing research. Where policy is inadequate or unrealistic, nurse professionals may increase the scope of their professional activities to function as advocates for the elderly.

AHO W R Participation of senior citizens in the swine flu inoculation program: an analysis of Health Belief Model variables in preventive health behavior. Journal of Gerontology 1979 Mar; 34 (2): 201–8

Albinsson G Services for the elderly: Sweden. World Hospital 1979 Feb; 15 (1): 54–7

Aurousseau P Services for the elderly: France. World Hospital 1979 Feb; 15 (1): 31

Barber J B Statement of the National Medical Association to the Select Committee on Aging and Congressional Black Caucus Brain Trust on Aging at the hearing on 'Needs of the minority elderly'. Journal of the National Medical Association 1979 Aug; 71 (8): 745–6

Binstock R H A policy agenda on aging for the 1980s. National Journal (Washington) 1979 Oct 13; 11 (41): 1711–7

Binstock R H Federal policy treated toward the aging — its inadequacies and its politics. National Journal (Washington) 1978 11 Nov; 10 (45): 1838–45

Eichhorn S Services for the elderly: German Federal Republic. World Hospital 1979 Feb: 15 (1): 36–8

Emlet C A A psychosocial approach to institutionalized aged. Journal of American Health Care Associations 1979 Sep; 5 (5): 19, 22

Fritz D The advocacy agency and citizen participation: the case of the Administration on Aging and the elderly. Journal of Health and Human Resource Administration 1978 Aug; 1 (1): 79-108

Hillestad B, Palmer H Services for the elderly: Norway. World Hospital 1979 Feb; 15 (1): 48-51

Kasschau P L Developing gerontology in a developing country: The case of San Paulo, Brazil. International Journal of Aging and Human Development 1977-1978; 8 (4): 325-37

Kleh J Needs of the elderly: changes in delivery systems needed. Internist 1978 Sep; 19 (7): 12, 14

Lamy P P The senior boom — ready or not (editorial). Hospital Formulary 1979 Apr; 14 (4): 510-2

Leu F Services for the elderly: Switzerland. World Hospital 1979 Feb; 15 (1): 58-9

Mancini M Medicare: health rights of the elderly. American Journal of Nursing 1979 Oct; 79 (10): 1810, 1812

Margan I Services for the elderly: Yugoslavia. World Hospital 1979 Feb; 15 (1): 65-8

McCoy J L Antecedents of mortality among the old-age assistance population. Social Security Bulletin 1979 Jul; 42 (7): 3-15, 37

McKay R Ageing Britain: when law of the jungle is reversed. Health Social Service Journal 1979 5 Jan; 89 (4623): 12-4

Mullooly J P, Freeborn D K The effect of length of membership upon the utilization of ambulatory care services. A comparison of disadvantaged and general membership populations in a prepaid group practice. Medical Care 1979 Sep; 17 (9): 922-36

Onuallain C Services for the elderly: Ireland. World Hospital 1979 Feb; 15 (1): 39-41

Peterson D A, Powell C, Robertson L Aging in America toward the year 2000. Gerontologist 1976 Jun; 16 (3): 264-75

Richmond J B Health promotion and disease prevention in old age. Aging 1979 May-June; (295-296): 11-5

Russell B Elderly persons' impact on social policy. Geriatrics 1977 Sep; 32 (9): 77-9

Schmicke S W Services for the elderly: German Democratic Republic. World Hospital 1979 Feb; 15 (1): 33-5

Services for the elderly: United Kingdom. World Hospital 1979 Feb; 15 (1): 60-4

Simola H Services for the elderly: Finland. World Hospital 1979 Feb; (1): 29-30

Somers A R The high cost of health care for the elderly: diagnosis, prognosis, and some suggestions for therapy. Journal of Health Politics and Policy Law 1978 Summer; 3 (2): 163-80

Stolte J B Services for the elderly: Netherlands. World Hospital 1979 Feb; 15 (1): 45-7

Toftemark C Services for the elderly: Denmark. World Hospital 1979 Feb; 15 (1): 27-8

Vetere C Services for the elderly: Italy. World Hospital 1979 Feb; 15 (1): 42-3

Weissert W G Rationales for public health insurance coverage of geriatric day care: issues, options, and impacts. Journal of Health Politics and Policy Law 1979 Winter; 3 (4): 555-67

Wershow H J The outer limits of the walfare state: discrimination, racism and their effect on human services. International Journal of Aging and Human Development 1979-80; 10 (1): 63-75

Wilcox F Development of the nursing services in Scotland. The elderly. Nursing Mirror 1978 4 May: 146 (18): xii-xiii

World Health Assembly (1979f) Collaboration with the United Nations System: health care of the elderly. Resolution 32.55. Geneva

World Health Organization (1977a) Nursing aspects in the care of the elderly: Report of a working group. Copenhagen

Yeaworth R C Political issues and health care to America's elderly citizens. Journal of Gerontologic Nursing 1978 Mar-Apr; 4 (2): 38-41

IMPAIRMENT AS A CONSEQUENCE OF AGING

Because the aging process is a changing process, literature on change, loss, and learning should be considered. Of major concern, as reported by a national group of consultants calling themselves 'Consultation Group on Strategies for Promoting Health for Specific Populations — Elderly Americans', headed by L. W. Green, are the outcomes of change and impairment for the elderly. Highest on the list are preventive health services for sensory deprivation control. In addition injury control as health protection and improved nutrition as health promotion were rated very high. All of these topics relate to change and the responses to change associated with aging.

(The full address of this group is: Consultation Group on Strategies for Promoting Health for Specific Populations — Elderly Americans, Chairperson, L. W. Green, Director of Office of Health Information, D.H.S.S. Health Promotion and Physical Fitness and Sports Medicine, Washington, D.C. May 1980.)

A sampling of other writings on impairment are given below:

Abrahams R B, Patterson R D Psychological Distress Among the Community Elderly: Prevalence Characteristics and Implications for Service. International Journal on Aging and Human Development 1978: 9 (1): 1-18

Aging Eye, The: facts on eye care for older persons. New York: National Society for the prevention of Blindness, Inc. 1977 Feb

Birren J E, Schaie K W Handbook of the Psychology of Aging. New York Van Nostrand Reinhold 1976: 771

Chauncey N H, House J E Dental problems in the elderly. Hospital Practice 1977 Dec: 12 (12): 81-6

Cohen S Mental Impairment in the Aged: Fable and Fact. Scientific Exhibit at the Gerontological Society's Conference 1978 (Dallas)

Debry G, Bleyer R, Martin J Nutrition of the elderly. Journal of Human Nutrition 1977 Jun; 31 (3): 195-203

Finch C E, Hayflick L Handbook of the Biology of Aging. New York: Van Nostrand Reinhold 1977: 771

Glasscote R, Gudeman J E, Miles D Creative Mental Health Services for the Elderly. Washington, DC Joint Information Service 1977: 190

McCartney J H; Nadler G How to help your patient cope with hearing loss. Geriatrics 1979 Mar; 34 (3): 69-71, 75-6

Riemer Y Dental care and the aging. NADL Journal 1977 Apr; 24 (4): 11, 13, 15

Schiffman S S Changes in taste and smell in older persons. Center Reports on Advances in Research. Durham North Carolina: Duke Center for the Study of Aging and Human Development 1978 Fall

Smith C E Influence of standards on the nutritional care of the elderly. Dolores Nyhus Memorial Lecture. Journal of American Dietary Association 1978 Aug; 73 (2): 115-9

Tempro W A Nutritional problems in the aged: diatary aspects. Journal of the National Medical Association 1978 Apr; 70 (4): 281-3

MEDICAL MANAGEMENT

Probably the largest numbers of citations are to be found in the area of medical management, which of course covers all aspects of care including those cases in which surgical intervention is necessary. But medical plans specifically for the elderly, conditions leading to the medical management of the elderly or conditions consequent on the medical care of the elderly are less evident in the literature. The problem of the elderly as a surgical risk is addressed, but medical management and associated nursing care tailored especially to the needs of the elderly, in which multi-problem conditions are aggravated by age or aging, are much needed in health literature. Below are examples of those in print, only a portion of which include a presentation of associated nursing care needs or plans.

Ferris P Surgical management of the elderly. Hospital Practice 1976 Jul; (7): 65–71
Haber P A Issues and trends in gerontology. Current Practice of Gerontologic Nursing 1979; 1: 229–37
House S M Post-traumatic nitrogen metabolism in the elderly. Nursing Times 1978 31 Aug; 74 (35): 1457–9
Kelsey J L, White A A 3rd; Pastides H, Bisbee G E Jr The impact of musculoskeletal disorders on the population of the United States. Journal of Bone and Joint Surgery (AM) 1979 Oct; 61 (7): 959–64
Kovar M G Health of the elderly and use of health services Public Health Report 1977 Jan-Feb; 92 (1): 9–19
Newman T F The setting up of a geriatric screening clinic in Cape Town. South African Medical Journal 1977 26 Mar; 51 (13): 427–30
O'Donnell T F, Darling R C, Linton R R Is 80 years too old for aneurysmectomy? Archives of Surgery 1976 Nov; 111 (11): 1250–7
Passeri M Therapy of chronic consequences of brain ischemia. Comparison between two drugs acting on brain circuation and metabolism. European Neurology 1978; 17 Suppl 1: 150–8
Pike L A Screening the elderly in general practice. Journal of Royal College of General Practice 1976 Sep; 26 (170): 698–703
Pratt M A Physical exercise: a special need in long-term care. Journal of Gerontologic Nursing 1978 Sept-Oct; 4 (5): 38–42
Riggle K L Physiological changes of aging and nursing assessment. Current Practice of Gerontologic Nursing 1979; 1: 39–63
Roquefeuil B (Resuscitation of the elderly brain). Annals of Anesthesiology Fr 1979; 20 (1): 55–62
Schuckit M A, Miller P L Alcoholism in elderly men: a survey of a general medical ward. Annals of New York Academy of Science 1976; 273: 558–71
Sorensen A A, Sorensen D I, Zimmer J G Appropriateness of vitamin and mineral prescription orders for residents of health related facilities. Journal of American Geriatric Society 1979 Sep; 27 (9): 425–30
Yerby A Community medicine in England and Scotland. Washington, DC DHEW(PHS) National Institutes of Health No. 76–1061. John E. Fogerty International Center for Advanced Study 1976

NURSING CARE AND NURSING SERVICES

The nurse writer, researcher, and administrator comes into prominance in the bibliographical entries of articles on nursing care and

SPECIALISED BIBLIOGRAPHIES

nursing services. These publications, represented only in part here, range in their emphases from those which challenge other nurses to accept their responsibility to the elderly to those which pioneer new nursing approaches and new nursing roles in this area of practice. In addition to giving the care, the professional nurse writer suggests methods of improving the assessment of the quality of the care in various settings. Perennial nursing problems such as feeding, rehabilitating, and ambulating the elderly person continue to be represented to the literature. Additionally, perennial problems which were never talked of or written about, such as the acknowledgement of the patient's sexuality, are now addressed. Significantly, many nurses write about the particular job satisfaction they find while working in settings in which the elderly live, and they describe their ability to be creative and innovate in planning and implementing patient care.

Alford D M The affluent elderly: problems in nursing care. Journal of Gerontologic Nursing 1978 Mar-Apr; 4 (2): 44–7
Barrowclough F, Pinel C All nurses must share in the care of the old. Nursing Mirror 1978 4 Jan; 148 (1): 13–6
Bawden M A caring experience. Canadian Nurse 1977 Apr; 73 (4): 24
Benson E R Observation on health care for the elderly in the USSR. Journal of Gerontologic Nursing 1978 Sept-Oct; 4 (5): 18–20
Burrows J The elderly: a challenge to nursing-2. The elderly in our society. Nursing Times 1977 27 Oct; 73 (43): 1670–4
Cairns J Treating long-term patients as individuals. Nursing Times 1979 21 Jun; 75 (25): 1058–9
Campbell M E, Browning E M Nursing assistants — an untapped resource in providing quality care to the elderly ill. Journal of Gerontologic Nursing 1978 Nov-Dec; 4 (6): 18–20
Castellanos M Complimentary education in nursing care for the aged (interview). Z Krankenpfl 1979 Jun; 72 (6): 262–4
Chisholm M K The nurse's responsibilities when caring for the elderly. Nursing Times 1977 29 Sept; 73 (39): 1509–10
Cruise V J, Wright W B Better geriatric care — making it happen. Nursing Times 1978 21 Sept; 74 (38): 1563–4
Daly J, Jones J, Rees J, Williams M Practical nursing: getting the elderly back on their feet after an accident. Nursing Mirror 1979 15 Mar; 148 (11): 28–30
Dufault K Recognition of a classic in gerontological nursing. Journal of Gerontologic Nursing 1979 May-Jun; 5 (3): 56–8
Eliopoulos C The gerontological nurse specialist. Current Practices in Gerontologic Nursing 1979; 1: 197–203
Friedeman J S Sexuality in older persons: implications for nursing practice. Nursing Forum 1979; 18 (1): 92–101
Gadow S Advocacy nursing and new meanings of aging. Nursing Clinics in North America 1979 Mar; 14 (1): 81–91
Joyce A, Krawczyk R Preventative nursing intervention with the elderly. Journal of Gerontologic Nursing 1978 Sep-Oct; 4 (5): 28–34
Kiesel M, Bininger C An application of psycho-social role theory to the aging: (role possibilities of the elderly in nurse-patient interactions). Nursing Forum 1979; 18 (1): 80–91
Kraning M J, Mumma C The implementation of holistic/humanist nursing concepts in a rehabilitation setting. ARN Journal 1978 Nov-Dec; 3 (6): 12–5

Kratz C R Sensory deprivation. 3. In the elderly. Nursing Times 1979 22 Feb; 75 (8): 330-2
Mackeprang B, Bentzon M W Minimum need for care in geriatric institutions. Scandinavian Journal of Social Medicine 1978; 6 (1): 25-9
Mantle J Nursing's contribution to the quality of care. Journal of Gerontologic Nursing 1978 Mar-Apr; 4 (2): 34-7
Mc Clelland M Japan's modern approach to an age-old problem. Nursing Mirror 1978 17 Aug; 147 (7): 13-5
McIver V Freedom to be: a new approach to quality care for the aged. Canadian Nurse 1978 Mar; 74 (3): 19-26
Millard F H To rehabilitate or to vegetate? Nursing Mirror 1978 16 Mar; 146 (11): 14-6
Moses D V The nurse's role as advocate with the elderly. Current Practices in Gerontologic Nursing 1979; 1: 221-6
Nurse could you care more? Nursing Times 1979 10 May; 75 (19): 776
The nursing services in Wales: nursing the elderly. Nursing Mirror 1978 21 Sep; 147 (12): x-xi
Quinn J L, Ryan N E OR nursing assessment of the older adult. Association of Operating Room Nurses Journal 1979 Feb; 29 (2): 235-46
Reinhardt A M, Quinn M D Current practice in gerontological nursing: preface. Current Practices in Gerontologic Nursing 1979; 1: xi-xiii
Schwab M Gerontological nursing: skilled nursing revisited. Journal of the American Health Care Association 1978 Sep; 4 (5): 82-6
Summary report of working group on nursing aspects in the care of the elderly. Journal of Advanced Nursing 1978 Jul; 3 (4): 407-12
Taggart M When your elderly patient is withdrawing . . . what can you do? Journal of Practical Nursing 1976 Dec; 26 (12): 16-9
Taylor K H, Harned T L Attitudes toward old people: a study of nurses who care for the elderly. Journal of Gerontologic Nursing 1978 Sept-Oct; 4 (5): 43-7
Wainwright H Feeding problems in elderly disabled patients. Nursing Times 1978 30 Mar; 74 (13): 542-3
Weiner M B Caring for the elderly. Sex and aging: myths and realities. Journal of Nursing Care 1978 Oct; 11 (10): 9
Wichita C The challenge of geriatric care. You can't change brain damage, but you can change their lives. Registered Nurse 1978 May; 41 (5): 52-3

PSYCHOLOGY OF THE AGING

Perhaps a disservice is done in listing the psychology of aging publications as distinct from other inextricable factors such as the physiology and sociology of aging. The citations given here focus attention on the particular needs of the aging as well as the aging experience itself. These references should be consulted in association with three listed under the heading of Aging and Change.

Bowling J H Significance of motivation. Australas Nurses Journal 1977 Aug; 7 (1): 8-10
Burnside I M Recognizing and reducing emotional problems in the aged. Nursing (Jenkintown) 1977 Mar; 7 (3): 56-9
Chang B L Generalized expectancy, situational perception, and morale among institutionalized aged. Nursing Research 1978 Sep-Oct; 27 (5): 316-24
Chang B L Locus of control, trust, situational control and morale of the elderly. International Journal of Nursing Students 1979; 16 (2): 169-81
Erickson R, English S, Halar E, Hibbert J Employing reality orientation in a short term treatment setting. American Registered Nurse 1978 Nov-Dec; 3 (6): 18-21

Esberger K Body image. Journal of Gerontological Nursing 1978 Jul–Aug; 4 (4): 35–8

Flood N Deprivation and existence or stimulation and life: our choice for the elderly. Nursing Homes 1976 Nov; 25 (6): 21–3

Foster J Social care: loneliness. The group solution to isolation. Nursing Mirror 1978 12 Oct; 147 (15): 28–9

Gayler G The importance of being human. Australas Nurses Journal 1977 Aug;. 7 (1): 10–2

Gilette E Apathy vs. reality orientation. Journal of Nursing Care 1979 Apr; 12 (4): 24–5

Haring P W Short-term adjustment of geriatric residents. Issues in Mental Health Nursing 1978 Spring; 1: 25–41

Henthorn B S Disengagement and reinforcement in the elderly. Research in Nursing and Health 1979 Mar; 2 (1): 1–8

Hill B Toward a continuum of life style. California Nurse 1977 Dec; 73 (6): 12–4

Jacobs B P Social care: loneliness. When age brings a crisis, the nurse can restore hope. Nursing Mirror 1978 12 Oct; 147 (15): 25–7

Junod J P, Landry D (Confusional states in geriatrics). Annals of Anesthesiology, France 1977; 18 (5–6): 467–70

Kane L, Anderson N A The elderly isolate. Australian Family Physician 1978 Mar; 7 (3): 244–51

Luker K A Measuring life satisfaction in an elderly female population. Journal of Advanced Nursing 1979 Sep; 4 (5): 503–11

Mooney C M Psychologic problems of the aged. Journal of the American Geriatric Society 1978 Jun; 26 (6): 268–73

Niemi T Effect of loneliness on mortality after retirement. Scandinavian Journal of Social Medicine 1979; 7 (2): 63–5

Oster C Sensory deprivation in geriatric patients. Journal of the American Geriatric Society 1976 Oct; 24 (10): 461–4

Pease R A Dependency and the double-bind in the aged. Journal of Gerontologic Nursing 1978 Jul–Aug; 4 (4): 24–30

Roscher C I Social and emotional needs of the aged. Address given during an inservice education course on the care of the aged. South African Nursing Journal 1978 Mar; 45 (3): 6–7

Ross H E, Kedward H B Psychogeriatric hospital admissions from the community and institutions. Journal of Gerontology 1977 Jul; 32 (4): 420–7

Skoglund J A comparative factor analysis of attitudes toward societal relations of the elderly. International Journal of Aging and Human Development 1977–1978; 8 (4): 277–91

Smith J Sensory deprivation — a primary concept of nursing. Nursing Mirror 1978 3 Aug; 147 (5): 7

Stenback A, Kumpulainen M, Vauhkonen M L On successful aging (summary). Gerontologist 1977; (21): 61–3

Thurmott P The elderly: a challenge to nursing-7. Isolation and loneliness. Nursing Times 1977 1 Dec; 73 (48): 1884–6

Toseland R, Sykes J Senior Citizens Center participation and other correlates of life satisfaction. Gerontologist 1977 Jun; 17 (3): 235–41

Turner R J, Sternberg M P Psychosocial factors in elderly patients admitted to a psychiatric hospital. Age and Ageing 1978 Aug; 7 (3): 171–7

Warshow H J Comment: reality orientation for gerontologists. Some thoughts about senility. Gerontologist 1977 Aug; 17 (4): 297–302

Weiner M B Caring for the elderly: the positive effect of negative emotions in the elderly. Journal of Nursing Care 1979 Mar; 12 (3): 11

Weuber N B Caring for the elderly: mental health in the elderly. Journal of Nursing Care 1979 Jul; 12 (7): 34

Whitbourne S K Psychological adaptation in old age. Long Term Care Health Services Administration Q 1977 Summer; 1 (2): 145–51

Whitehead T Confusing causes of confusion. Nursing Mirror 1978 21 Sep; 147 (12): 29–30

Weiner M B, Wilensky H A psychotherapeutic approach to emotional problems of the elderly. Journal of Nursing Care 1978 May; 11 (5): 14–5, 27–8

Williams L M A concept of loneliness in the elderly. Journal of the American Geriatric Society 1978 Apr; 26 (4): 183–7

Yondorf B The declining and wretched. Public Policy 1975 Fall; 23 (4): 465–82

Youmans E G Attitudes: young-old and old-old. Gerontologist 1977 Apr; 17 (2): 175–8

RESEARCH AND THE PROTECTION OF HUMAN SUBJECTS

Related to ethical considerations are the specific concerns for the safety of clients of all ages. Research and non-research settings are asked to consider reasonable preventable risk. Professor Lowrance of Harvard University states that preventable risk is not reasonable (a) when consumers do not know that the risk exists; (b) when, though aware of it, consumers are unable to estimate its frequency and severity; (c) when consumers do not know how to cope with it, and hence are likely to incur harm unnecessarily; or (d) when risk is unnecessary in that it could be reduced or eliminated at a cost in money or in the performance of the product that consumers would willingly incur if they knew the facts and were given the choice. Application of these criteria to the aging population is particularly evident in the consideration of the protection of the elderly in all settings in which they live.

Axelsen D, Wiggins R A An application of moral guidelines in human clinical trials to a study of a benzodiazepine compound as a hypnotic agent among the elderly. Clinical Research 1977 Jan; 25 (1): 1–7

Berkowitz S Informed consent, research, and the elderly. Gerontologist 1978 Jun; 18 (3): 237–43

Cooper, Hartman Aging: research. Issue brief number 1B74097 Washington, D.C. Congressional Research Service, Library of Congress 1974; 29 Jul: 1978; 6 Dec

Kerdig H L, Warren R The adequacy of census data in planning and advocacy for the elderly. The Gerontologist 1976; 16 (5): 392–396

Lowrence W W Of acceptable risk. Science and the determination of society. 1976 Los Angeles, Calif.

Reich W T Ethical issues related to research involving elderly subjects. The Gerontologist 1978 Aug; 18 (4): 326–337

Wales J B, Treybig D L Recent legislative trends toward protection of human subjects: implications for gerontologists. Gerontologist 1978 Jun; 18 (3): 244–9

West H Researcher applies biofeedback therapy to nursing home residents. Journal of Gerontologic Nursing 1978 May–Jun; 4 (3): 19

SETTINGS IN WHICH THE AGING LIVE

Health publications often use the settings in which the aging person lives as an organizing concept for studying his situation, needs, and quality of life. These publications may be concerned with any of the following: the aging in the community, housing for the aging, family and aged members living at home, the aging in hospitals, the aging in nursing homes. (The term 'nursing home' is defined differently in the United States than, for example, in the United Kingdom. In the USA the term is a broad one meaning a place of residence for the aged or elderly. Although the adjective "nursing' is applied, the level of care at these homes ranges from independent and ambulatory with a minimum amount of supervision by personnel to nearly intensive care conditions in which complex nursing needs require highly skilled professional nursing care.)

Setting as an organizing concept not only reminds us of the housing conditions and varied needs of the older person, but also defines the meaningful or significant others: depending on the setting they may be spouse, family members, fellow club members, fellow church members, professional colleagues, known and unknown community members, or total strangers. Hence, a discussion of the setting brings us into contact with both the psychology of aging and the assessment of the vulnerability of the client.

Aged and community

An ageing population. Community Outlook 1978 10 Aug: 221-3

Benson E R, BoDevitt Jz Know your community resources: nursing service and nursing education: co-action to meet the health needs of the elderly. Journal of Gerontologic Nursing 1978 May-Jun; 4 (3): 20-4

Blomerus E K Ten years of preventive geriatric services in the city of Germiston. Tracing the aged in a community. Curationis 1979 Mar; 1 (4): 25-6

Breslow R W, VanDyk M W Developing group homes for older people: a hand book for community groups. Rockville, Maryland-Jewish Council for the Aging of Greater Washing, Inc. 1978 Oct

Clark G Community psychiatric nursing. Community Outlook 1978 9 Nov: 356

Cross R Community nursing: a fight for independence. Nursing Mirror 1979 Mar; 1 (4): 23-6

Erasmus C A Ten years of preventive geriatric services in the city of Germiston: introduction. Curationis 1979 Mar; 1 (4): 23-5

Gunter L M, Estes L A Tomorrow's aged: impact of transgenerational trends on nursing education. American Nurses Association Publication 1979; (G-135): 86-95

Hassett P Community nursing: no substitute for love and trust. Nursing Mirror 1978 28 Sept; 147 (13): 39-40

Hunt P Community nursing. Dementia in the elderly: the caring family needs support. Nursing Mirror 1979 2 Aug: 149 (5): 24-5

Keywood O Community nursing: preparing the elderly to return home. Nursing Mirror 1978 7 Sept; 147 (10): 42-4

Sudding L J Ten years of preventive geriatric services in the city of Germiston. A member of the community geriatric team. Curationis 1979 Mar; 1 (4): 26-7

Sullivan J A, Armicnacco F Effectiveness of a comprehensive health program for the well-elderly by community health nurses. Nursing Research 1979 Mar-Apr; 28 (2): 70-5

Tobiason S J, Knudsen F, Sieagel J C; Giss M Positive attitudes toward aging: the aged teach the young. Journal of Gerontolic Nursing 1979 May-Jun; 5 (3): 18-23

Housing for the aging

Craigmile W M, Fordvce Id, Mooney G H Domiciliary care of the elderly. Nursing Times 1978 2 Feb; 74 (5): suppl 13–5

Harel Z, Harel B B On-site coordinated services in age-segregated and age-integrated public Housing. Gerontologist 1978 Apr; 18 (2): 153–8

Harris H, Lipman A, Slater R Architectural design: the spatial location and interactions of old people. Gerontology 1977; 23 (5): 390–400

Jordan J J Designing interiors for the elderly. Executive Housekeeper 1979 Aug; 26 (8): 14–5

Mackeprang B, Bentzon M W Some aspects concerning admittance to and accommodation in geriatric institutions housing persons with varying degrees of need for care. Scandinavian Journal of Social Medicine 1978; 6 (2): 59–62

Newcomer R J, Newcomer S R, Gelwicks L E Assessing the need for semi-dependent housing for the elderly. Gerontologist 1976 Apr; 16 (2): 112–7

Sabatino J S Designing a modern home for the elderly. Journal of Long Term Care Admitting 1979 Summer; 7 (2): 29–39

Spivack M, Grayson P, Morris G The Elizabeth Seton Residence and the patient bedroom module. Aging Leisure Living 1979 Jan; 2 (1): 13–7

Struyk R J The housing expense burden of households headed by the elderly. Gerontologist 1977 Oct; 17 (5 PT1): 447–52

Families and aged members at home

Alvermann M M Toward improving geriatric care with environmental intervention emphasizing a homelike atmosphere: an environmental experience. Journal of Gerontologic Nursing 1979 May-Jun; 5 (3): 13–7

Asiel M (Housing and accommodation of able-bodied aged). Archives of Belgium Medical Society 1978 Mar; 36 (3): 162–72

Brody, Stanley, et al The family caring unit: a major consideration in the long-term support system. The Gerontologist 1978 18 (6): 556–561

Christiana S, Genevieve S, Lambert C, Maisonneuve A, Trencic N, Vasseur E Relationship with the patient's family in the geriatric milieu. Soins 1979 5–20 Jul; 24 (13–14): 71–4

Dobrof R, Litwak E Maintenance of family ties of long term care patients: theory and guide to practice. USA-DHEW. National Institute of Mental Health. 1977

Lawton M P Institutions and alternatives for older people. Health Social Work 1978 May; 31 (2): 108–34

O'Kelley F, McNulty C Survey of patients seen in their own homes and in nursing homes in a group practice population. Ireland Medical Journal 1978 21 Dec; 71 (18): 621–4

Packer L Quality of life for the elderly. Nursing Times 1979 30 Aug; 75 (35): 1502–3

Pepper C Are we turning the elderly out of their homes? Family Health 1979 Mar; 11 (3): 6

Smith R G, Lowther C P Follow-up study of two hundred admissions to a residential home. Age Ageing 1976 Aug; 5 (3): 176–80

Veylon R Home care and maintenance of the aged patient. Nouvelle Presse Medicale 1977 10 Sept; 6 (29): 2611–4

Weiner M B Caring for the elderly. Helping families visit the older patient. Journal of Nursing Care 1978 Aug: 11 (8): 8

Aged in hospitals

Alexander J R, Eldon A Characteristics of elderly people admitted to hospital, Part III homes, and sheltered housing. Epidemiology Community Health 1979 Mar; 33 (1): 91–5

Anderson O W Reflections on the sick aged and the helping systems. Journal of Gerontologic Nursing 1977 Mar–Apr; 3 (2): 14–20

Cronj'e A S Living in a geriatric hospital. Some suggestions for improving the quality of life. South American Nursing Journal 1978 Mar; 45 (3): 22–3

Dent R V Geriatric care in hospital. Nursing Times 1977 29 Sep; 73 (39): 1507–9

Lewis K Practical illustrations of nurse-social worker collaboration and teamwork in a long-term health care facility. Journal Gerontologic Nursing 1979 May–Jun; 5 (3): 34–9

Naus P J Institutions for the aging, instruments of growth? Catholic Hospital 1978 May–Aug; 6 (3–4): 17–8

Noelker L, Harel Z Predictors of well-being and survival among institutionalized aged. Gerontologist 1978 Dec; 18 (6): 562–7

Thursfield P J Community Nursing: the hospital that doesn't say 'good-bye'. Nursing Mirror 1979 8 Feb; 148 (6): 50–2

Ward A B Are we improving hospital care of elderly patients? Ann Arbor Michigan. Professional activity study. PAS Reporter 1977 19 Sept; 15 (9)

Weissert W G Two models of geriatric day care: finding from a comparative study. The Gerontologist 1976 16 (5): 420–427

Wylie C M Hospitalization for fractures and bone loss in adults. Why do we regard these phenomena as dull? Public Health Report 1977 Jan–Feb; 92 (1): 33–8

Aged in nursing homes

Barney J L Community presence as a key to quality of life in nursing homes. American Journal of Public Health 1974 Mar; 64 (3): 265–268

Burge J M Stereotyped attitudes toward the aged in nursing homes. Issues of Mental Health Nursing 1978 Spring; 1: 53–61

Dudley C J, Hillery G A Jr Freedom and alienation in homes for the aged. Gerontologist 1977 Apr; 17 (2): 140–5

Larson L E Who belongs in a nursing home? Long Term Care Health Service Administration Quarterly 1977 fall; 1 (3): 249–53

Lipman A, Slater R Homes for old people: toward a positive environment. Gerontologist 1977 Apr; 17 (2): 146–56

Lipman A, Slater R Status and spatial appropriation in eight homes for old people. Gerontologist 1977 Jun; 17 (3): 250–5

McKnight E M Nursing home research study: quantitative measurement of nursing services. Washington, DC DHEW publication no (NIH) 72-223 1972 Jan

Moss F E, Halamandaris V J Too old, too sick, too bad. Nursing Homes in America. Germantown, Maryland. Aspen Systems Corp. 1977

Vicker R L Attitudes of nursing home personnel toward aging the aged. Long Term and Health Services Administration Quarterly 1978 Fall 2 (3): 197–219

VULNERABILITY

The elderly are especially sensitive and vulnerable in terms of their particular needs associated with identity, communication, independence/dependence, pain, privacy/dignity, interpersonal relationships, memory, and reduced energy and vigor. The available literature indicates that these needs have been attended to by a variety of individuals, including community health team members, clergy, family, and neighbors. Nevertheless, the increasing vulnerability of the elderly has been demonstrated in the reports of battering and abuse within the home as well as in the fears for the elderly as potential victims of a variety of confidence and street crimes. These latter subjects are beginning to appear in professional health journals.

Barney J L The prerogative of choice in long-term care. Gerontologist 1977 Aug; 17 (4): 309–14

Barrowclough F Ward accidents. Danger! Why old people fall. Nursing Mirror 1979 14 Jun; 148 (24): 28–9

Clark C C, Mills G C Communications with hearing impaired elderly adults. Journal of Gerontologic Nursing 1979 May-Jun; 5 (3): 40–4

Cook F L, et al Criminal victimization of the elderly: the physical and economical consequences. The Gerontologist 1978 Aug; 18 (4): 338–354

Donahue W T The Donald P. Kent Award Lecture: What about our responsibility toward the abandoned elderly? Gerontologist 1978 Apr; 18 (2): 102–11

Feist R R A survey of accidental falls in a small home for the aged. Journal of Gerontologic Nursing 1978 Nov-Dec; 4 (6): 15–7

Goldsmith J, Tomas N Crimes against the elderly: a continuing national crisis. Aging 1974 Jun-Jul

Gryfe C I, Amies A, Ashley M J A longitudinal study of falls in an elderly population: I. Incidence and morbidity. Age of Ageing 1977 Nov; 6 (4): 201–10

Hugonot R Participation of elderly persons: not only a right but above all a duty. Bruxton Medicine 1977 Jan; 57 (1): 5–11

Hulebroeck G Participation . . . a right of our senior citizens. Bruxton Medicine 1977 Jan; 57 (1): 17–20

Marois M Participation and quality of life. Bruxton Medicine 1977 Jan; 57 (1): 13–6

Moherg D O Needs text by the clergy for ministries to the aging. The Gerontologist 1975 Apr; 170–174

Maxwell R J Doomed status: observations on the segregation of impaired old people. Psychiatry Quarterly 1979 Spring; 51 (1): 3–14

O'Brien M A 'Battered grandparents': does this term apply to elderly people in New Zealand? New Zealand Nursing Journal 1979 Mar; 72 (3): 3–4

Pelizza J J Suicide in the elderly: can it be prevented? Long Term Care Health Service Administrative Quarterly 1979 Summer; 3 (2): 85–91

Reynolds B J Suddenly blind at 80. Nuring (Horsham) 1979 Jul; 9 (7): 46–9

Shulman K Suicide and parasuicide in old age: a review. Age of Ageing 1978 Nov; 7 (4): 201–9

Weiner M B, Wilensky H A psychotherapeutic approach to emotional problems of the elderly. Journal of Nursing Care 1978 May; 11 (5): 14–5, 27–8

Weuber N B Caring for the elderly: mental health in the elderly. Journal of Nursing Care 1979 Jul; 12 (7): 34

Whitbourne S K Psychological adaptation in old age. Long Term Care Health Service Administrative Quarterly 1977 Summer; 1 (2): 145–51

Whitehead T Confusing causes of confusion. Nursing Mirror 1978 21 Sep; 147 (12): 29–30

Williams L M A concept of loneliness in the elderly. Journal of the American Geriatrics Society 1978 Apr; 26 (4): 183–7

Yondorf B The declining and wretched. Public Policy 1975 Fall; 23 (4):465–82

Youmans E G Attitudes: young-old and old-old. Gerontologist 1977 Apr; 17 (2): 175–8

WELLNESS

The trend toward health promotion and disease prevention has yielded many articles about these concepts as associated with the elderly. The increased interest in physical fitness has meant an increase in fitness programs for the elderly. Health, as the World Health Organization has defined it, is more than the absence of disease. This awareness on the part of health professionals and clients alike are influencing care patterns, procedures, and practices associated with the aging.

Dresden S E Staying well while growing old: autonomy: a continuing developmental task. American Journal of Nursing 1978 Aug; 78 (8): 1344–6

Evans L K Maintaining social interaction as health promotion in the elderly. Journal of Gerontologic Nursing 1979 Mar-Apr; 5 (2): 19–21

Fitness challenge in the later years. Administration on Aging 1975 Jun

Handle yourself with care. Accident prevention for older Americans. Department of Health Education and Welfare Administration on Aging 1977 Feb

Mcglone F B, Kick E Health habits in relation to aging. American Geriatrics Society Newsletter 1978 Nov; XXVI (11): 481–489

Index

Activities of daily living (ADL), 127–128, 182–183
Activity theory, 50
Adults, older, 114, 115–117
  financial problems of, 116
  health care problems of, 116
  mortality rate of, 115
  see also Aging
Age Concern, 47
Age, losses associated with, 140
Ageism, 116–117
Aging
  and change, 210
  and dying, 138, 140
    see also Death, aging and
  and where they live, 227–228
  dementia of *see* Dementia of aging
  developments in, 25–27
  economics and law affecting, 213
  epidemiology of, 215–216
  impairment due to, 222
  psychobiology of, 28
  psychology of, 225
  research *see* Research, of the aging
Alzheimer's disease, 22
American Nurses' Association (ANA), 120–121
Assessment
  see under various types of assessment
Australia *see* Geriatric nursing in Australia
Autonomy, 40

Beautitudes Campus of Care, 153
Behavior
  neurological basis of, 23–24
  research *see* Research, behavioral therapy, 24
Bereavement support, 148
Bioethics, 38
Biofeedback, 24

Care
  British perspective, 168–189
  community-based, 17–20
  cost of, 78–79
  day, 18–19
  evaluation, 168–189
  family-centered, 29, 177
  home, 142
  hospital, 46–72
    in Britain, 47–53
    long-term, 58–64

  see also Geriatric wards, longstay *and* Long-term care
  short-term, 56–58
    see also Hospital
  institutional *see* Institutional care
  long-term *see* Long-term care
  residential *see* Residential homes, care in
  round-the-clock, 142
  tender loving, 46–72
Cognitive impaired and families, 159–165
Consent, informed, 194–196
Consultants, behaviour of, 63–64
Costs
  containment of, 148–149
  relative, 48
Creativity, 23

Death, 137
  aging and, 138
  and dying, 211
  attitudes towards, 138–141
    of aging, 139–140
    of health care professionals, 139
    of society, 138–139
  fear of, 139, 140
  reluctance to accept, 138
Decision-making, 41–45
  ethical, 44–45
    see also Ethical decisions
Demands of daily living (DDL), 127–128
Dementia of aging, 22
Deontology *see* Formalism
Department of Health and Social Security (DHSS), policy, 49–53
Directors of Nurses (DN), 75–90
  attributes of, 79–80
  employment measures, 79
  experience, 88–89
  interpersonal network, 80
  job satisfaction of, 80, 86–88
    correlates of, 87–88
  potential social support indicator, 80, 89
  professional level of, 79–80
  psychological environment of, 77–78
  response to environment, 80
  role
    ambiguity of, 77, 82
    conflict of, 77–78, 82
    conformity of, 79
    frustration of, 77, 82

INDEX 235

Directors of Nurses (contd)
  stress of, 76–90
  correlates of, 84–86
  salary of, 79
  staff consensus on responsibilities of, 79
Disengagement theory, 50, 140
DNA, 21–22
Drugs, 22–23, 212
  for pain control, 146–147
Dying see Death

Ethical decisions, 139
  see also Decision-making, ethical
Ethical issues, 38–45, 200–202, 218
Ethical pluralism, 39
Ethical reasoning, 38–39
Ethics, 38
  and the care of the elderly, 41–44
  see also Research, and ethical standards
Ethnicity, 219

Fear
  financial, 145
  of abandonment, 144
  of becoming a burden, 144
  of death see Death, fear of
  of pain see Pain, fear of
  of prolonged illness, 141
Fogarty Fellowship, 28–29
Footdrop, 24
Formalism, 39
Funding, fragmentation of, 10

Genetics and aging, 21–22
Georgetown University Hospital, 153
Geriatric Functional Rating Scale (GFRS), 8
Geriatric nurse practitioner (GNP), 29–30, 114–115, 119–123
  education of, 120–121
  responsibilities of, 121–122
  role and function of
    in clinic, 131–132
    in hospital, 132–134
    in independent practice, 134–135
    in nursing home, 129–131
    in Public Health Department, 134
Geriatric nursing
  education, 68, 95–96, 98–101, 214
  in Australia, 92–113
  post-basic courses in, 68, 95–96, 99–101
  see also Gerontological nursing
Geriatric wards, 46–72, 179
  longstay, 177–178
  nurses in, 180–182
  organisation of work in, 53–64
Geriatrics, 51
Gerontological nursing, 29, 120, 121
  see also Geriatric nursing
Gerontology, 119–120
Grey Panthers, 117

Health assessment, 123–129
  environment, 126–127
  functional ability, 127–129
  health habits, 126
  holistic, 123–124
  medical problems, 126
  medications, 126
  nutritional, 125
  occupation and activities, 125
  physical, 124
  psychosocial, 124–125
  sociodemographic, 125
Health care, 26
  see also Adults, older, health care problems of
Health care assessment, 6–9
Health care data, long-term, 9–10
Health, planning and policy, 220
Hillhaven Hospice, 154
HMO, 30–31
Home, 175–176
  see also Care, home and Hospice, care in the home
Hospice, 137–156
  care in the home, 148–149
  concept, 141–149
  free-standing, 153–154
  implications of
    for financial wellbeing, 151
    for physical wellbeing, 149–150
    for psycho-social wellbeing, 150–151
    for spiritual wellbeing, 151–152
    for survivors, 155
    for the aging, 149–155
  in hospital settings, 154–155
  in nursing homes, 153
  in private homes, 152–153
  interdisciplinary team, 142
  setting, 141–142
Hospital, 177–178

Hospital (contd)
  psychiatric, 180
  quality of life in, 186–187
  staffing levels, 179–180
  see also Residential homes
Hospital Innovation Project, 180
Housing, sheltered see Sheltered housing

Immunology, 28
Incontinence, 24
  survey, 105
Informed consent see Consent, informed
Institutional care, 10–11, 68
  inappropriate use of, 11–12
  see also Care, hospital and Residential homes
Intelligence, 23

Johnson, Robert Wood, Foundation Program, 16–17, 30–31
Justice, distributive, 43–44

Knowledge base, 41–42

Life
  expectancy, 3
  quality of, 171–172, 183–187
Lifestyle, 128–129
Longevity, cultural and historical value of, 39–40
Long-term care, 4–31, 49–72
  assessment techniques for use in, 7–9
  costs of, 5, 48
  definition of, 4
  education for, 29–31
  financing for, 10
  in hospital see Care, hospital, long-term and Geriatric wards, longstay
  problems in, 5–14
  solution of problems in, 14–25
Long-term care services
  management of, 12
  quality control in, 12–14

Management, 11, 12
Medical assessment, 105
Medical management, 223
Mental illness, 6
Mental Status Questionnaire (MSQ), 9
Multi-disciplinary committee, 102–105
  organisational structure, 102–103
  study objectives, 103
Multi-disciplinary groups, attitudes of, 101–102

National Health Service (NHS), 71
National Institute on Aging, 21
Nurses
  as research informants, 199–200
  attitudes of, 93–97
  stereotyping by, 96–97
  stress in see Stress, in nurses
  see also Geriatric wards, nurses in and Registered nurse
Nursing, 65–69
  education, 98–101
  geriatric see Geriatric wards, nurses in and Geriatric nursing
  in research, 201–202
Nursing care, 179–182
  and nursing services, 223–224
  primary, 100–101, 114, 117–119
Nursing care plans, 98
Nursing homes, 75–76
  see also Residential homes
Nutrition, 24–25
  see also Health assessment, nutrition

OARS Multidimensional Functional Assessment Questionnaire, 8–9, 160
Old-old, 114

Pain
  assessment of, 145–146
    method, 146
    objectives, 145–146
  control, 146–147
  due to anger, 145
  fear of, 144
  of grief, 145
  physical, 145–147
    acute versus chronic, 145
    intractable, 145
  psychological, 144

Pain (contd)
  social, 143
  spiritual, 143–144
Pan American Health Organization (PAHO), 27
Patient
  and family, 142
  care goals for, 55–56
Patient Appraisal and Care Evaluation (PACE), 8
Patient Classification for Long-term Care, 8
Patient-nurse dependency study, 104–105
  see also Research, into patient-nurse dependency
Patient Status Instrument (PSI), 9
Personhood, concept of, 41
Personnel resources, 78
Persons, respect for, 42–43
Population, percentage of elderly in, 3, 92, 115, 174
Primary care see Nursing care, primary
  family-centered see Care, family-centered
Professional workers, attitudes of, 93–96

Quality control, 12–13

Registered nurse (RN), 75–76
  post-basic course for, 99–100
Rehabilitation, 177
  see also Research, into stroke rehabilitation
Research
  and education, 149
  and ethical standards, 200–201
  and protection of human subjects, 227
  behavioral, 20–21, 23–24
  biomedical, 20
  British, 169–174, 178–187
  clinical, 192–202
  evaluation, 178–187
  genetical, 21–22
  into activities of daily living, 182–183
  into families coping with cognitive impaired see Cognitive impaired and families
  into patient-nurse dependency, 179–182
  into quality of life, 183–187
  into role stress, 75–90
  findings, 82–90
  sample and method, 80–82
  summary and conclusions, 88
  into stroke rehabilitation, 182–183
  into work organization in geriatric wards, 53–64
  liability for, 198–199
  of the aging, 20–21
  patient's rights to see Rights, of patients, to research
  risks of, 198
  social, 17–20, 20–21
Residential homes, 176–177
  care in, 69–72
  quality of life in, 183–186
Rights
  of patients, 192
    to know, 194
    to refuse, 196–198
    to research, 193–194
  of the dying, 152
Role see Directors of Nurses, role and Geriatric nurse practitioner, role and function
Romania, 28
Royal Victoria Hospital (Edinburgh), 182
Royal Victoria Hospital (Montreal) Palliative Care Service, 141, 154

Sensory perception, 24
Sheltered housing, 175
Short Portable Mental Status Questionnaire (SPMSQ), 159–160
Social workers
  qualifications for, 71
  resident, 71
Society, attitudes of, 92
Staff stability measures, 78
St Christopher's hospice, 141, 153–154
Stress
  in nurses, 75–90
  total role, 78, 82
Suicide, 140
Symptom control, 143

Therapy
  activation, 105–111
    questionnaire, 107–109
TRIAGE, 17

United Nations (UN), 25-27
U.S.S.R., 27
Utilitarianism, 38-39

Volunteers, 147-148
Vulnerability, 230-231

Ward sisters, work scheduling by, 62-63

Warehousing
  minimal, 58-59, 61-64, 66
  personalised 59-61, 61-64, 65-69
Wellness, 231-232
Women, older, 25
World Health Assembly (WHA), 25-27, 32-33
World Health Organization (WHO), 25-27

Young-old, 114